MW01222700

Teacher's Guide

PATHWAYS

Listening, Speaking, and Critical Thinking

3

Becky Tarver Chase
Robyn Brinks Lockwood

ESL Institute
University of New Hampshire
Hamilton Smith Hall
95 Main St
Durham NH 03824
USA

NATIONAL GEOGRAPHIC LEARNING | HEINLE CENGAGE Learning

Australia • Brazil • Japan • Korea • Mexico • Singapore • Spain • United Kingdom • United States

Pathways 3 Teacher's Guide
Listening, Speaking, and Critical Thinking

Publisher: Sherrise Roehr

Executive Editor: Laura Le Dréan

Acquisitions Editor: Tom Jefferies

Development Editor: Lydia Sheldon

Director of Global Marketing: Ian Martin

Marketing Manager: Caitlin Thomas

Marketing Manager: Emily Stewart

Director of Content and Media Production: Michael Burggren

Content Project Manager: Daisy Sosa

Manufacturing Manager: Marcia Locke

Manufacturing Buyer: Marybeth Hennebury

Cover Design: Page 2 LLC

Cover Image: Terry W. Eggers/CORBIS

Interior Design: Page 2 LLC, Cenveo Publisher Services/Nesbitt Graphics, Inc.

Composition: Cenveo Publisher Services/ Nesbitt Graphics, Inc.

© 2013 National Geographic Learning, a part of Cengage Learning

ALL RIGHTS RESERVED. No part of this work covered by the copyright herein may be reproduced, transmitted, stored, or used in any form or by any means graphic, electronic, or mechanical, including but not limited to photocopying, recording, scanning, digitizing, taping, Web distribution, information networks, or information storage and retrieval systems, except as permitted under Section 107 or 108 of the 1976 United States Copyright Act, without the prior written permission of the publisher.

For permission to use material from this text or product, submit all requests online at **cengage.com/permissions**
Further permissions questions can be emailed to
permissionrequest@cengage.com

ISBN-13: 978-1-111-83082-3

ISBN-10: 1-111-83082-7

National Geographic Learning
20 Channel Center St.
Boston, MA 02210
USA

Cengage Learning is a leading provider of customized learning solutions with office locations around the globe, including Singapore, the United Kingdom, Australia, Mexico, Brazil, and Japan. Locate your local office at: **international.cengage.com/region**

Cengage Learning products are represented in Canada by Nelson Education, Ltd.

Visit Heinle online at **elt.heinle.com**
Visit our corporate website at **www.cengage.com**

Printed in the United States of America
3 4 5 6 7 8 15 14 13 12

TABLE OF CONTENTS

Advantages of *Pathways Listening, Speaking, and Critical Thinking*

In *Pathways Listening, Speaking, and Critical Thinking*, real-world content from *National Geographic* publications provides a context for meaningful language acquisition. Students learn essential, high-frequency vocabulary, review important grammatical structures, and practice listening and speaking skills that will allow them to succeed in both academic and social settings.

Pathways Listening, Speaking, and Critical Thinking can be used in a wide variety of language-learning programs, from high schools and community colleges to private institutes and intensive English programs. The high-interest content motivates students and teachers alike.

The following features are included in *Pathways Listening, Speaking, and Critical Thinking*:

- Academic Pathways give students and teachers clear performance objectives for each unit.
- Opening pages introduce the unit theme and provide key vocabulary and concepts.
- Interesting content is used to present target vocabulary and to spark discussions.
- Extensive audio programs include lectures, interviews, conversations, and pronunciation models that expose students to many different kinds of speakers.
- Clear grammar charts present key grammar structures and explain language functions such as asking for clarification and sustaining a conversation.
- Presentation Skills boxes highlight skills for planning and delivering successful oral presentations.
- Student to Student boxes provide real-world expressions for making friends and working with classmates.
- An *Independent Student Handbook* and vocabulary index at the end of each level serve as tools to use in class or for self-study and review.

Teaching Language Skills and Academic Literacy

Students need more than language skills to succeed in an academic setting. In addition to teaching the English language, the *Pathways* series teaches academic literacy, which includes not only reading, writing, speaking, and listening skills, but also visual literacy, classroom participation and collaboration skills, critical thinking, and the ability to use technology for learning. Students today are expected to be motivated, inquisitive, original, and creative. In short, they're expected to possess quite an extensive skill set before they even begin their major course of study.

Using *National Geographic* Content in a Language Class

The use of high-interest content from *National Geographic* publications sets the *Pathways* series apart. Instead of working with topics that might seem irrelevant, students are engaged by fascinating stories about real people and places around the world and the issues that affect us all.

High-interest content is introduced throughout each unit—as context for target vocabulary, as content for lectures and conversation—and provides the information students need for lively discussions and interesting presentations.

The topics in the *Pathways Listening, Speaking, and Critical Thinking* series correspond to academic subject areas and appeal to a wide range of interests. For example:

Academic Subject Area	Unit Title	Unit Theme
Health Science	*Inside the Brain*	the physiology and psychology of the human brain
History/Archaeology	*Learning from the Past*	recent underwater discoveries and the lessons they impart about the value of history
Anthropology/Sociology	*Culture and Tradition*	traditions from cultures around the world, from cowboys to Caribbean music
Earth Science	*Fascinating Planet*	the geography and geology of national parks in China, Brazil, Madagascar, and New Zealand
Economics/Business	*Making a Living, Making a Difference*	economic development including cooperatives, cottage industries, entrepreneurs, and charitable organizations

Increasing Visual Literacy

Photographs, maps, charts, and graphs can all convey enormous amounts of information. Lecturers and professors rarely give oral presentations without some kind of visual aid. Helping students to make sense of visuals is an important part of preparing them for academic success.

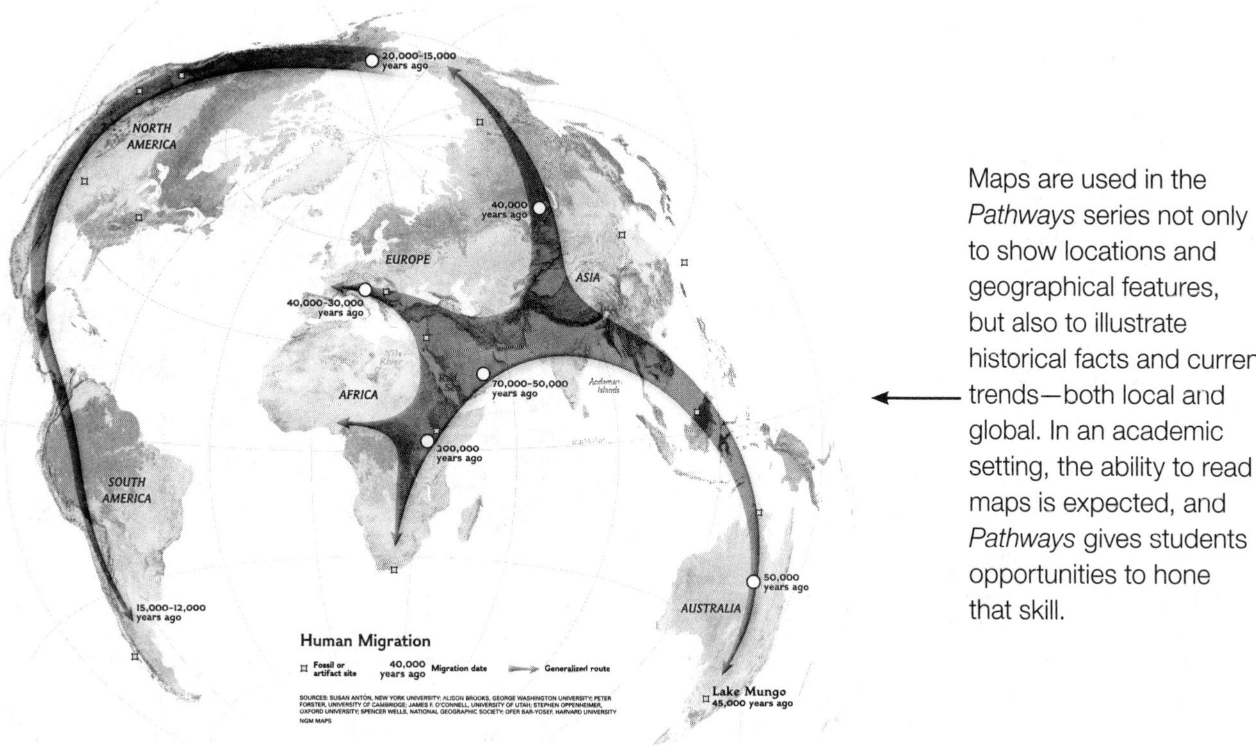

Maps are used in the *Pathways* series not only to show locations and geographical features, but also to illustrate historical facts and current trends—both local and global. In an academic setting, the ability to read maps is expected, and *Pathways* gives students opportunities to hone that skill.

Charts and graphs present numerical data in a visual way, and the *Pathways* series gives students practice in reading them. In addition to the standard pie charts and bar graphs, *Pathways* includes more unusual visuals from the pages of *National Geographic* publications.

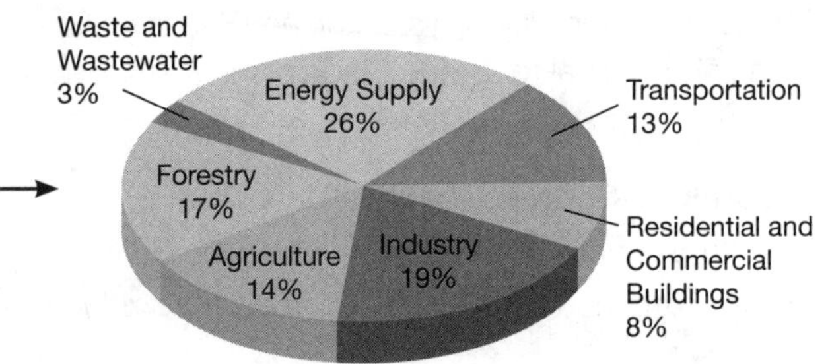

Graphic organizers have several functions in the *Pathways* series. They appeal to visual learners by showing relationships between ideas in a visual way. So, in addition to texts and listening passages, *Pathways* uses graphic organizers to present interesting content. Students are asked to use graphic organizers for a number of academic tasks such as generating topics or organizing notes for a presentation.

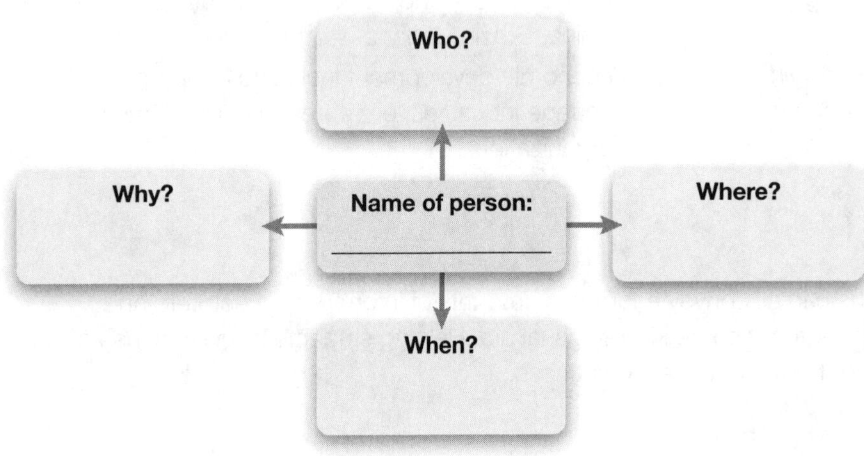

The photographs in the *Pathways* series go far beyond decorating the pages. Photographs introduce the unit theme and provide necessary background information for understanding listening passages and texts. Teachers will also want to exploit the photographs in *Pathways* to initiate discussions and reinforce the target language.

Building Critical Thinking Skills

Critical thinking skills are explicitly taught and practiced in *Pathways Listening, Speaking, and Critical Thinking*. One reason for this is that critical thinking—the ability to make judgments and decisions based on evidence and reason—is an essential skill for students in an academic setting, where they're expected to reflect on and analyze information rather than simply remember it. Students need to be prepared to think critically while listening, reading, writing, and participating in discussions. The skills of critical thinking do not develop on their own; they need to be taught, learned, and practiced.

The ability to think critically is also required in most careers, and critical thinking contributes to language acquisition by requiring deep processing of the language. In order to consider an idea in relation to other ideas and then articulate a response or an opinion about it, we must make complex associations in the brain. This in turn leads to better comprehension and retention of the target language.

Here are just a few examples of the academic tasks that require critical thinking skills:

- deciding which material from a lecture to take notes on
- determining a speaker's purpose when assessing the content of a talk
- forming an opinion on an issue based on facts and evidence
- relating new information to one's personal experiences
- giving specific examples to support one's main idea
- assessing the credibility of a source of information

The *Pathways* series gives explicit instruction on and practice of critical thinking skills. Each unit has a Critical Thinking Focus and several practice exercises. For example:

Critical Thinking Focus: Drawing Conclusions

When you draw a conclusion, you make a logical judgment about something based on the information you have. For example, *I might stop by your house. If there are no lights on, and when I knock on the door nobody answers, I'll probably conclude that nobody is home. I can't know this for certain since I can't go into the house and look around, but I do have enough information to reach a logical conclusion.*

A | In a group, discuss the information from this unit about Angkor and the Khmer Empire and list some conclusions you can draw based on this information. Consider the topics below.

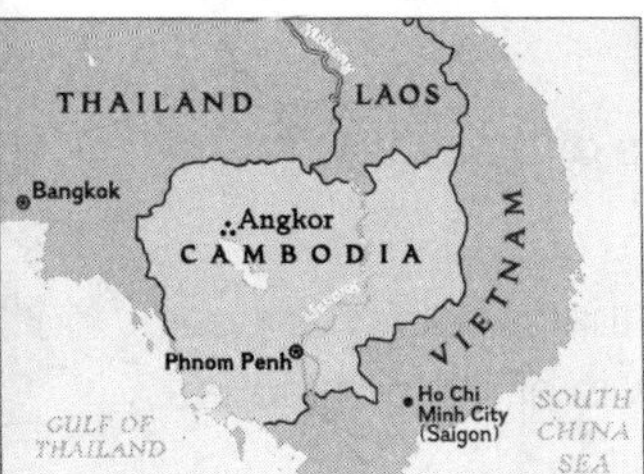

- The length of time that Angkor was the capital of the Khmer Empire
- The art and architecture that can be seen at Angkor
- The number of temples built at Angkor
- The size and sophistication of the water control systems in and around Angkor
- The fact that Angkor's wealth and power declined after losing river access to the sea
- The fact that Angkor Wat is on UNESCO's World Heritage site list

We can conclude that there were a lot of workers in Angkor. Somebody had to construct those huge man-made lakes.

Teaching with *Pathways Listening, Speaking, and Critical Thinking*

Using the Opening Pages

Each unit of *Pathways Listening, Speaking, and Critical Thinking* begins with a unit opener and a two-page spread called Exploring the Theme. These opening pages serve the important functions of raising student interest in the unit theme and introducing key vocabulary and concepts.

The Unit Opener

Every unit opener features a stunning photograph that draws students into the unit theme. You'll want to direct students' attention to the photograph and the unit title. Give students a chance to react to the photograph and give the class some of the background information that you'll find in the Teacher's Guide.

Every unit opener also includes Think and Discuss questions that encourage students to interact with the photograph and to relate it to their own lives.

The unit opener also lists the Academic Pathways for each unit. These are clearly stated performance objectives that preview some of the main culminating activities in the unit. The Academic Pathways are also useful in assessing students' progress at the end of each unit.

Exploring the Theme

After you've worked with the unit opener, go on to the two-page Exploring the Theme section, which provides information in the form of maps, captioned photographs, charts and graphs, and short articles. This section gives students the background information and key terms they need before beginning the unit.

The Exploring the Theme questions check students' comprehension of the information and give them a chance to respond to it in a meaningful way.

Building Vocabulary

Each level of *Pathways Listening, Speaking, and Critical Thinking* contains approximately 200 target vocabulary words in addition to footnotes for less frequently used words. The target vocabulary words in the *Pathways* series are . . .

- **High-frequency:** Students are likely to use high-frequency words on a regular basis, which leads to greater acquisition and better fluency.
- **Level-appropriate:** The target vocabulary words in each level of the *Pathways* series are appropriate for the students studying in that level.
- **Useful for discussing the unit theme:** The vocabulary words in each unit are introduced in the vocabulary sections, used in the listening passages, and recycled in many of the activities.
- **Informed by the Academic Word List:** The *Pathways* series contains a high percentage of the words found on the Academic Word List.*

*The Academic Word List (AWL) is a list of the 570 highest-frequency academic word families that regularly appear in academic texts. The AWL was compiled by researcher Averil Coxhead based on her analysis of a 3.5-million-word corpus (Coxhead, 2000).

Developing Listening Skills

Each unit of *Pathways Listening, Speaking, and Critical Thinking* contains two listening sections. The listening passage in Lesson A takes place in a relatively formal context such as a lecture, a meeting, or a formal presentation. Lesson B presents an informal speaking situation such as a conversation between friends or a group project with classmates.

The language in the listening passages represents realistic situations, yet the language is controlled for level, and students may listen to each passage more than once. This guided listening gives students the chance to practice listening and note-taking skills and to develop the confidence and fluency they'll need before they are immersed in an academic setting.

Each listening section contains three parts:

- **Before Listening** activities provide background information and explicit instruction in listening skills.
- **While Listening** activities give students practice in listening for main ideas and smaller details and in making inferences.
- **After Listening** activities are designed to reinforce listening skills and to allow students to discuss and react to the listening passage.

Pronunciation

The pronunciation lessons are designed to increase students' listening comprehension as well as the comprehensibility of their own speech. The focus is on supra-segmentals, such as rhythm and intonation patterns, rather than on individual sounds.

Note-Taking

Pathways Listening, Speaking, and Critical Thinking takes a scaffolding approach to building note-taking skills. Students begin by listening for specific information to fill in blanks. Later they complete partial notes and practice independent note-taking.

Listening Critically

Since critical thinking is an essential part of listening, skills such as identifying a speaker's purpose and summarizing the main points from a talk are part of the *Pathways* listening program.

Listening Homework

Extensive listening can play an important role in increasing listening comprehension. Students can expand on the listening they do in class by using the Audio CD, the Online Workbook, and the Presentation Tool CD-ROM.

Developing Speaking Skills

Every section of *Pathways Listening, Speaking, and Critical Thinking* provides opportunities for classroom speaking and discussion, often in pairs or in small groups. The Exploring Spoken English sections focus entirely on speaking. Striking images and brief stories about real people and places often provide the content for engaging interactions.

Accurate Speech

Clear and succinct grammar lessons give students a single language structure to concentrate on for each Exploring Spoken English section. The grammar points lend themselves to discussion of the unit theme and can be recycled throughout the unit.

Fluent Speech

Frequent classroom discussions and interactions prepare students to participate in class and succeed in an academic setting. Language Function boxes address the situations in which stock expressions or target grammatical structures are commonly used, increasing the students' level of comfort and confidence in dealing with common speaking situations.

Speaking activities are designed with a scaffolding approach. They progress from controlled activities to guided activities to free activities. Early confidence-building motivates students to attempt activities that increase in difficulty, taking them to their ultimate goal—participation in authentic speaking activities such as classroom presentations, formal discussions, and debates.

Presentation Skills boxes appear at points where students give presentations, so they provide immediate practice of skills needed for planning and delivering successful oral presentations.

Student to Student boxes provide tips and expressions to help students develop the informal, one-on-one speaking skills they will need for class work and in their day-to-day exchanges.

Engage is a consolidating speaking activity. It is a task or project involving collaboration with a partner or a group as well as an oral presentation of results or ideas.

Using Videos in the Language Classroom

The video clips in *Pathways Listening, Speaking, and Critical Thinking* come from the award-winning *National Geographic* film collection and act as a bridge between Lesson A and Lesson B of each unit. The videos consolidate content and skills from Lesson A and illustrate a specific aspect of the unit theme in a visually dynamic way.

What is the Lesson A and B Viewing section?

The viewing section features a video on a theme related to the whole unit. All video clips are on the Online Workbook and the Presentation Tool CD-ROM, as well as on the classroom DVD.

Why teach video-viewing skills?

In daily life, non-fiction videos can be found on television, on the Internet, and in movie theaters in the form of documentaries. Just as *Pathways* provides a wide variety of listening passages to build students' listening skills, the series also builds viewing skills with videos from *National Geographic*. *Pathways* promotes visual and digital literacy so learners can competently use a wide range of modern media.

Videos differ from listening texts in important ways. First, students are processing information by viewing and listening simultaneously. Visual images include information about the video's setting as well as clues found in nonverbal communication, such as facial expressions and body movements. The video may also include animated maps and diagrams to explain information and processes. The soundtrack contains narration, conversations, music, and sound effects. Some contextual words may appear on screen in signs or as identification of people or settings. In addition, full English subtitles (closed captions) are available as a teaching and learning option.

What are the stages of viewing?

Before Viewing prepares students for the video, engages their background knowledge about the topic, and creates interest in what they will watch. Effective ways of previewing include:

- brainstorming ideas and discussing what the class already knows about the topic;
- using photographs and the video's title to predict the content;
- pre-teaching key vocabulary essential to understanding the video content;
- skimming the summary reading.

While Viewing may occur multiple times and at different speeds while:

- picking out and understanding the main ideas of the video;
- watching and listening closely for detail;
- watching and listening for opinion and inference.

After Viewing activities include:

- describing the main points and the sequence of events in the video;
- completing the cloze summary with provided target vocabulary;
- answering discussion questions that relate the video to the students' own lives or experiences.

How should teachers use the videos to teach?

The narration on each video has been carefully graded to feature vocabulary items and structures that are appropriate for students' proficiency level. Here are techniques for using video in class:

- Have students preview the video by reading the transcript or the summary paragraph.
- Pause, rewind, or fast-forward the video to focus on key segments or events.
- Pause the video midway to allow students to predict what will happen next. Resume the video so students can check their predictions.
- Have students watch the video with the sound off so they can focus on what they see. If this approach is used, follow-up discussion helps students share their ideas about the content of the video. Then play the video with the sound on for students to check their ideas.
- Have students watch without subtitles after which they discuss what they hear; then play with subtitles for students to check their ideas.
- Have students follow the script as they listen to the video to help with intonation, pitch, and stress. Stop and replay key phrases for students to repeat.
- Have students watch the video independently and complete the comprehension questions on the Online Workbook.
- To extend viewing skills to speaking and writing skills, have students make a presentation or create a written report about a short video of their choice, using language they have learned from the Student Book and video narration.

All video scripts are printed at the back of the Teacher's Guide. Teachers have flexibility in how or whether they want students to use the scripts. See individual units in this Teacher's Guide for specific teaching suggestions for each video.

Features of the *Pathways* Teacher's Guide

The *Pathways* Teacher's Guide contains teaching notes, answer keys, and the audio and video scripts. There are also warm-up activities to help teachers present the material in the textbook and overviews of the unit theme and the video clip to help turn teachers into "instant experts."

Academic Pathways Boxes

Each unit in the Teacher's Guide begins with a preview of the Academic Pathways. A description of each pathway is then given at the point where it occurs in the unit along with helpful information for the teacher. Teachers are also directed to the online and the Assessment CD-ROM with Exam*View*® resources that will help to reinforce and assess the skills learned for each pathway.

Ideas for... Boxes

Throughout the *Pathways* Teacher's Guide, you will find boxes with ideas to help both novice and experienced teachers. There are four types of Ideas for... boxes:

- **Ideas for Presenting Grammar** boxes provide a variety of ways to introduce grammatical structures and utilize the grammar charts.
- **Ideas for Checking Comprehension** boxes remind teachers of the need to continually assess students' comprehension during every class session.
- **Ideas for Expansion** boxes suggest ways to expand on the content of the book when students need extra instruction or when they have a high level of interest in a topic.
- **Ideas for Multi-level Classes** boxes provide techniques to use in mixed-ability classrooms, where learner diversity can benefit everyone in the class. On the other hand, providing the right kind of help for all the students in any classroom can be a balancing act. When different types of instruction are needed for different learners, teachers must be careful not to embarrass lower-level learners in any way or detract from the learning experience of higher-level learners.

Tips

Tips for instruction and classroom management are provided throughout the *Pathways* Teacher's Guide. The tips are especially helpful to less-experienced teachers, but they are also a resource for more experienced teachers, providing new ideas and adding variety to the classroom routine.

UNIT 1

Gender and Society

Academic Track
Interdisciplinary

Academic Pathways:
Lesson A: Listening to a Lecture
Giving a Presentation about a Name
Lesson B: Listening to a Conversation between Classmates
Participating in a Mini-Debate

Unit Theme

Everyone is born with a biological sex, either male or female. In contrast, we learn our gender from the people around us, and each culture has different ideas about what is appropriate for men and women, and girls and boys.

Unit 1 explores the topic of gender as it relates to:

- male and female roles at work and at home
- societal expectations
- physical attractiveness
- natural abilities

Think and Discuss *(page 1)*

5 mins

In sports, the biological differences between the sexes seem obvious, and sports teams often consist of only female participants or only male participants. Some sports even exclude one sex altogether.

Wrestling is one such sport. It's normally reserved for men or boys, but in El Alto, Bolivia, the "fighting *cholitas*," all of them women, combine wrestling with theater. The women's clothing identifies them as "good" or "bad" characters in this unusual sport with very few rules.

- Discuss the questions.
- Give students some background information about the photo. If they're curious about the word *cholita*, explain that many people in Bolivia have Aymara Indian ancestors. The word refers to a woman with indigenous ancestors.

Exploring the Theme: Gender and Society *(pages 2-3)*

15 mins

The opening spread features a world map. Check students' knowledge of the English names for countries and continents as you look at the most popular male and female names of the labeled countries. For example:

T: In Australia, Isabella and Jack were popular names. Let's look at the next two names. Where were Lena and Lukas popular?
S: In Austria.
T: OK, and where is Austria?
S: Here (points to book), in Europe.
T: Good, and what's another country labeled on the map that's in Europe? Which names were popular there?

- Discuss the questions.
- Have students read and listen to the introductory information.

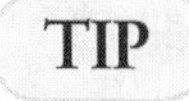

Give students enough time to read the photo captions and ask questions.

Pronunciation Note
Kamchatka: kam-**chaht**-kuh

30 mins

Building and Using Vocabulary *(pages 4-5)*

WARM-UP

The Lesson A target vocabulary is presented in the context of theater and film, where male actors have often played female roles. Occasionally, female actresses have also played male roles.

- Ask students to name a few of their favorite actors and actresses.
- Discuss whether any of the actors and actresses could play the role of a person of the opposite gender.

Building Vocabulary

track 1-2 **Exercise A. | Meaning from Context** Make sure students know that a word's context is everything around it. In this case, the context includes the language in the boxes, the pictures, and other information in this unit on gender.

- For each information box, give students time to read the text without stopping to look up words in the dictionary.
- Discuss the contents of each box before discussing the target vocabulary words. For example:
  T: Are there a lot of female actresses in kabuki theater?
  S: No, in fact, there aren't *any* actresses.
  T: No actresses? Which sentence tells us that?
- After discussing content and checking comprehension, write each vocabulary word on the board. Find out whether students have a sense of each word's meaning and write down any context clues or synonyms that students suggest.

Using Vocabulary

Exercise B. | Students might want to use their dictionaries at this point to clarify the meanings of the target vocabulary words and to complete the exercise.

Answer Key

1. generally
2. role
3. behavior
4. female
5. characteristic
6. gender
7. feminine
8. reverse
9. masculine
10. male

TIP **As you go over the answers in exercise B, have students identify the context clues in each sentence that helped them choose the correct word.**

Exercise C. | Each student circles his or her own opinions.

Exercise D. | Discussion

- Put students into small groups.
- Suggest that students talk about each sentence before moving on to the next sentence (rather than talking about all of one person's opinions before moving on to the next person).

Exercise E. | Ask students to identify one statement for which everyone in the group had the same opinion. Have a representative from each group tell the class which statement all the members agreed upon and what opinion they shared.

IDEAS FOR... Checking Comprehension

Have each group report to the rest of the class something interesting from their discussion. Monitor students' use of the target vocabulary and ask follow-up questions that require students to use the target words. For example:

T: So you think boxing is too masculine a sport for women to play. What are some of the characteristics of boxing that make it a very masculine sport?

Pronunciation Note

onnagata: on-uh-**gah**-tuh

45 mins

Developing Listening Skills *(pages 6-7)*

Exercises A and B. | Students may already have a note-taking system they like, but any note-taking system makes use of key words and abbreviations.

Answer Key *(Answers may vary.)*

A. 1. ~~In~~ some cultures, men ~~and~~ women ~~are expected to~~ follow ~~very~~ strict rules ~~about~~ gender roles
2. Children learn ~~about~~ gender roles ~~when they watch the~~ behavior ~~of the~~ people ~~around them.~~

B. 1. yr. **2.** w/o **3.** < **4.** >

Before Listening

Exercise A. | Prior Knowledge

- Have students discuss the questions in pairs to prepare them to listen to information about a female ruler.

Listening: A Lecture

track 1-3

Exercises A and B. | Listening for Main Ideas
The lecture is divided into two parts. The first part of the lecture is about how children learn gender roles.

- Have students listen and cross out unnecessary words.
- Give students a second chance to listen and make any changes to their work.

Answer Key *(Answers may vary.)*

track 1-4

Exercise C. | Listening for Details

- Have students listen and fill in the blanks in the notes.

Answer Key *(Answers may vary.)*

- We ask: baby boy or girl? b/c later role in world depends on *gender*
  1. gender roles today *changing*
  2. some people don't *follow usual gender pattern*
- In ancient Egypt, Hatshepsut became *female king* (ca. 150 yrs. aft. Tut)
- While H ruled (*15* yrs.) constructed/repaired *buildings + monuments* (wanted to be remembered)
- Early art: H w/ *female* characteristics. Later art: *male characteristics* (reason? maybe easier to keep power w/♂ looks)

IDEAS FOR... Multi-level Classes

Pair higher-level students with lower-level students to compare notes from exercise **C**. Higher-level students benefit from guiding others and lower-level students can get information they missed.

After Listening

Critical Thinking | Critical thinking questions encourage students to apply higher-order thinking skills to a topic. Here, students move beyond simply remembering the content of the lecture to understanding and evaluating the information, and even suggesting additional explanations for the information.

TIP **At the beginning of a course, it's important that students get to know each other. Have students get into small groups with different classmates from the ones they worked with during the vocabulary lesson.**

IDEAS FOR... Expansion

As a class, brainstorm a list of women who have not followed the usual gender pattern for their time (e.g., pilot Amelia Earhart; prime minister Indira Gandhi; scientist Marie Curie). For each person, ask students:

1. *What characteristics do people need in order to be successful in this profession?*
2. *Do you usually think of these characteristics as masculine or feminine?*

Pronunciation Note Hatshepsut: hat-**shep**-soot

45 mins

Exploring Spoken English *(pages 8-10)*

Language Function: Talking about Rules and Expectations

IDEAS FOR... Presenting Grammar

- Write the following words and phrases on the board and discuss their meanings:
  must *have to* *must not*
  T: What is something you <u>must not</u> do in this classroom?
  S: We must not smoke here.
- Then write on the board and discuss the meanings of the following phrases:
  be (required / forbidden / allowed) to
  T: <u>Are</u> you <u>required to</u> do anything before you get on an airplane?
  S: Yes, you're required to go through security and show them your boarding pass.
- Repeat the procedure with these expressions:
  be (supposed / expected) to
- Go over the grammar chart.

Exercise A. | Critical Thinking

- Briefly discuss the photo and caption and have students do the matching exercise.

Answer Key	**1.** d **2.** e **3.** a **4.** c **5.** b

Exercise B. | After partners have compared answers and asked any questions they have about the grammar, read the first discussion question aloud and model a conversation. Use two different voices and change your position to indicate two people talking. For example:

S1: Would it be hard to wear a uniform?
S2: No. I always wore a uniform at school.
S1: So which rule would be the hardest for you to follow?
S2: I don't enjoy exercising very much. It would be hard for me to do it every day.

Exercise C. | Using a Graphic Organizer

- Go over the information on T-charts on page 214 of the *Independent Student Handbook.*
- Encourage students to use several expressions from the grammar chart.

Exercise D.

- Ask students to talk about the information in their charts (rather than show it to their partners).
- Remind students to write down only key words and to use abbreviations as they take notes.

Exercise E.

- Students use their notes to report their partner's ideas to the group.

Grammar: Indefinite Pronouns

IDEAS FOR... Presenting Grammar

- Write the following sentences on the board and discuss the differences between them:
  Bill and Tomoko are giving a presentation on Monday.
  Everyone in the class is giving a presentation on Monday.
- Go over the grammar chart.

Exercise A. | The focus of this exercise is on the meaning of the indefinite pronouns.

Answer Key	**1.** everywhere **2.** anything **3.** nothing **4.** everybody **5.** anyone

Exercise B. | This exercise focuses on subject-verb agreement with indefinite pronouns.

Answer Key	**1.** has **2.** is **3.** Is **4.** is **5.** Is

Exercise C. | After students have read the story, ask them if it reminds them of a real situation at work, at home, or at school. Going through the story with a real job in mind—for example, buying some milk at the grocery store—can give the story more meaning.

Exercise D. | This exercise presents the problem of gender in language, particularly in English pronoun usage.

- Elicit students' ideas about the three sentence options.

30-45 mins

Speaking *(page 11)*

Giving a Presentation about a Name

Exercise A. | Discussion Partners interview each other in order to generate information for a brief presentation.

TIP **If you don't have an even number of students, you can take the role of a student and do your presentation first as a model.**

Exercise B. | Organizing Ideas The T-chart is the graphic organizer that was used on page 9 of the Student Book. Here, it's used to separate main ideas from details.

Be sure to tell students how long each presentation should be (based on your class size and the amount of time available).

TIP **Let students know that they won't simply be reading their notes aloud. They will be speaking in a natural way during their presentations, and the notes are meant to help them remember the topics they want to talk about.**

TIP **The Presentation Skills boxes provide useful tips for effective public speaking. The activities in the Student Book allow for immediate practice of the presentation skill. In this case, students should write their T-chart notes in a way that makes them easy to use while speaking to the class.**

Exercise C. | Presentation

- Ask students to stand up and to hold their notes down and away from their faces while they speak.
- Encourage students to talk for the full time allotted to them without going much over that amount of time.

IDEAS FOR... **Multi-level Classes**

Challenge higher-level students by asking them more detailed questions.

Exercise D. | Discussion Since this is the first formal presentation in the course, use this discussion time to set a comfortable and enjoyable tone for the semester and to stress the importance of students' listening carefully to each other.

TIP **Ask for a student volunteer to read the speech bubble aloud.**

30 mins

Viewing: Wodaabe *(pages 12-13)*

Overview of the Video | When it comes to physical attractiveness, both genders are under pressure. Our faces, the shape of our bodies, our height, and our hair all play a role in whether we're seen as attractive in our culture.

On the other hand, in cultures that hold beauty pageants (where physical attractiveness is formally judged), women and girls are usually the only contestants. But in the Wodaabe culture's *geerewol* festival, it's the young men who compete in a beauty pageant.

Before Viewing

- Ask students to look at the map and photos and answer these questions:
  1. Where do the Wodaabe people live?
  2. Is the video probably about their everyday lives or a special event?

Exercise A. | Critical Thinking Understanding one's own culture is the first step to understanding another person's culture. It allows us to identify similarities and differences and to understand our reactions to people from other cultures.

- After partners discuss the questions, get a sampling of their ideas by asking one or two students in the class each question.

Exercise B. | Using a Dictionary

- After students have read the story while they listened to the audio, give them time to read the passage again and use their dictionaries.

IDEAS FOR... Checking Comprehension

Ask questions to check students' comprehension. For example:

T: Tom, is your family **nomadic**, or not?
S1: We're not nomadic. We live in an apartment in Hong Kong!
T: Good, and Laura—when you get a new piece of clothing or jewelry, do you like to **show it off**?
S2: Definitely. I wear it to school the next day so that everyone can see it.

While Viewing

3:16

Exercise A. | Note-Taking

- After students watch the video and take notes, ask them to tell the class about their reactions or have students share their reactions with a partner.

3:16

Exercise B.

Answer Key

1. makes his white teeth stand out
2. brings out his charm & personality; makes him irresistible
3. The three most beautiful women of the clan act as judges.
4. only the most handsome men

Give students time to read through the questions in the exercise before they watch the video.

After Viewing

Critical Thinking

- If you have enough class time, ask each group to choose one person to be their "reporter." Then, after the discussion, ask the reporters to tell the class about their group's ideas.

Pronunciation Note

Wodaabe: Woo-**dah**-bey
geerewol: gare-eh-wol

30 mins

Building and Using Vocabulary *(pages 14-15)*

WARM-UP

The Lesson B target vocabulary is presented in the context of two news articles. Both articles discuss the fact that boys seem to do better than girls in certain competitions involving geography.

- Have students look at the pictures. Ask which school subject the two articles are probably about (geography).
- Ask students to list school subjects they think boys are better at than girls (perhaps math, etc.). Then ask for subjects girls are better at (perhaps language, etc.).

Building Vocabulary

track 1-6
track 1-7

Exercise A. | Meaning from Context

- Refer to page 204 in the *Independent Student Handbook* for tips on understanding meaning from context.
- Have students read and listen to both articles without using a dictionary.

IDEAS FOR... Checking Comprehension

Call on individual students to answer questions about the article. If students aren't sure how to answer, point out the necessary information in the article. For example:

T: Bobby, what is a "gender gap"?
S1: I think it's a difference . . . like how girls and boys are different.
T: That's right. Are scientists sure about the reasons for the gender gap in geography? Leona?
S2: I think so. They give a lot of reasons at the end of the second article.
T: That's true, but look carefully at the language there. Do you notice anything?
S3: It says, "might" and "maybe" and "possibly." That means they're not sure.

Using Vocabulary

Exercise B.

- Have students match the vocabulary words to the definitions.

Answer Key	**1.** h **2.** a **3.** e **4.** b **5.** i **6.** g **7.** c **8.** j **9.** d **10.** f

Exercise C. | Giving Reasons This exercise asks student to do two things. First, they must locate information in the article. Second, they must use their own critical thinking skills to come up with additional reasons for the gender gap in geography.

- Remind students that their own reasons in the second part of the exercise don't have to be "right." The goal is to brainstorm ideas.

Answer Key

1. Boys may be taught to be more assertive.
2. Boys might feel more pressure from parents.
3. Boys might have a better ability to use maps.
4. Teachers might encourage boys more in geography classes.

Your own ideas: (Answers will vary.)

Exercise D. | Critical Thinking This exercise asks students to compare their ideas with their partner's ideas and then decide which idea is the best explanation for the gap.

- Talk about the ideas students chose in the exercise. Encourage students to give reasons for their choices.

Exercise E. | Discussion The discussion provides an opportunity to recycle the target vocabulary words and to practice giving reasons.

45 mins

Developing Listening Skills *(pages 16-17)*

Before Listening

- Draw a T-chart on the board. Label one side "women" and the other "men."
- Elicit from the class as many types of jobs as possible. Have the class tell you which side of the chart to put each job in.
- For question 2, ask students to give examples of men's and women's work 100 years ago, 20 years ago, and today.

IDEAS FOR... Multi-level Classes

As you fill in the T-chart, call on your lower-level students. This is an opportunity for them to participate by supplying simple responses such as "nurse" or "police officer."

Listening: A Conversation between Classmates

track 1-8

Exercise A. | Listening for Main Ideas

The conversation in this listening section is divided into three separate sections, with each section corresponding to one exercise.

Answer Key *(Answers may vary.)*

1. Dylan worked for his uncle in Toronto for two months.
2. Mia took a summer school course.
3. Gender and Sociology
4. ways he disagrees with the professor

Allow time for students to read the questions before they listen.

track 1-9

Exercise B.

Answer Key **1.** a **2.** c **3.** b

TIP **Make sure that everyone in the class understands the three graphs in exercise B. First, point out the color key (blue for women and red for men), the X-axis (amount of weight lifted), and the Y-axis (number of people). Then go through each chart and discuss its implications. For example, in the first chart, all men can lift more weight than all women.**

track 1-10

Exercise C. | Listening for Details

Answer Key

1. F (Mia thinks both men and women can do many jobs.) **2.** F (She said it was "awful.") **3.** T **4.** F (Dylan thinks male flight attendants can lift heavier bags.) **5.** F (Mia isn't angry with Dylan.)

TIP **As you go over the answers in exercise C, ask students to make the necessary changes to turn the false statements into true statements.**

After Listening

Collaboration | Students work together in pairs to discuss the three graphs and then create a new graph to share with the class.

If the class is large, have students share their graphs with another pair.

track 1-11
track 1-12

Pronunciation: Can/Can't

It's difficult for learners to distinguish between "can" and "can't" in spoken English, so it's helpful to know that the /t/ sound is not the only difference in the way the two words are pronounced: "Can't" is pronounced with the full vowel sound /æ/, while "can" usually has the reduced schwa sound /ə/.

Answer Key **1.** can **2.** can't **3.** can **4.** Can **5.** can't **6.** can

30 mins

Exploring Spoken English
(pages 18-19)

Language Function

TIP **As you go over the Language Function box, make sure students understand that the sentences marked with a red X would *not* be acceptable in an academic setting.**

Exercise A. | Each sentence contains a crossed-out "error." Students replace the exclusive language with more inclusive terms.

Answer Key

1. business executives **2.** mail carrier **3.** nurse
4. chair **5.** server **6.** salesperson

Exercise B. | Discussion

- Encourage discussion of the sentences in exercise **B**. Students may have learned that these examples are "correct," or they may notice that at times there's a reason to emphasize gender.

Answer Key *(Answers may vary.)*

1. businesspeople / business executives
2. Patients should always ask doctors for their advice . . .
3. no change (speaker uses "female directors" to make a point)
4. Early humans / People lived in caves . . .
5. Parents should feed their children . . .

Exercise C. | Discussion

- As groups discuss different jobs, walk around the classroom and listen for inclusive language.

IDEAS FOR... Multi-level Classes

When forming groups, one strategy is to place lower-level learners with higher-level classmates. This allows the higher-level learners to "teach" by example and to provide occasional help and language suggestions.

Language Function: Talking about Rules and Expectations in the Past

This box provides expressions for talking about rules and expectations in the past.

IDEAS FOR... Presenting Grammar

- Write the following words and phrases on the board and discuss their meanings:
  were *had to* *were not*
  T: What is something you <u>had to stop doing when you got sick and wanted to feel better?</u>
  S: I had to stop eating unhealthy food.
- Then review the meanings of the following vocabulary: *be (required / forbidden / allowed) to*
  T: <u>Was there anything your doctor required you to do?</u>
  S: Yes, he/she required me to take medicine.
- Repeat the procedure using the different words and phrases.
- Go over the grammar chart.

Exercise A. | The sentence starters in this exercise contain expressions from the Language Function box.

Answer Key *(Answers will vary.)*

1. Women were expected to stay at home and take care of children.
2. Women were not supposed to wear pants.
3. Men were not expected to help clean the house.
4. Men were supposed to work and earn money for the family.

Exercise B. | Partners share and discuss their sentences from exercise **A**.

Exercise C.

TIP **Ask each group to choose three group members to be discussion leaders. Each leader facilitates discussion of one of the three questions.**

45 mins

Engage: Participating in a Mini-Debate *(page 20)*

WARM-UP

Remind students of the term "gender gap" and the apparent difference between boys and girls when it comes to geography (see page 14).

- Draw a T-chart on the board and label the two sides "culture" and "biology." Elicit reasons that scientists and your students suggested for the gender gap and list the reasons in the chart.
- Elicit other ways in which our culture and our biology make men and women or girls and boys different from each other.

TIP **Tell the class that in a formal debate, two teams or two individuals take turns presenting two sides of an issue; for example, "Climate change is a natural process" versus "Climate change is caused by human activity." Each side usually has a set time to (1) present their own arguments, (2) respond to their opponents' arguments, and (3) present their final arguments.**

Exercise A. | Brainstorming Before you put students into pairs, give them a few tips on brainstorming. Remind them that the goal of brainstorming is to come up with many ideas quickly. They shouldn't worry about being "wrong" or using incomplete sentences at this point.

Exercise B. | Collaboration Partners continue to work together to evaluate the reasons they generated in the brainstorming activity, to choose the three strongest reasons, and to think of an example for each reason.

Exercise C. | Note-Taking An essential part of any debate is predicting what the opposing side will say and being prepared to respond. The notes students take in this part of the lesson should be short; they will be used in exercise **D**.

Exercise D. | Discussion In this activity, students plan their rebuttals (i.e., the arguments they will use to refute their opponents' opinions).

Exercise E. | Organizing Ideas Students prepare their notes for the debate.

TIP **Refer students to the Presentation Skills box on page 11. Once again, students will be preparing notes that will be useful during a presentation.**

Exercise F. | Presentation

- Write on the board the amount of time students will have for the debate. For example, each team might have two minutes to present their arguments, then two minutes to respond, and finally one minute for final arguments (for a total of 10 minutes).
- As the groups are debating, walk around the classroom and take notes on some of the arguments you hear. After students have wrapped up their debates, share the arguments you took notes on with the whole class as a final consolidating step.

Reproducing Life

Academic Track
Life Science

Academic Pathways:
Lesson A: Listening to a Conversation about a Documentary
Discussing Species Conservation
Lesson B: Listening to a Conversation between Classmates
Creating and Presenting a Group Plan

Unit Theme

Reproduction is a biological process that produces new life. All forms of life are produced from parents, but some species face more challenges during the reproduction process. Others use a different type of process altogether.

Unit 2 explores the topic of reproduction as it relates to:

– challenges to reproduction
– global warming
– processes
– conservation

5 mins

Think and Discuss *(page 21)*

In the animal kingdom, groups of animals have names; for example, a group of bears is a "sleuth" or "sloth." Likewise, offspring also have a name. In addition, some species are only found in certain habitats or locations.

Young polar bears are called "cubs," and they live with their parents on sea ice in the frigid climates near such places as the Arctic Circle and Newfoundland Island. Because they feed on seals, they tend to live near the edge of the ice and follow the seals as they migrate.

- Discuss the questions.
- Initiate the discussion by providing students with names for some other young animals, such as "kitten" (cat), "calf" (cow), and "chick" (chicken). Challenge them to think of lesser-known vocabulary as well: "fawn" (deer), "infant" (monkey), or "tadpole" (frog or toad).
- Explain that Arctic animals can live in extreme conditions. The list of Arctic animals includes penguins, seals, and reindeer. Challenge students to think of others.

Encourage students to use picture dictionaries or other sources to participate in the discussion.

15 mins

Exploring the Theme: Reproducing Life *(pages 22-23)*

The opening spread features photos illustrating the three types of reproduction. Prepare students to discuss the three types of reproduction by focusing their attention on the theme. For example:

T: Reproduction can be challenging for penguins. What is one challenge penguins face?
S: Keeping the eggs warm.
T: OK, why is that hard?
S: It's really cold.
T: Right. Let's look at some other types of reproduction and talk about challenges other species might have.

- Discuss the questions.
- Have students read the introductory information.

30 mins

Building and Using Vocabulary *(pages 24-25)*

WARM-UP

The Lesson A target vocabulary is presented in photos and captions about the challenges to reproduction for the King Penguin, including space limitations, predators, cold temperatures, and climate change.

- Ask students to name a few challenges of living in their city. Help students start by writing *transportation* or *weather* on the board. Accept any reasonable answers.
- Discuss options they have for handling those challenges. Ask them to think about what they would do if they had no other options available.

Building Vocabulary

track 1-13

Exercise A. | Meaning from Context Remind students that understanding a word's context helps them figure out its meaning.

- For each caption, give students time to read the text without looking up new words in their dictionaries.

IDEAS FOR... Expansion

Write the following words on the board:
reproduction *predator*
Draw students' attention to the suffixes. Underline *-tion* and *-or*. Ask students if they can think of other words that end in *-tion*. If they need help, write the words *caption* and *actor* on the board. Using these two words as column headings, make a list on the board of the other words students come up with. Remind students that words having the same suffix are the same part of speech. For example, if they don't know the word *predator*, they can still figure out that it is a noun by comparing it to the word *actor*. This skill can be helpful when looking at answer choices on quizzes and tests.

Exercise B. | Challenge students to narrow down their choices without using their dictionaries and by using the context of the captions.

Answer Key

1. adult	**5.** predators	**9.** reproduction
2. weigh	**6.** colony	**10.** challenge
3. depend	**7.** mate	
4. defend	**8.** territory	

TIP **As you go over the answers, have students identify the context clues and suffixes that helped them complete the exercise.**

Using Vocabulary

Exercise A. | Have students read the text and fill in the blanks with a word from the box.

Answer Key **1.** adult **2.** mate **3.** colonies **4.** territory

Exercise B. | Have students select *T* or *F*. Go over the answers with the class.

Answer Key **1.** F **2.** F **3.** F **4.** F **5.** T

IDEAS FOR... Checking Comprehension

Have each student make the necessary changes to turn each false sentence into a true sentence.

Exercises C and D. | Critical Thinking
Encourage students to give reasons and explanations for their answers. Allow class time for students to work together. Solicit volunteers to share answers.

45 mins

Developing Listening Skills *(pages 26-27)*

Before Listening

track 1-14

Exercises A and B. | Meaning from Context
Explain that the skill of deriving meaning of new words from context is just as important while listening as it is while reading. Tell students to follow along as they listen to the audio. Give them time to choose the correct answer.

Answer Key **1.** a **2.** b **3.** a **4.** a **5.** b

Listening: A Conversation about a Documentary

track 1-15

Exercise A. | Listening for Main Ideas The conversation is about making a documentary about King Penguins.

- Have students listen to the conversation and choose the best answer to each question.

Answer Key **1.** b **2.** a

track 1-15

Exercise B. | Listening for Details

- Have students listen and write answers to the questions in their notebooks.

Answer Key

1. four hours **2.** They are a part of a penguin's life. **3.** to show how cold it is **4.** The penguins aren't there in the winter. **5.** one hour

> **IDEAS FOR... Multi-level Classes**
> Before going over answers with the class, pair higher-level students with lower-level students to compare answers. This gives the higher-level students a chance to explain their answers and serve as a peer tutor.

After Listening

Make sure students know the definition of *relevance*. Give the example that knowing math is not *relevant* to this English class. Read the information in the box aloud.

Exercise A. | Ask students to identify which footage the speakers chose.

Answer Key R, NR, NR, R, R

Exercise B. | Discussion Ask students to make decisions about what footage to include in a documentary. Tell them to be prepared to discuss their reasons.

Answer Key R, R, NR, R, NR, R

Exercise C. | Collaboration Ask students to continue working with their partner. Remind them that they will be sharing their ideas and suggest they take good notes.

TIP If time and resources allow, ask students to do online research about their subject at home or in your school's computer lab.

Exercise D. | Presentation Schedule time in class for students to share their ideas.

> **IDEAS FOR... Expansion**
> Watch an excerpt from a documentary such as *An Inconvenient Truth*. Have students write a dialog about what they thought was interesting.

Exploring Spoken English

45 mins *(pages 28-30)*

Pronunciation: Stress Patterns Before Suffixes

track 1-16

It is important for students to notice that the syllable stress can change when a suffix is added, but the changes follow a pattern.

Exercises A and B. | Play the audio and have students identify the stressed syllables and suffixes.

Answer Key

genetic	technical	reproduction

Exercise C. | Have students work in pairs to determine the parts of speech and stress patterns.

Answer Key

-ic, adjective	*-ical*, adjective	*-tion*, noun
genetic	ethical	extinction
specific	practical	connection
problematic	mechanical	conservation
characteristic	psychological	reproduction

TIP Brainstorm other words to go in each column of the chart.

Exercise D.

- Draw students' attention to the illustration on page 29. Make sure they understand the concept of a flow chart.
- Tell students that flow charts are used to simplify difficult ideas.
- Brainstorm a list of processes that could be illustrated in a flow chart.

TIP As you go over the Language Function box, make sure students understand that transition words could be inserted between the steps in the flow chart. Ask students to suggest places to insert them.

IDEAS FOR... Expansion

Inform students that there are other transition words. Give examples, such as *later* or *finally*. Put students in groups to see which group can think of the most transition words. Allow students sufficient time to create a list of four or five words and then have each group read their list. Encourage students to keep a list of all the transition words all the groups came up with in their notebooks.

Language Function

Exercise A.

- Tell students they are going to listen to the information about cloning again.
- Remind them to focus on writing the words and phrases used to transition from one step to another.
- Have students compare their lists with a partner and add any words or phrases they missed.

Exercise B. | Walk around the classroom to make sure students are using transition words and phrases.

IDEAS FOR... Expansion

Have students take notes about a process they are familiar with. They might consider the steps involved in cooking a favorite recipe, completing a science experiment or math problem for another class, or playing a game. Ask them to write the steps of the process using transition words and phrases. If time allows, have students present their process to the rest of the class.

Exercise C. | Discussion Have students work in small groups to discuss the questions.

Grammar: Adjective Clauses

IDEAS FOR... Presenting Grammar

- Write these two sentences on the board:
  I have a hardworking brother.
  I have a brother who works hard.
  T: What is the adjective in the first sentence?
  S: *Hardworking.*
  T: What is the adjective in the second sentence?
  S: *Who works hard.*
  T: Notice that the adjective in the first sentence comes before the noun and consists of one word. The adjective in the second sentence follows the noun and consists of several words. This second type of adjective is called an adjective clause.
- Go over the grammar chart.

Exercise A. | Remind students to think about whether the noun being described is a person or thing.

Answer Key	**1.** that **2.** that **3.** that **4.** that **5.** who **6.** that

IDEAS FOR... Expansion

Ask students to bring in a picture of someone they know or something from their house. Have them work in groups. Students each take a turn holding up their picture and the other students write a sentence guessing who or what it is and describing something about the subject using an adjective clause. For example, if the picture is of a young woman sitting on a beach, a student might write: *The woman is Marco's sister who is on vacation in Florida.* After everyone reads his or her guesses, the owner of the picture can give the answer using an adjective clause: *She is my cousin who lives in Hawaii.*

Exercise B. | Critical Thinking Remind students that each answer will create a complex sentence.

Answer Key	*(Answers will vary.)*

TIP Draw attention to the photo and speech bubble. Ask students if they knew that platypuses are mammals that lay eggs before today. Explain that new and interesting facts are a good way to create complex sentences and use adjective clauses.

Exercise C. | Discussion Read the topics aloud. Give students a few minutes to jot down a few ideas. Then have them talk about their ideas with a partner. Walk around the classroom to make sure students are using adjective clauses. After partners discuss both topics, ask each person to share the one fact they found most interesting or didn't know before they talked with their partner.

30-45 mins

Speaking *(page 31)*

Discussing Species Conservation

Exercise A. | Read the information in the box.

IDEAS FOR... Multi-level Classrooms

Ask a higher-level student to read the information in the box aloud. By listening to a higher-level student read, lower-level students have the chance to listen to the language as they read the text.

Exercise B. | Discussion Make sure students understand the discussion topic of species extinction. Have them work in groups and encourage them to generate enough ideas to share in a brief presentation.

Exercise C. | Presentation Ask a member of each group to report the group's ideas to the class.

Exercise D. | Critical Thinking Ask pairs to rank the arguments. Survey the class to compare results.

Exercise E. | Discussion After students complete the sentences, ask them to discuss their reasons for agreeing or disagreeing with each other.

Remind students to use the expressions in the Student to Student box if they need to ask for repetition.

Pronunciation Note
skua: **skyoo**-uh

30 mins

Viewing: Turtle Excluder

(pages 32-33)

Overview of the Video | Species that are endangered have a population that is dwindling, so much so that they are at risk of extinction. Species face varying levels of threat: near threatened, vulnerable, endangered, critically endangered, only in captivity, or extinct.

Sea turtles are reptiles that live in all the world's oceans except the Arctic. Sea turtles can live up to 80 years, but they are decades old before they can reproduce. All sea turtles are threatened, but some are endangered, such as the Kemp's Ridley.

Before Viewing

- Ask students to look at the video title, map, and photo and answer these questions:
  1. Have you ever visited or are you familiar with any of the areas shown on the map? What is something you know about one of the areas?
  2. What kinds of animals do you know of that live in this part of the world?

Exercise A. | Critical Thinking Reasons for population decreases vary. Some are environmental, such as climate change affecting habitats; others are human, such as fishing or deforestation.

- After partners discuss the questions, have them write their list of threats on the board.

Exercise B. | Self-Reflection

- Give students time to discuss the questions.

Exercise C. | Using Adjective Clauses

- Review adjective clauses before students complete the activity.

Answer Key	**1.** c **2.** e **3.** d **4.** a **5.** b

IDEAS FOR... Checking Comprehension

- Go around the room and ask each student one question. For example:

  T: Would you want to be a **biologist**?
  S1: No. I want to be an engineer.
  T: What **device** do you use every day?
  S2: I use a microwave to cook dinner.

While Viewing

2:51

Exercise A.

- After students watch the video and answer the questions, go over the answers.

Answer Key

1. a device that allows turtles to escape from being caught by fishermen

2. The funnel allows water to move quickly. Anything caught is pushed against the bars. Anything smaller goes through the bars, but anything larger can escape.

3. shrimp fishermen

2:51

Exercise B. | Note-Taking

- Remind students that a T-chart is a good way to organize ideas. Tell students they will watch the video again.

Answer Key

Disadvantage: holes cause fishermen to lose a significant portion of their catch

Advantage: excludes anything large, so fishermen can pull nets for longer and get a higher percentage of shrimp

Give students time to review the T-charts they completed in Unit 1 on pages 9 and 11.

After Viewing

Collaboration | Explain that this activity simulates teamwork often found in academic settings and in workplaces. Have students read their letters to the other teams.

30 mins

Building and Using Vocabulary *(pages 34-35)*

WARM-UP

Students are asked to read and listen to information about orchids and how they reproduce. The article is presented in a question and answer format. Let students know this format is used frequently in documents and during formal discussions. Ask students where they have seen a question and answer document before. If students have trouble thinking of ideas, suggest common question and answer information forms such as insurance, banking, health, or education documents. Bring in samples if you have them or show some online.

Building Vocabulary

track 1-19

Exercises A and B. | Meaning from Context

- After students read the text and listen to the audio, ask them if any of the information was new or interesting. Encourage them to answer using adjective clauses.
- Review page 204 in the *Independent Student Handbook* and ways to determine parts of speech. Do not let students use a dictionary for this activity. Encourage them to rely on the context.

Answer Key

Nouns: insects, shelter, scents, instinct
Verbs: trick, attract, imitate, resemble, obtain
Adjectives: fascinating

IDEAS FOR... Checking Comprehension

- Call on individual students to answer questions using the vocabulary and information in the article. Make sure every student has a chance to answer one question.

T: What is a great way to **trick** birds?
S1: Offering food.
T: Yes. Have you ever **tricked** anyone?
S1: Yes, I have. One time I **tricked** my little brother into giving me some money.

Using Vocabulary

Exercise A. | Using a Dictionary Let students use a dictionary if necessary. Walk around the classroom to help as needed or allow students to work with a partner to complete the sentences. Ask volunteers to read their answers for the class.

Answer Key

1. attracting . . . **2.** fascinating . . . **3.** obtain . . .
4. insects . . . **5.** trick . . . **6.** scent . . . **7.** shelter . . .
8. instincts . . . **9.** resemble . . . **10.** imitate . . .

Exercise B. | Critical Thinking Have students work in small groups to discuss the questions. Encourage them to think of as many ideas as they can.

Answer Key *(Answers will vary.)*

IDEAS FOR... Expansion

Have students plan a question and answer discussion using one of the questions from exercise **B**. Ask them to start with the original question, write two additional questions, and then answer all three. If time allows, have students stage the discussion in front of the class.

Developing Listening Skills *(pages 36-37)*

45 mins

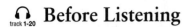

Before Listening

track 1-20

It can be difficult for second language learners to distinguish between stressed and unstressed words. Before playing the audio, have students try reading the sample sentences.

> IDEAS FOR... **Multi-level Classes**
> Call on higher-level students to read the sample sentences in the box or the dialog from exercise **A**. This gives them a chance to practice a challenging skill while allowing lower-level students to listen to examples.

track 1-21

Exercises A and B. | Have students work independently to complete the activity. After playing the audio for students, survey the class to see if their predictions were correct. Discuss any differences and reasons for the stressed words.

Answer Key greenhouse, together, before, fascinating, world, tropical

Listening: A Conversation between Classmates

track 1-22

Exercise A. | Listening for Main Ideas The conversation in this listening section is a conversation between two students.

Answer Key **1.** b **2.** b

TIP Remind students to listen to the entire conversation before answering the questions.

track 1-22

Exercise B. | Listening for Details

Answer Key

1. from the air
2. high up on trees in tropical places
3. There is more light and fewer animals to eat them there.
4. They have parts that attach to the tree.
5. A lot of orchids are epiphytes.

TIP **Remind students that they don't need to understand the technical words to be able to answer the questions. It doesn't help to panic when they hear a new word, such as *epiphyte;* instead, they should keep listening to the audio to get the main ideas and details.**

After Listening

Self-Reflection | Have students work with a partner to discuss questions 1 and 2.

Answer Key

Students should check: a class lecture, the greenhouses, knowledge of orchids

Before question 3, reinforce the idea that students don't have to know someone well to have a conversation. Have pairs select a topic to talk about.

TIP **Bring a stopwatch or timer to class and set it for two minutes. Have pairs begin at the same time.**

> IDEAS FOR... **Multi-level Classes**
> Pair students together who have the same approximate level, so that lower-level students are not intimidated by the speed or quantity of content of the higher-level students.

Pronunciation Note
epiphyte: **ep**-uh-fahyt

30 mins

Exploring Spoken English *(pages 38-39)*

Language Function: Making Suggestions

IDEAS FOR... Presenting Grammar

Present this question to the students: *What advice would you give a new student joining an English class?* Elicit answers such as *buy the book* or *talk to current students.* Write students' ideas on the board.

Go over the information in the Language Function box. Make sure everyone understands. Discuss ideas about when to be direct and when to be more indirect.

Revisit the list of suggestions on the board and have students rewrite them to reflect directness or indirectness and correct grammar.

Exercise A. | Have students work together to complete the dialog. Remind them that answers can vary.

Answer Key *(Answers may vary.)*

could, We could, why don't we, should

Exercise B. | Have students practice reading the conversation aloud. Solicit volunteers to read for the class.

TIP **Revisit the pronunciation lesson about stressing content words or new information. Ask students which words they would emphasize in the conversation.**

Exercise C. | Tell students to shift their attention to more direct language to complete this exercise.

Answer Key *(Answers may vary.)*

recommend, suggest, Let's get together to

Exercise D. | Ask students to practice reading the conversation aloud. Solicit volunteers to read for the class.

Exercise E. | Collaboration Explain that committees and teamwork are an important part of the academic and professional world and that this activity will allow students to work as a committee to solve problems. Read the situation aloud and inform students that they will read their responses to the class. Walk around the classroom as students are working to help with grammar and to answer any vocabulary questions. After students have written their responses, allow time to compare the suggestions and hold a whole-class discussion about why they chose to be direct or indirect.

IDEAS FOR... Expansion

Ask students to write a question or problem they are curious about on an index card. Tell them this is an anonymous activity and they should not write their name on the card. Collect the cards and redistribute them, making sure no student receives his or her card. Ask students to form groups and read the questions or problems to each other. Then have them create a list of suggestions for the question or problem and write them on the back of the card. After sufficient time, re-collect the cards and read the suggestions to the class or have each student present the question or problem and read the group's list of suggestions.

45 mins

Engage: Creating and Presenting a Group Plan *(page 40)*

WARM-UP

Explain that many university students earn grants to help fund research. Grants can be hard to get, but winning them allows the applicants to move forward with innovative research projects. Ask students if they are familiar with any research projects in their own fields.

TIP **Provide information about grants and how they work to students. Consider bringing in a few grant applications to show students how important grants are in academic study and how detailed plans need to be in order to earn funding.**

Exercise A. | Ask students to read the information about winning a grant.

Exercise B. | Have students complete the questionnaire. Then encourage them to brainstorm a list of potential topics. Review brainstorming from Unit 1 and remind students that the goal of brainstorming is to come up with many ideas quickly and that quantity matters more than quality at this stage.

Have students prioritize their ideas and then agree on a species to study.

Exercise C. | Organizing Ideas Tell students that organizing ideas is an essential component of any good academic project. Have them summarize their discussion from exercise **B** into the Study Plan form.

TIP **Refer students to the Presentation Skills box at the bottom of the page. Inform students that using specific details helps the audience understand the content. Specific details are usually the content words. Review the information about emphasis on key words on page 36.**

Exercise D. | Presentation Write on the board the amount of time students will have for their group presentation. Encourage them to add specific details about why they chose their species, location, travel method, study length, and any other details about their research project.

Allow time in class for students to formally present.

Show a sample PowerPoint presentation from a formal grant presentation.

IDEAS FOR... Expansion

Tell students that after their study plan was announced, the representatives in charge of funding had to divide the money between students at several schools. Therefore, they will still get grant money, but not nearly as much as they had anticipated. Have students reconvene in their groups and give them a more restrictive budget (suggestion: $10,000). Ask them to discuss how their study plan needs to be revised and resubmitted to the representatives (the class).

Human Migration

UNIT 3

Academic Track
Sociology

Academic Pathways:
Lesson A: Listening to a PowerPoint Lecture
Discussing Case Studies
Lesson B: Listening to a Small Group Discussion
Giving a Group Presentation

Unit Theme

Emigration is the act of leaving a home country to go live in another. Emigration is studied from the perspective of the person's home country. Immigration is the same action, but studied from the perspective of the new country.

Unit 3 explores the topics of emigration and immigration as they relate to:
- reasons for emigration and immigration
- places to emigrate from or immigrate to
- analyzing information
- telling stories

5 mins

Think and Discuss *(page 41)*

Reasons for emigration vary, but some people emigrate to avoid wars, seek religious freedom, go to school, get married, live in better climates, or find jobs.

- Initiate the discussion by asking students to think of reasons why people may want to move to another country. Make a list of ideas on the board. Then focus students' attention on the picture and ask about Hong Kong specifically.

There are a variety of reasons people may move to Hong Kong. Some people have moved there to work in the many businesses located in the city. A lot of businesses prefer Hong Kong for the taxation benefits or free trade. Other people have moved there to attend school.

- Ask students to talk about where they are from and their experiences with immigration or emigration.

TIP **This topic might be sensitive or personal for some students. It is best to solicit answers only from volunteers.**

15 mins

Exploring the Theme: Human Migration *(pages 42-43)*

The opening spread features a world map that highlights several human migration patterns. Get students involved by asking them to notice the arrows and photo captions. For example:

T: It looks like people migrate to and from many places. Which migration was the longest?
S: From Europe to Australia.
T: OK, why did people leave Europe?
S: The caption says they were displaced after World War II.
T: Good, and what is an example of a short migration?
S: India to Saudi Arabia.
T: What was the reason for that migration?
S: People went to Saudi Arabia to work.

- Discuss the questions.
- Have students read and listen to the introductory information.

30 mins

Building and Using Vocabulary *(pages 44-45)*

WARM-UP

The Lesson A target vocabulary is presented in context. Remind students that paying attention to the other words in the sentence can help them determine definitions without using a dictionary.

Building Vocabulary

track 1-23

Exercise A. | Meaning from Context Have students read and listen to the sentences before matching the words to their definitions. Point out that sometimes words have to change form or tense to be correct.

Answer Key

a. trend **b.** abroad **c.** emigrate **d.** temporary
e. immigrant **f.** permanent **g.** original **h.** negative
i. community **j.** native

Exercise B. | Using a Dictionary Remind students that the root of a word carries the meaning and the suffix changes the part of speech. Let them know that different dictionaries may have slightly different wording.

Answer Key *(Answers may vary.)*

immigrate: to come to live in a new country
immigration: the process of immigrating
emigrant: a person who emigrates
emigration: the process of emigrating
temporarily: lasting only a limited time
permanently: lasting forever
originally: being the first or earliest
negatively: being bad, unpleasant, or harmful
trendy: being part of a general pattern

IDEAS FOR... Checking Comprehension

Ask each student to write one or two sentences using two of the vocabulary words. Give them one example:

T: I want to go **abroad** to the United States to visit family. They live there **permanently**.

Using Vocabulary

Exercise A. | Draw attention to the picture in the box. Give students time to answer the questions.

Exercise B. | Inform students that they may need to change the form of the vocabulary word to correctly complete the sentence.

Answer Key

1. trend	**5.** community	**9.** immigrants
2. abroad	**6.** native	**10.** negative
3. emigrated	**7.** permanent	
4. temporary	**8.** original	

Exercise C. | Give students time to write answers to the questions.

TIP **Consider allowing students to do online research at home or give them time in class to go to the school's computer lab to find answers to question 1.**

Exercise D. | Discussion Have students form small groups to discuss their answers.

45 mins

Developing Listening Skills
(pages 46-47)

Before Listening

Exercise A. | Predicting Content Explain that predicting content is a good habit because it improves comprehension. Remind students that it is not important if their prediction is correct. It's more important that they are thinking about the topic and activating their prior knowledge. Give them time to make predictions.

Exercise B. | Have each pair of students join another pair to compare predictions.

IDEAS FOR... Multi-level Classes

Assign a higher-level student in each group to be the group leader. The leader can help organize the discussion and summarize the group's answer.

Listening: A PowerPoint Lecture

track 1-24

Exercise C. | Listening for Main Ideas Tell students they are going to hear a lecture, but the slides in the book are not in the correct order. Challenge them to number the pictures in the correct order.

Answer Key 3, 1, 5, 6, 2, 4

track 1-24

Exercise D. | Listening for Details Tell students it is challenging to take notes when visual aids are used. They have to listen to the words as well as look at the visuals. Play the audio again and have students take notes. Tell students to look at the numbers on the slides from exercise **C** to help them navigate the order.

Answer Key

Slide 1. had farmland that many immigrants were looking for, people are leaving, especially rural areas

Slide 2. **1.** travel was easier **2.** when railroad companies finished building, they sold extra land for cheap

Slide 3. **1.** several years of very dry, windy weather **2.** economic crisis of the 1930s forced farmers to sell land and leave

Slide 4. 75, 6

Slide 5. larger cities, not small towns

Slide 6. communities, poets

After Listening

Critical Thinking | Have students form groups to discuss the questions. Solicit volunteers to share their answers.

TIP Walk around the classroom to answer questions about North Dakota or other regional information the students might not be familiar with.

IDEAS FOR... Expansion

Tell students to imagine their group is the city council for the city your school is located in. Population is declining and they must think of a plan to save the city. Have the groups work together to develop a list of reasons why people should immigrate to the town. If time permits, have students create a brochure about the town. The brochure should list appealing reasons for someone to move from another country to live in your town.

45 mins

Exploring Spoken English *(pages 48-50)*

Grammar: Adjectives with *Enough*, *Not Enough*, and *Too*

IDEAS FOR... Presenting Grammar

- Tell students that sometimes English can be like math: putting things together equals a new meaning. Write these "equations" on the board:
  adjective + enough =
  not + adjective + enough =
  too + adjective =
  T: If I add an adjective with the word *enough*, it means "sufficient."
- Write *sufficient* on the right side of the first equation.
  T: What does the second equation equal?
  S: Insufficient.
- Write *insufficient* on the right side of the second equation.
  T: Right. What does the third equation equal? For example, if I have too much food, what do I have?
  S: More than you need.
  T: More than I need or excessive.
- Write *excessive* on the right side of the third equation.
- Go over the grammar chart.

Exercise A. | Point out the words in parentheses. Tell students to use those words to write a sentence with *enough*, *not enough*, or *too*.

Answer Key

1. I'm too busy to see a movie.
2. It's too small for me.
3. It's not loud enough.
4. They're old enough to make dinner.
5. It isn't interesting enough for a vacation.
6. The land is too dry.
7. It's big enough to hold my laptop and my books.

Exercise B. | Have two students read the speech bubbles. Give students adequate time to practice.

IDEAS FOR... Multi-level Classes

Ask two lower-level students to read the speech bubbles aloud.

Exercise C.

- Encourage students to be creative.
- Have each pair read one of their dialogs to the class.

IDEAS FOR... Presenting Grammar

- Tell students there are three new equations. Write these on the board:
  enough + noun =
  not enough + noun =
  too + much/many + noun =
- Ask students to guess the "answers."
- Go over the grammar chart.

Exercise A. | Give students a few minutes to complete the exercise before going over the answers.

Answer Key

1. not enough **2.** too much **3.** too much
4. too many, not enough **5.** enough

Exercise B. | **Discussion** Have students discuss the topics and remind them to use the language from the boxes. Have one student read the speech bubble. Then ask a volunteer from each group to present an idea or opinion for one of the three topics.

Language Function: Asking for Reasons

Explain that asking for reasons is a valuable skill. Go over the information in the box.

> **IDEAS FOR... Multi-level Classes**
>
> Give each student an index card. Have them write three facts about themselves on the card. Give some examples: *My favorite singer is Lady Gaga. I like pizza. I visited New York City last summer.* Then have them give their card to a partner. Assign students partners of similar levels, so that their dialogs can be appropriately challenging for both. Partners should choose one fact and ask for a reason. The writers should answer. Partners can reverse roles. Students should change partners to exchange cards again.

Exercise A.

- Tell students that questionnaires are popular ways to ask for information.
- Have students add two questions of their own.

Exercise B. | Give students time to interview a partner and complete the questionnaire.

TIP **Explain that people giving questionnaires take notes on their forms, so they can use the data later. Have students write their partner's answer onto the form, so they can use it to keep a conversation going after they've both completed the questionnaire.**

> **IDEAS FOR... Expansion**
>
> Have students find someone outside of the classroom who is not originally from the city or country to interview. Have them use the questionnaire as it is or adapt it as necessary to use during their interview. If time allows, have students prepare a short presentation about the person they interviewed and share the person's reasons for moving.

30-45 mins

Speaking *(page 51)*

Discussing Case Studies

Exercise A. | Have students read the case studies silently.

TIP **Assign the reading as homework so students can more carefully think about what information is the most important to highlight.**

Answer Key *(Answers will vary.)*

Exercise B. | Collaboration Review the information about T-charts in Unit 1. Have students create a T-chart for each of the three case studies.

Exercise C. | Discussion Challenge students to make a decision for each of the three case studies. Tell them that all members of the group should share reasons and agree on a recommendation.

Exercise D. | Presentation Ask each group to present their recommendations to the rest of the class. Remind them that having reasons for their recommendations is required.

> **IDEAS FOR... Expansion**
>
> Have students work in pairs to "create" a case study. Their person can be based on someone they know or can be someone they make up. Have them exchange case studies with other pairs. They should create a T-chart and then make a recommendation for the new person. Case studies can be exchanged more than one time if desired. When both pairs have discussed each other's case studies, they should get their original case study back and see what the other group recommended. Have students share their case study and talk about what the other groups recommended.

30 mins

Viewing: Turkish Germany

(pages 52-53)

Overview of the Video | Guest worker programs allow workers to work in a country that is not their own. These programs have advantages and disadvantages for both the workers and the countries.

Germany and Turkey have had a guest worker treaty for 50 years. As a result of this treaty, Turks moved to Germany to work, but never returned to their native land. Consequently, several generations of Turks have been born in Germany, but many Germans still consider them to be foreigners.

Before Viewing

Ask students if they are familiar with guest worker programs. Generate a class discussion about what students predict about the type of information they will hear in the video.

track 1-25

Exercise A. | Open a class discussion about working in a country that is not your native country. Solicit volunteers to talk about what countries they worked in and what kind of work they did.

- Have students read the text as they listen to the audio about Germany's guest worker program.
- Draw attention to the line graph and map.

Exercise B. | Understanding Visuals

- Ask students to list other types of visual aids they are familiar with. Write a list on the board. Make sure everyone understands how a line graph is read.
- Give students time to discuss the questions.

Exercise C. | Review the grammar on pages 48 and 49.

Answer Key	**1.** not enough **2.** enough **3.** too **4.** not enough

While Viewing

2:23

Exercise A. | Have students watch the video and mark the aspects of culture they see.

Answer Key
Students should check the following boxes: food, music, clothing, religion, language, other (work, history)

2:23

Exercise B.

Tell students they will watch the video again.

Answer Key	**1.** together **2.** higher **3.** two languages **4.** higher

TIP **Watch the part about Rixdorfer Elementary School again so students can see why they missed any answers.**

After Viewing

Read the Critical Thinking Focus box aloud. Make sure students understand what an inference is.

Critical Thinking | After students discuss the issues, have each group summarize their discussion.

30 mins

Building and Using Vocabulary *(pages 54-55)*

WARM-UP

Teach students that often phrases can be condensed into one word or changed to a better word. Such changes can make information more concise. Let students know that concise information sounds more academic. Give an example. Write *mother, father, three brothers, and grandmother* on the board. Ask students if they can think of one word to replace all of those. Solicit the answer, *family*. Remind them that the words they use to replace others must retain the same meaning.

Building Vocabulary

track 1-26

Exercise A. | Give students time to read the sentences and choose a word from the box for each one. Ask volunteers to read the sentences aloud.

Answer Key

1. ancestors	**5.** settle	**9.** discrimination
2. minority	**6.** retain	**10.** attitude
3. generation	**7.** ethnic	
4. positive	**8.** assimilate	

IDEAS FOR... Checking Comprehension

Call on individual students to fill in the blanks in your statements. Make sure every student has a chance to answer.

T: My grandmother is one of my _______.

S: ancestors

T: Right. Now someone else try the next one.

My children are the next generation.

You need to study to retain your vocabulary!

Sometimes people who look different face discrimination.

I love ethnic food like Italian and Chinese.

A good attitude helps you succeed.

I want to settle in Mexico because I like the food.

I am positive that you can all learn English.

It is hard to assimilate to a new culture.

Only four out of 20 people have blond hair. Blonds are the minority.

Exercise B. | Self-Reflection Walk around the classroom to help as needed or allow students to work with a partner to discuss the questions. Ask volunteers to read their answers to the class.

Using Vocabulary

Exercise A. | Divide the class into two groups, A and B. Give each group one set of information.

track 1-27
track 1-28

Exercise B. | Note-Taking Have a member of Group A find a partner from Group B. Tell students to take notes as their partners tell them about the information they read.

Exercise C. | Using a Graphic Organizer Draw a Venn diagram on the board. Refer students to page 214 of the *Independent Student Handbook* for more information. Tell them to create a Venn diagram using their notes and to answer the questions in the book.

Exercise D. | Critical Thinking Ask students to use their notes and diagrams as they discuss the questions.

IDEAS FOR... Expansion

Have students find a partner from a country different from their own. Ask them to create a Venn diagram about their two countries to present to the rest of the class.

Pronunciation Note

Hmong: hmawng

45 mins

Developing Listening Skills *(pages 56-57)*

Before Listening

TIP **Explain that activating prior knowledge is helpful because it enables listeners to make connections between the topic and what they already know.**

Prior Knowledge Have students look at the pictures and questions. Allow them ample time to discuss the questions.

Listening: A Small Group Discussion

track 1-29

Exercise A. | Using a Graphic Organizer Review T-charts and Venn diagrams. Then introduce charts as another type of graphic organizer. Tell students they are going to listen to an instructor give a discussion assignment. Direct them to pages 214–215 of the *Independent Student Handbook* for more information.

Answer Key	**2.** come from **3.** go to **4.** Why **5.** assimilate

TIP **Prepare students for the fact that they're going to hear four voices and a lot of details. Encourage them to take notes on another piece of paper and then transfer the information into the graphic organizer.**

track 1-30-33

Exercise B. | Listening for Details

Answer Key

Josh's grandparents	Nasir's father	Emily's uncle	Sunisa's ancestors
Poland	Pakistan	England	China
Chicago	Saudi Arabia	Australia	Thailand
war	work	girlfriend	population
no	no	no	yes

After Listening

Discussion | Have students complete their graphic organizers before discussing the questions.

track 1-34

Pronunciation: Fast Speech

Tell students that native English speakers often talk quickly. Teach the information in the box about reductions and linking. Have students practice reading the examples.

track 1-35

Exercise A. | Prepare students to take dictation.

Answer Key

1. Why'd [Why did] they leave?
2. Did he earn a lot of money there?
3. You can go see your relatives in Australia.
4. And how'd [how did] he like it?
5. D'you [Do you] know why?

Exercise B.

Answer Key

1. Why'd they leave?
2. Did he earn a lot of money there?
3. You can go see your relatives in Australia.
4. And how'd he like it?
5. D'you know why?

Exercise C. | Ensure that students correctly transcribed the sentences. Ask them to practice reducing and linking.

30 mins

Exploring Spoken English *(pages 58-59)*

Grammar: Using the Past Continuous Tense

> **IDEAS FOR... Presenting Grammar**
>
> Ask students to finish this sentence: *Once upon a time, an English student was . . .*
>
> Go over the information in the grammar box and discuss situations for which past continuous is used.
>
> Solicit volunteers to read their sentence aloud.

Exercise A. | Have students work together to ask and answer the questions. Walk around the classroom to make sure they are using the tense correctly.

Exercise B. | Have students complete the sentences in their own ideas. Solicit volunteers to read their answers to the class.

Answer Key *(Answers will vary.)*

> **IDEAS FOR... Expansion**
>
> Ask students to write a short story beginning with the line *Once upon a time, an English student named [their name] was studying when . . .* Tell them the last line of their story will be *After that, the English student was going to live happily ever after.* Remind them to use the past continuous tense as often as they can. Solicit volunteers to read their stories to the class.

TIP Revisit the pronunciation lesson about reductions and linking. Have students mark any places in the sentences in the book or in the stories where sounds would be reduced or linked.

Language Function: Telling a Personal History

Exercise A. | Brainstorm Remind students that brainstorming is used to generate a large quantity of ideas. Have them keep their list in their notebook.

Exercise B. | Using a Graphic Organizer Introduce students to the new type of graphic organizer. Have them choose one person they know well and complete the graphic organizer about that person. Allow time for students to share their graphic organizers with others.

Storytelling Tips | Ask students what kinds of stories they like and why they like them. Elicit answers such as, "It was exciting", "It had a surprise ending", or any other reasonable answers. Have students follow along as you read the information and examples in the book.

Exercise C. | Ask students to review their graphic organizers and write a short story about the person they chose. Encourage them to include details so that their audience will be interested.

Exercise D. | Presentation Have students present their stories in small groups. Give them time for a question and answer period after each story.

Student to Student: Asking Sensitive Questions | Explain that native speakers try to be polite when asking sensitive questions. They sometimes preface a question with a remark to soften the question. Ask students if they can think of other expressions to add to the list.

> **IDEAS FOR... Expansion**
>
> Tell students to imagine they are winning an award for having the best English scores in the school. They must have a short autobiography printed in the award ceremony's program. Ask them to write a short story about their life.

45 mins

Engage: Giving a Group Presentation *(page 60)*

WARM-UP

Explain that many conferences and workshops have visual presentations. Explain that posters and slides are visually appealing because they include text, pictures, and graphs. As students move forward in their academic career, they will likely encounter this type of presentation often. Have a student read the information in the box aloud. Make sure everyone understands the details about the assignment.

TIP **Show students sample posters so they have an idea of what they need to do. Many samples are available online.**

IDEAS FOR... Expansion

Have students find a sample visual presentation for a subject or discipline that they are interested in. Ask them to show an image or bring in a copy to share with a group. Have students talk about what they like about each one. Encourage them to consider their likes and dislikes when they create their visual presentation for class.

TIP **Groups of four are ideal for this activity.**

Exercise A. | Encourage students to brainstorm a list of ideas for their topic. Give them time to narrow their ideas down until they all agree on one group of people. Ideas you can offer include Mexicans to the United States, Bangladeshi to Saudi Arabia, Polish to Ireland, or Lebanese to France.

Note: This can be a sensitive topic. Groups that migrate tend to be from difficult socio-economic circumstances. If students choose any of the topics that are listed above, encourage them to be thoughtful and considerate as they research these migrations.

TIP **If students participated in the Expansion activity, consider using the same groups. Or, consider having students complete the Expansion activity at this point.**

Exercise B. | Researching Make sure students know which topic they are researching. Encourage them to use online sources as well as other secondary sources such as books or journals.

Exercise C. | Planning a Presentation Have students work together to plan and organize information about their topic. Remind them to practice their presentation and give them time in class if possible.

TIP **Refer students to the Presentation Skills box at the bottom of the page. Inform students that listeners need to be directed by the speakers to the most important part of the visuals. This is especially true in a presentation that has a lot of pictures and graphs. Encourage students to include several types of visuals in their presentations.**

Exercise D. | Presentation Write on the board the amount of time students will have for their presentations. Encourage them to prepare some remarks. They should include the phrases and nonverbal cues in the Presentation Skills box.

Allow time in class for students to make their presentations. Also consider having a question and answer period after each presentation so students can practice asking and answering questions about their topic.

Fascinating Planet

Academic Track
Earth Science

Academic Pathways:
Lesson A: Listening to a Documentary
Explaining Causes and Effects
Lesson B: Listening to an Informal Conversation
Doing and Discussing Internet Research

Unit Theme

Earth science is a general term to describe the study of the planet. This unit looks at some places on the planet that have fascinating formations, and it discusses World Heritage sites, which are places of special cultural or physical significance.

Unit 4 explores the topic of earth science as it relates to:

- fascinating locations and formations
- causes and effects
- the World Heritage program
- national parks

Think and Discuss *(page 61)*

5 mins

Tongariro was the first national park in New Zealand and only the fourth in the world. The park has lakes, fields, and forests, but it is well known for several other reasons, namely its Maori culture and volcanic characteristics. The park was founded in 1887.

National parks are owned by the government and are protected from human exploitation. They are open to the public, but only for educational, cultural, or recreational purposes.

- Discuss the questions.
- Extend the discussion by asking students if they have ever visited a national park. Ask what they liked about the park and why they think that land was made into a national park.
- Explain that land must meet certain requirements before it can be declared a national park. Ask students to guess what features it must have.

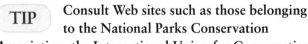

Consult Web sites such as those belonging to the National Parks Conservation Association, the International Union for Conservation of Nature, or the National Park Service.

Exploring the Theme: Fascinating Planet *(pages 62-63)*

15 mins

The opening spread features a map and pictures from Tsingy de Bemaraha National Park. Check students' comprehension and activate their prior knowledge.

T: Where is Tsingy de Bemaraha National Park?
S: In Madagascar.
T: OK, and on what continent can I find Madagascar?
S: In Africa.
T: Yes. What is one kind of animal that lives there?
S: Dragonflies.

- Discuss the questions.
- Have students read the introductory information.

Pronunciation Note

Tongariro: tahn-ga-**reer**-oh
Tsingy de Bemaraha: zing-ee day behm-ah-ra-ha

30 mins

Building and Using Vocabulary *(pages 64-65)*

WARM-UP

The Lesson A target vocabulary is presented as individual words in a box. Explain that it is a good idea to think about vocabulary before seeing it in context.

- Explain that looking at the words in advance and thinking about what you already know saves time because not all the words need to be looked up later.
- Tell students to look up words they don't already know. Doing so means the words won't be encountered for the first time when they see or hear them in context.

Building Vocabulary

Exercise A. | Using a Dictionary Ask students to identify the words they already know. Remind them that everyone will have different answers.

track 1-36

Exercise B. | When everyone has had enough time to look up the words they don't know, have students complete the sentences. Encourage them not to use their dictionaries anymore. Point out that sometimes words have to change form or tense to be correct.

Answer Key

1. stone	**5.** form	**9.** lack
2. crack	**6.** rare	**10.** protect
3. deep	**7.** dissolve	
4. sharp	**8.** eroded	

IDEAS FOR... Expansion

Have students bring in a paragraph from another textbook. Ask each student to create an exercise like exercise **A** for a classmate. Students should choose 10 words from the paragraph to write on a piece of paper and then exchange the paper with a partner. The partners will identify the words they already know and look up new words. After the activity, students should share the original paragraph so their partners can see the context.

track 1-37

Exercise C. | Meaning from Context Challenge students to complete the activity without using a dictionary.

Answer Key	lack, deep, dissolved, rare, protected

IDEAS FOR... Checking Comprehension

Have each student write a sentence using the incorrect answer choices so they can clearly see the difference between each set of two words.

Using Vocabulary

Exercise D. | Discussion Give students time to discuss the questions. Have them share answers with the class.

track 1-38

Exercise E. | Meaning from Context Challenge students to complete the activity without using a dictionary.

Answer Key	formed, stone, sharp, erode, cracks

Exercise F. | Discussion Give students time to discuss the questions. Have them share answers with the class.

Exercise G. | Critical Thinking After students discuss the questions, ask them to talk about their answers to one of the questions as a class.

IDEAS FOR... Multi-level Classes

Have students of similar levels work together. For summation of discussions, have the lower-level students summarize question 1 since it is easier than the other three questions.

Pronunciation Note

Jiuzhaigou: jo-jai-go

45 mins

Developing Listening Skills *(pages 66-67)*

Before Listening

Exercise A. | Explain that often listeners have to apply the words they hear to pictures or other visuals.

TIP Read the sentences aloud and have students mark the answers as you read them.

Answer Key	**1.** b **2.** e **3.** a **4.** c **5.** f **6.** d

Tuning Out Distractions | Ask one student to read the information. Open a discussion about distractions. Ask students to discuss and compare the locations where they study.

track 1-39

Exercise B. | Warn students that the conversation contains distractions.

Answer Key	**1.** b **2.** c **3.** c **4.** b

Listening: A Documentary

track 1-40

Exercise A. | Ask students to first notice the distractions and list any they hear.

Answer Key

1. daughter's voice **2.** honking car horns
3. window closing **4.** door opening and closing

Note: Some students might also list music as a distraction.

track 1-40

Exercise B. | Note-Taking Have students listen to the audio again and complete the notes. Require students to take notes for the whole passage to be used in exercise **C**.

Answer Key

1. it's a national park **2.** impossible for people to go there; walk barefoot **1.** stone peaks are sharp as knives **2.** caves and water to deal with

IDEAS FOR... Multi-level Classes

Pair a higher-level student with a lower-level student to compare notes. This technique ensures the lower-level students have enough information to complete more exercises.

Critical Thinking Focus | Read the information in the book and review the previous graphic organizers.

track 1-40

Exercise C. | Using a Graphic Organizer Have a volunteer write the answers on the board.

Answer Key

Effects: **1.** lack of visitors/tourism **2.** lack of money
3. no funding for scientific research on Tsingy

After Listening

Exercise A. | Review cause and effect. Remind students that certain words can signal cause and effect. *Because* is one word that commonly signals a cause and effect relationship.

Answer Key

1. The animals in the Tsingy are protected because it's a national park.

2. The peaks in the Tsingy are very sharp because rain has eroded the stone.

3. Because the Tsingy is almost impossible to get to, not many tourists visit it.

4. The caves became larger because the stone that had divided them collapsed.

5. Because there is little money for research, scientists aren't sure how climate change is affecting the Tsingy.

Exercise B. | Discussion Have students work together to notice the placement of causes and effects.

45 mins

Exploring Spoken English *(pages 68-70)*

Grammar: The Simple Past Tense with the Past Continuous Tense

Exercise A. | Prior Knowledge Challenge students to answer the questions. Tell them they can use knowledge they already have to get the right answers.

> **IDEAS FOR... Presenting Grammar**
>
> Ask students to think about the verb tenses used in exercise **A.** Elicit answers about the forms including the past tense and the *-ing* form of the verb. Go over the information and examples in the box. Ask students to write a sentence about the picture of eco-tourists in the book. Make sure everyone understands that their sentences should include a past tense form and a past continuous form. Have students form groups to write sentences about themselves.
>
> Draw a time line on the board. Ask one student from each group to write one of their sentences on the board. Have a volunteer mark the time line for the activities in the student's sentence. Repeat the process. See page 215 of the *Independent Student Handbook* for an example of a time line.

Exercise B. | Go over the directions. Ask two students to read the speech bubbles. Give students time to complete the activity.

Answer Key *(Answers may vary.)*

1. While I was doing research in the Tsingy de Bemaraha last September, I discovered a new species of frog.
2. My neighbor was painting the front of her house when I got home from work.
3. Debora saw a bear while she was hiking at the national park.
4. The train arrived while Mitch and Jean were buying tickets at the ticket counter.
5. Last night while we were watching TV, the dog started to bark.

> **IDEAS FOR... Expansion**
>
> Draw attention back to the speech bubbles and point out there is often more than one way to write sentences. Have students rewrite their sentences from exercise **B** another way.

Language Function: Talking about Historical Events

Read the information in the box aloud. Ask students in what classes they might talk about historical events.

Draw a time line for the example in the book.

TIP **Bring in sample paragraphs from textbooks in other disciplines so students can see how widely used the past continuous tense is.**

> **IDEAS FOR... Expansion**
>
> Ask each student to bring in a paragraph or page from one of his or her textbooks for another class. Have them highlight the uses of past tense in one color and past continuous in another. See who has the most highlights of each color. Open a discussion about what each passage was about and compare the disciplines, topics, and reasons for use of the verb tenses.

Exercise A. | Draw attention to the box. Have a student volunteer read the information aloud.

- Give students time to think about the four dates and descriptions.
- Have pairs of students talk about their lives or countries.
- Have students draw a time line for the four dates and their activities.

TIP **Arrange for students to use the school computer lab or assign this exercise as a research task so students can better discuss the answers in class.**

Pronunciation Note

Lençóis Maranhenses: lain-soice mah-rahn-yain-sayce

Exercise B. | Give students time to read the information and chart.

TIP **Walk around the classroom to help students with vocabulary questions. Consider assigning the reading passage as homework so students will be prepared to participate in exercise C in class.**

Exercise C. | Remind students there is more than one possible correct answer for each question.

Answer Key

1. When *Citizen Kane* was released, World War II was going on.
2. The first computer was built while the United Nations was creating an education and cultural organization.
3. Miguel Alemán became Mexico's president while UNESCO was holding its first session.
4. UNESCO countries were discussing ways to conserve places of importance when Martin Luther King, Jr. was killed.
5. While Neil Armstrong walked on the moon, UNESCO was discussing ways to conserve important places on Earth.

30-45 mins

Speaking *(page 71)*

Explaining Causes and Effects

IDEAS FOR... Presenting Grammar

Before class, write the causes and effects from the sample sentences on the board. Scramble the order. Ask students to identify whether each one is a cause or an effect. Mark *C* by clauses students identify as *causes* and *E* by those they designate as *effects*.

Review clauses and the use of the word *because* in cause-and-effect statements. Tell students there are other words that can be used as well. Go over the examples in the box.

Revisit the sentence halves on the board and make any corrections.

Exercises A and B. | Draw students' attention to the flow charts and ask students to pay special attention to the arrows. Have students work in pairs to talk about the flow charts. Ask them to reverse roles and then explain the other chart.

IDEAS FOR... Expansion

Ask students to work in groups to create a flow chart about the advantages and disadvantages of the city they live in. Ask each group to present their flow charts to the rest of the class.

Exercise C. | **Critical Thinking** Have partners join another pair of students to answer the critical thinking questions.

IDEAS FOR... Expansion

Divide the class into two teams for a debate. Assign one team to argue the advantages and the other to argue the disadvantages of World Heritage status. Let students use their notes from the discussion and give them time to prepare their remarks. Give each team two minutes to present an introduction, two minutes for each argument, one minute to rebut arguments from the other team, and two minutes for closing arguments (summary). Let students choose who will be the speakers, but encourage them to have enough arguments that each person can speak at least once.

TIP **Research different debate structures in advance and adjust the debate to fit your class time and students' abilities.**

IDEAS FOR... Multi-level Classes

Mix the levels for the debate so that one team does not have more higher- or lower-level students than the other.

30 mins

Viewing: The Giant's Causeway *(pages 72-73)*

Overview of the Video | In modern times, a causeway is a road or railway, usually elevated, that extends across water. Some more well-known causeways include the roads connecting Singapore and Malaysia, and Venice to mainland Italy.

The Giant's Causeway, in Ireland, is not man-made. It is the result of a volcano and there are many legends associated with its history. Today, it is one of the most visited sites in Ireland.

Before Viewing

Remind students that it is helpful to think about vocabulary before viewing a video so that new words won't slow down or hinder comprehension.

Exercise A. | Using a Dictionary Inform students that the video may have some words they are not familiar with and that several words are scientific.

Answer Key	**1.** d **2.** e **3.** f **4.** c **5.** a **6.** b

Exercise B. | Critical Thinking Remind students that two answers are required for each set of causes and effects.

Answer Key *(Answers may vary.)*

1. Because pressure built up in a volcano, hot lava . . . ; Pressure built up in a volcano, so hot lava . . .
2. Since the lava cooled slowly, the basalt . . . ; The basalt cracked and formed columns because the lava . . .
3. The basalt columns eroded. As a result, some of the stones . . . ; Some of the stones look like steps because the basalt columns . . .
4. The stones looked like a causeway, so people made up . . . ; People made up a story about a giant since the stones looked like a causeway.
5. The giant decided to go to Scotland, so he built . . . ; The giant built a stone causeway since he decided . . .
6. The Giant's Causeway is interesting. Therefore, many people visit it each year; Many people visit the Giant's Causeway since it is . . .

Exercise C. | Using the Simple Past with Past Continuous Tell students to use the information in exercise **B** to answer the questions.

Answer Key

1. Pressure was building up in the volcano before it erupted.
2. While the lava was cooling, the basalt cracked and formed columns.

While Viewing

2:37

Exercise A. | After students watch the video and answer the questions, go over the answers as a class.

Answer Key	**1.** 40,000 **2.** 25 **3.** 60 **4.** 1800s

2:37

Exercise B. | Note-Taking Encourage students to use a T-chart to take notes.

Answer Key

According to the legend: Finn was angry with a Scottish giant. Because he was not a good swimmer, he used rocks to build a road to Scotland.

According to geologists: A volcano erupted, spewing lava quickly and making flows that were very thick. The lava dried and shrunk, making the many-sided columns.

Exercise C. | Give students time to talk and encourage them to use their notes.

After Viewing

Exercises A and B. | Collaboration Explain to students that this activity allows them to be creative. Have students tell their stories to another group.

30 mins

Building and Using Vocabulary *(pages 74-75)*

WARM-UP

Students are asked to read and listen to information about New Zealand's Tongariro National Park. The information is presented in text and illustrations. Point out that this presentation is similar to what is in academic textbooks. Ask students what they like and dislike about this format.

Building Vocabulary

track 1-41

Exercise A. | Meaning from Context Give students time to read the information and direct them to pay special attention to the vocabulary words being used in context.

Using Vocabulary

Exercise B. | After students read, review parts of speech and emphasize how a word's part of speech can help students determine the correct answers. Remind them that they might have to change the form of a word to match the definition.

Answer Key

1. compromise	**5.** surface	**9.** balance
2. threat	**6.** options	**10.** basis
3. edge	**7.** sufficient	
4. constantly	**8.** features	

IDEAS FOR... Checking Comprehension

Call on individual students to answer questions using the vocabulary and information in the article. Make sure every student has a chance to answer at least one question.

T: What is a **compromise**?
S1: It's an agreement.
T: Yes. Have you ever had to make a **compromise**?
S1: Yes. One time I **compromised** with my lab partner.

Exercise C. | Have students complete the dialog and then read it aloud.

Answer Key **1.** basis **2.** balance **3.** options **4.** threat **5.** compromise

IDEAS FOR... Expansion

Have students write new dialogs using the vocabulary words. Allow time for them to perform their dialogs for the class.

Exercise D. | Brainstorming Have students work in small groups to brainstorm answers to the questions.

IDEAS FOR... Expansion

Use the brainstorming activity as a game. See which group can think of the most answers. Give everyone the same amount of time. After the time limit, have each group read their answers. If another team has the same idea, both teams cross it off their lists. Each idea that no other team has is worth one point. After three questions, the team with the most points "wins" the brainstorming challenge.

Developing Listening Skills

45 mins

(pages 76-77)

Before Listening

Exercise A. | Make sure students read the question in the direction line before reading and listening to the passage.

Answer Key

The park is unusual because it has characteristics of both a desert and a seascape.

IDEAS FOR... Multi-level Classes

Call on higher-level students to give examples of how the Lençóis is like a desert and how it is like a seascape. Doing so keeps the higher-level students engaged.

Exercise B. | Define intonation for the students (*variation in pitch*). Explain that native English speakers use a lot of intonation when they speak. Play the passage again and ask students to pay special attention to the underlined sentences.

Pronunciation: Intonation for Choices and Lists

track 1-43

Continue talking about intonation. Teach students that different intonation patterns serve different purposes. Go over the information in the box and explain rising and falling intonation when giving two and three choices. Have students practice the examples with each other.

Exercises C and D. | Tell students to mark the sentences with arrows as they listen. Then give them time to practice reading them aloud with a partner.

Answer Key

1. We have coffee, tea, and lemonade.
2. Do you think the salary they're offering is sufficient, or will you ask for more?
3. We could stay home, or we could stay out late, or we could compromise.
4. Would you rather go to Spain or to Portugal?
5. She's going to Korea, Japan, and China.

Listening: An Informal Conversation

Exercise A. | **Listening for Main Ideas** The listening passage in this section is a conversation.

Answer Key

1. vacation destination
2. New Zealand, Australia
3. one week in New Zealand and one week in Australia

Exercise B. | **Listening for Details**

Answer Key **1.** a **2.** a **3.** b **4.** a **5.** b

After Listening

Self-Reflection | Have students work with a partner to discuss the questions.

TIP Walk around the classroom to make sure students are using correct intonation.

IDEAS FOR... Expansion

Have students write dialogs for one of the questions. Give them time to perform their conversations.

30 mins

Exploring Spoken English *(pages 78-79)*

Grammar: *So* + Adjective + *That*

Exercise A. | Prior Knowledge Challenge students to read the conversation and answer the questions. Reinforce the benefits of activating prior knowledge.

Answer Key **1.** b **2.** b

> **IDEAS FOR... Presenting Grammar**
>
> Write the first half of this sentence on the board: *Our English class is so good that . . .* Ask students to write the second half on a piece of paper or on an index card.
>
> Go over the information and examples in the box. Ask students to write a sentence about the picture in the book: *The polar bear is so...* Ask volunteers to read their sentences about the picture.
>
> Give students time to make sure their sentence about the English class is grammatically correct. Collect all the sentences and read them aloud.

Exercise B. | Have students write at least two endings to each sentence with a partner. Solicit volunteers to share their answers with the class.

Answer Key *(Answers will vary.)*

TIP Consider having students work in teams to brainstorm adjectives to use in exercise C.

Exercise C. | Allow students adequate time to write new sentences.

Presentation Skills: Making Eye Contact | Ask students to list reasons why a presenter who doesn't make eye contact is not as strong as one who does. Elicit answers such as *eye contact makes me pay attention* or *eye contact makes the speaker less boring/ more interesting*. Direct students to review pages 211–213 of the *Independent Student Handbook*.

Exercise D. | Presentation Have each student read two sentences from exercise **C**, making sure to make eye contact.

Exercise E. | Brainstorming Have students think of places that match each description.

Exercise F. | Ask students to use each of their places in a sentence that includes *so + adjective + that + noun*. Have two students read the speech bubbles as examples.

Language Function: Responding to Suggestions

Go over the information in the box.

Practice using the phrases from the box when discussing the topics.

> **IDEAS FOR... Expansion**
>
> Have students form small groups. Ask students if they can think of other ways to go along with or not go along with suggestions. After sufficient time, ask each group to write their additional words and phrases on the board. Encourage students to write any new phrases in their notebooks.

45 mins

Engage: Doing and Discussing Internet Research *(page 80)*

WARM-UP

Ask students what kinds of research they do on the Internet. As they share answers, begin to focus their attention on academic projects and research. Continue the discussion by asking students if they've used the Internet for research. Ask them to talk about their methods, favorite research sites, and good search engines. Explain that many academic projects involve doing and presenting Internet research.

TIP **As you present the questions students should ask themselves when doing Internet research, consider having your own "rules" or school "rules" for students to follow. For example, some instructors prefer that information be no older than five years old and prohibit the use of unreliable Web sites such as Wikipedia.**

As you go through each question, ask students to think of specific sources for each one. For example, for accurate and reliable information, elicit answers such as *CNN* or *The Wall Street Journal*. Ask students to think of sources that they need to more carefully analyze, such as *YouTube*.

Exercise A. | Give students time to work in the school's computer lab to find the answers for the parks online. Or, assign the research as homework and have them compare answers with a partner in class.

Answer Key

Note that these numbers are approximate.

Jiuzhaigou National Park:
1982
448 sq mi (720 sq km)
2 million
yes/1982

The Tsingy de Bemaraha:
1998
600 sq mi (965 sq km)
1765
yes/1990

Tongariro National Park:
1887
300 sq mi (790 sq km)
800,000
yes/1993

Lençóis Maranhenses National Park:
1981
600 sq mi (965 sq km)
60,000
no

Exercise B. | Discussion Have students work together to compare answers. After checking answers, see what sources students used and which key word searches generated the best information. Open a class discussion to see if the sites they used are recent, relevant, accurate, and reliable.

IDEAS FOR... Expansion

Ask students to keep a log of their sources. Consider having them write their sources in MLA format or the citation format most used in their own discipline.

IDEAS FOR... Expansion

Have students work in small groups to brainstorm a list of other national parks. Ask them to do Internet research and compile a short presentation on their park for the rest of the class. Depending on your class time and schedule, require them to make a presentation about their national park to review the presentation materials from Unit 3.

Making a Living, Making a Difference

Academic Track
Economics/Business

Academic Pathways:
Lesson A: Listening to a Guest Speaker
Making Comparisons
Lesson B: Listening to a Class Question and Answer Session
Giving a Presentation Based on Internet Research

Unit Theme

Economics is the study of the way in which money, industry, and commerce are organized in a society. It includes the everyday work of people who are producing, buying, and selling goods and services. It also looks at how those products and services are used by consumers. This unit looks at a variety of businesses, goods, and workers around the world.

Unit 5 explores the topic of economics as it relates to:

- making a living
- impacting the world
- making comparisons
- asking questions

5 mins

Think and Discuss *(page 81)*

There are many types of employment, such as full-time, part-time, or self-employment. There are also many types of companies, including large and established companies or small and new companies.

- Initiate a discussion about companies that students are familiar with. Make a list on the board. Have students classify them into two categories: large and small.
- Continue the discussion by asking students what benefits large and small companies have. Also ask what they think the drawbacks are.
- Discuss the questions in the book and ask students to think about the benefits and drawbacks to self-employment.
- Have students talk about whether they would prefer to work for a large company or a small company.

TIP **Focus attention on the picture. Ask students to think about a large city they've been in and what other types of self-employed people they saw there.**

15 mins

Exploring the Theme: Making a Living, Making a Difference *(pages 82-83)*

The opening spread features a picture of a marketplace in Morocco and explains the difference between entrepreneurs and people who participate in cooperatives. Make sure students understand the difference between the two. Examples of entrepreneurs are Bill Gates and Oprah Winfrey.

- Discuss the questions.
- Have students read the introductory information.

IDEAS FOR... Expansion

Have students form small groups. Ask them to imagine their group is a cooperative. Have them brainstorm ideas for their business and discuss where their business will be. Open a class discussion to compare ideas.

45 mins

Building and Using Vocabulary *(pages 84-85)*

WARM-UP

The Lesson A target vocabulary is presented in a similar way as the vocabulary in Unit 4 is presented. Remind students of the reasons for identifying words they already know.

- Ask students to list some well-known businesspeople that they are familiar with. Elicit answers such as Ray Kroc (McDonald's), Mark Zuckerberg (Facebook), or Meg Whitman (eBay).
- List their answers on the board to refer to later.

Building Vocabulary

Exercise A. | Using a Dictionary Ask students to check the words they already know. Encourage them to use a dictionary to look up new words.

> IDEAS FOR... **Checking Comprehension**
>
> Refer back to the list of businesspeople on the board. Ask students which vocabulary words can be used to describe them.

Exercise B. | Give students time to read the article and fill in the blanks

Answer Key	**1.** enterprises **2.** owners **3.** cooperate **4.** wealth **5.** diverse

TIP As you go over the answers, have students identify the context clues and suffixes that helped determine the answers.

track 2-2

Exercise C. | Play the audio for the class.

Exercise D. | Discussion Have pairs summarize their answers.

Using Vocabulary

Exercise E. | Using a Dictionary Emphasize that the identification strategy is effective in expanding vocabulary and improving comprehension. Have students complete exercise **E**.

> IDEAS FOR... **Checking Comprehension**
>
> Ask students to work in groups to answer these questions: *Who is a successful entrepreneur? What is an effective study strategy? What is one way to help someone in poverty? How much do you think teachers earn? How should business owners assess their employees?*

Exercise F. | Give students time to read the article and fill in the blanks.

Answer Key	**1.** poverty **2.** entrepreneurs **3.** earn **4.** effective **5.** assess

track 2-3

Exercise G. | Play the audio for the class.

Exercise H. | Discussion Have students summarize their answers.

Exercise I. | Give students adequate time to reverse roles.

> IDEAS FOR... **Expansion**
>
> Begin a word form chart on the board for students to use with the vocabulary words from exercises **A** and **E**. Have them change the suffixes to make the words into nouns, verbs, adjectives, and adverbs. Remind them that not every word has every form and they should put an *X* in the boxes with no answer.

45 mins

Developing Listening Skills *(pages 86-87)*

Before Listening

track 2-4

Exercise A. | Explain that activating prior knowledge before listening helps comprehension. Point out that a good way to activate knowledge is to read something about the topic.

Exercise B. | Discussion Emphasize that discussing topics also activates prior knowledge. Give students time to discuss the questions.

Critical Thinking Focus: Identifying the Speaker's Purpose | Point out that identifying the speaker's purpose is another way to improve listening comprehension.

> **IDEAS FOR... Multi-level Classes**
>
> Put students in small groups. Ask higher-level students to read the Critical Thinking Focus box aloud and lead the group in discussion for exercise **C**. This strategy will keep higher-level students engaged and challenge them with leadership responsibilities.

Exercise C. | Critical Thinking Give students time to work together and challenge them to think of more than one answer for each situation. To extend the discussion, ask them for specific examples. For instance, students might say that the purpose of a stand-up comedian is to entertain and a specific example of a stand-up comedian might be Ricky Gervais.

Listening: A Guest Speaker

track 2-5

Exercise A. | Listening for Main Ideas The passage is a speech being given by a guest speaker. Have students listen and answer the questions.

Answer Key

1. Marsha Nolan, director of Worldwide Co-op
2. members of wildlife organizations
3. to explain that the ideas behind the Irulas's co-op can be used in many places

Exercise B. | Walk around the classroom to elicit reasons for students' answers to question 3.

track 2-5

Exercise C. | Listening for Details Play the segment again and tell students to focus on details, including numbers.

Answer Key	**1.** b **2.** b **3.** a **4.** c

> **IDEAS FOR... Checking Comprehension**
>
> Ask students questions using information from exercises **A** and **B**.
>
> T: Who is Marsha Nolan?
>
> S1: She is the speaker and the director of Worldwide Co-op.
>
> T: In what country do 30,000 people die from snake bites each year?
>
> S2: India.

After Listening

Critical Thinking | Have two students read the speech bubbles. Ask students to form teams to write similar dialogs.

TIP If time allows, have students do an online search for more endangered animals that are being killed by humans.

> **IDEAS FOR... Expansion**
>
> Watch an excerpt from a documentary about endangered animals, such as *Arctic Tale*, or a clip from *YouTube*. In groups, have students write a short movie script about one of the animals they saw in the documentary or clip. Ask them to perform their script or actually videotape the script to show in class.

45 mins

Exploring Spoken English *(pages 88-90)*

Language Function: Using Numbers and Statistics

It is important for students to be able to understand spoken numbers and visualize the numerals when they hear the words.

Exercises A and B. | Read the numbers in the box aloud and have students repeat them before asking them to write the numbers in exercise **B**.

TIP **Remind students that there are some variations in the way native speakers say numbers. Give the example *620,000* and say it with and without *and*: *six hundred twenty thousand; six hundred and twenty thousand.***

Answer Key

1. fifty thousand
2. three million two hundred thousand
3. four hundred
4. seven hundred forty thousand
5. eight billion
6. one million, two hundred ninety-seven thousand, three hundred

Exercise C. | Give students time to practice the numbers in exercise **B**.

IDEAS FOR... Expansion

Demonstrate some of the patterns and pauses native speakers use when giving long strings of digits, addresses, and phone numbers. Have students come up with more examples, write them down, and then read them to a partner. After students have exchanged numbers, give them time to check their answers.

track 2-6

Exercise D. | Draw students' attention to the photo and ask students if they are familiar with kudzu. Activate their prior knowledge by talking about the picture. Tell them to listen for statistics.

Answer Key

1. 300
2. 70,000,000
3. 20,000
4. 150,000
5. 8,000,000

TIP **Tell students to write the numeric version of the numbers.**

Exercise E. | Have students follow the instructions and practice dialogs.

IDEAS FOR... Expansion

Have students write the numbers they hear in exercises **D** and **E** in word form.

IDEAS FOR... Expansion

Explain that a fun party game or warm-up activity in the United States is called "Two Truths and a Lie." As homework, have students do some research and write two truths and a lie about a business or businessperson they find interesting. Have them read their truths and lie to the class and see if students can guess which statements are true. The student who "tricks" the most people wins.

Exercise F. | Give students time to read the story or ask volunteers to read it aloud. Answer any vocabulary questions that students may have.

Exercise G. | Discussion Have students work in small groups to discuss the questions.

Draw students' attention to the Small Business Statistics box. Remind students that boxed text and statistics are often a large part of academic writing.

TIP **Show examples of other charts of statistics from books or journals.**

Exercise H. | Draw students' attention to the Quick Facts statistics on page 90. Tell students to refer to this information as they work with their partner to ask and answer the questions. They will need to use arithmetic for some of the answers.

Answer Key

1. 1,275,000
2. 60,300,000
3. 9,800,000
4. 670,058
5. 599,333
6. 19,695
7. Bankruptcies increased between 2006 and 2009.
8. Start-ups declined between 2006 and 2009.

Exercise I. | Discussion Give students time to discuss the statistics. Prepare them to summarize their answers for the rest of the class.

Grammar: Making Comparisons with *as . . . as*

IDEAS FOR... **Presenting Grammar**

Have students work in pairs. Ask them to make a list of three things they have in common. Then ask them to make a list of three things they do not have in common. Go over the information in the Grammar box. Solicit one volunteer to come stand by you. Ask students to make comparisons.

T: What comparisons can you make?
S: Julio is not as tall as you are.
T: That's true. What is another one?
S: Julio doesn't talk as loudly as you.

After several examples, have students work with their partner to write sentences using the lists they made earlier.

Have students write sentences with the words in the book. Emphasize that all of the statements must be true.

30 mins

Speaking *(page 91)*

Making Comparisons

Exercise A. | Draw students' attention to the pictures and captions. Ask students to read the speech bubbles and then write their own dialogs.

IDEAS FOR... **Multi-level Classes**

Have students of similar levels work together. Higher-level students can write longer dialogs.

Exercise B. | Discussion Require students to use comparison language in their answers. Walk around the classroom to make sure the language is grammatically correct.

Exercise C. | Presentation Ask a member of each group to share ideas. Allow time for students to discuss differences of opinion.

IDEAS FOR... **Expansion**

Put students in groups. You may consider grouping students with similar majors or interests. Ask students to find a textbook in their field or a reliable Web site with a box or table of statistics. Have them bring their examples to class. Within their groups, have them compare and contrast the statistics and presentation of statistics. Then compile a new box or table with statistics to present to the class.

30 mins

Viewing: The Business of Cranberries *(pages 92-93)*

Overview of the Video | Cranberries are a large commercial crop in some parts of the United States, especially northern states such as Maine, Michigan, and Wisconsin, as well as in Canada, especially the provinces of Nova Scotia and British Columbia. Cranberry bushes grow low to the ground and in bogs.

Cranberries have a variety of uses. They're often seen in the form of juices or sauces or dried fruit. Cranberry sauce is often served with roasted turkey at American Thanksgiving dinners.

Before Viewing

- Ask students to look at the title and photo and answer these questions:

  1. Have you tasted cranberries? Did you like the taste or not?
  2. In what forms have you had cranberries (juice, pie)?

Exercise A. | Using a Dictionary Tell students that the words in the exercise are used in the video. Allow them to use a dictionary if necessary.

Answer Key	**1.** d **2.** h **3.** a **4.** e **5.** f **6.** c **7.** b **8.** g

IDEAS FOR... **Checking Comprehension**

Go around the room and ask each student a like or dislike question.

T: Would you like to **harvest** cranberries?
S1: No, I don't think so.
T: Why not?
S1: It sounds like a lot of work.
T: If you were a farmer, would you like a **bumper crop**?
S2: Yes.
T: Why?
S2: Because it means I have a large harvest.

Exercise B. | Prior Knowledge Give students time to discuss the answers to the quiz. Remind them that quizzes like this will help them start thinking about the topic. Thinking in advance about the topic improves listening comprehension.

Answer Key	**1.** a **2.** c **3.** a **4.** b **5.** c

While Viewing

3:59 **Exercise A. |** After students watch the video, discuss how they knew the answers were true or false.

Answer Key	**1.** T **2.** T **3.** T **4.** T **5.** F **6.** T

3:59 **Exercises B and C. |** Play the video again. Check students' answers in exercise **B** before they work on exercise **C**.

Answer Key	5, 3, 1, 2, 4

After Viewing

Exercise A. | Ask students to write sentences using their own opinions. Remind them there are no right or wrong answers. They should use *as . . . as* or *not as . . . as*.

Exercise B. | Discussion Give students time to share their ideas.

Exercise C. | Critical Thinking Have pairs from exercise **B** join another pair to discuss the questions. Have one student summarize answers for the group.

IDEAS FOR... **Expansion**

Have students continue working in groups. Ask them to think of a new food business, such as a restaurant, grocery store, or a catering service. Ask students to discuss and share the advantages and disadvantages of owning such a business and have them estimate how much money it will take to start the business.

30 mins

Building and Using Vocabulary *(pages 94-95)*

WARM-UP

Students are asked to read and listen to a conversation about a charity. Ask students if they have ever done anything charitable. Solicit answers such as *donating old clothing, helping to build a house,* or *teaching someone to read.* Accept any reasonable answers.

Building Vocabulary

track 2-7

Exercise A. | Meaning from Context Tell students to pay special attention to the words in blue.

IDEAS FOR... Checking Comprehension

Have students use each word in a sentence they write on their own.

Exercise B. | Discussion Have students discuss the three questions. Ask a volunteer from each group to write the charities they are familiar with on the board.

Exercise C. | Using a Dictionary Have students read the conversation aloud.

TIP **Encourage students to record themselves and play the recording back, comparing it to the original.**

IDEAS FOR... Multi-level Classes

Pair students of similar levels. Give them time to read the conversation with their partner. Lower-level students will feel more comfortable after they hear it.

track 2-8

Exercise D. | Meaning from Context Draw students' attention to the book review. Remind students to pay attention to the words in blue.

Using Vocabulary

Exercise E. | Encourage students to try the activity without using a dictionary.

Answer Key

1. cash	**3.** outcome	**5.** transfer
2. responsible	**4.** payment	

Exercise F. | Have students fill in the blanks. Go over the answers as a class.

Answer Key

1. cash	**4.** rate, drop	**7.** transfer
2. responsible	**5.** fundamental	**8.** charity
3. payment	**6.** concept	**9.** outcome

Exercise G. | Ask a pair of volunteers to read one of the dialogs aloud.

IDEAS FOR... Expansion

Have students write original dialogs using the vocabulary items. Then have them write the dialog on the board, drawing lines where the vocabulary items should be. Remind them to provide enough context so that other students can fill in the blanks correctly. Ask the rest of the students to complete the dialogs on the board with the vocabulary items.

45 mins

Developing Listening Skills
(pages 96-97)

track 2-9

Pronunciation: Contractions

It can be difficult for second language learners to understand contractions. Explain that native speakers often combine two or more words. Emphasize that it is important to notice contractions because they often carry significant meaning. Go over the examples in the book.

Give students time to listen to and then practice reading the contractions and sentences. Have them write sentences of their own using contractions.

Before Listening

Review the information on page 86 about identifying the speaker's purpose.

Listening: A Class Question and Answer Session

track 2-10

Exercise A. | The conversation in this listening section is a question and answer session. Review the question and answer format in Unit 2.

Answer Key

1. Donald Yates, someone with a lot of experience with charity organizations
2. to answer questions about charitable organizations

track 2-10

Exercise B.

Answer Key

1. I'd = I would
2. I'm = I am
3. professor's = professor is
4. I've = I have

track 2-11

Exercise C. | Tell students that this is a challenging activity. Let them know you are willing to play the audio more than once.

Answer Key

1. people really use the money for important things
2. you don't ask people to work for the money
3. makes decisions about the money
4. communities get things like new schools and roads

IDEAS FOR... Checking Comprehension

Give a "pop quiz" on contractions. Say the contractions used in this unit and have students say the two words that make the contraction. If time allows, say two words and ask students to say the contraction they form. Contractions from this unit include *I'd* (*I would*), *don't* (*do not*), *I'm* (*I am*), *I've* (*I have*), and *professor's* (*professor is*). For an additional challenge, use contractions from the box on page 96 or create your own.

track 2-11

Exercise D. | Note-Taking Remind students that note-taking is an important part of listening in English. Give an example of how notes may not be exact and answers may not be complete sentences.

Answer Key *(Answers may vary.)*

1. people make good decisions, buy things for children, farmers buy tools
2. people already working hard: families with children, crops, more than one job
3. money given to large group or governments or same payment given to every adult in village
4. charities decide or villages pool money to build something, still learning what works best

After Listening

Critical Thinking | Have students work together to discuss the questions. Make sure they explain their answers.

30 mins

Exploring Spoken English
(pages 98-99)

Grammar: Indirect Questions

IDEAS FOR... Presenting Grammar

Write two questions on the board: *Why should I study English?* and *Can you tell me why I should study English?* Ask students what question is being asked in each. Make sure they notice the question is exactly the same.

Go over the information in the Grammar box. Make sure that students can tell the difference between direct and indirect questions. Open a discussion about situations in which indirect questions are more appropriate. List the situations on the board. Have students give examples of indirect questions for each situation.

Exercise A. | Have students rewrite the questions. Call on volunteers to share their questions. Challenge students to use a variety of phrases from the Grammar box. Point out the indirect questions that do not use a question mark.

Answer Key *(Answers may vary.)*

1. Do you know where the cash for the payments comes from?
2. Can you tell me when the final exam will be given?
3. I'd like to know if there are any poor people in Japan.
4. Can you please explain why you gave me a C on this paper?
5. I was wondering how much money elderly people in Namibia get.
6. Do you know who the director of that organization is?

Exercise B. | Have students vote on an imaginary topic for a speaker to talk about. Have students prepare questions.

Student to Student: Showing Interest in What a Speaker Is Saying | Go over the information and phrases in the box. Remind students that being in the audience is just as important as being the speaker. Ask if students have any other phrases they would add to those listed in the book.

Exercise C. | Have students role-play with one student playing the role of the imaginary speaker, and the others asking questions and showing interest.

Language Function: Using Indirect Questions

Exercise A. | **Collaboration** Have students follow the steps. Explain that the objective of this exercise is to practice the language and grammar from the unit.

TIP Walk around the classroom to help students with questions about the charities or about vocabulary.

Exercise B. | Have groups join together to share the questions they wrote.

IDEAS FOR... Expansion

Have students work in groups to prepare a role play. Ask each group to think of an entrepreneur to research. One student in the group will act as the entrepreneur who is coming to the school to give a talk. The other students will act as audience members and will ask questions. Give students time in the computer lab (or assign as homework) to do online research. Schedule time in class for the skits.

45 mins

Engage: Giving a Presentation Based on Internet Research *(page 100)*

WARM-UP

Explain that a non-governmental organization (NGO) is an organization that doesn't have any government representatives as members and doesn't usually use government funding. Some NGOs are international; even more are national. Although some are very large, such as the Red Cross and the Red Crescent, there are thousands more that are very small and operate in only a region, such as a city or state. Ask students to name any NGOs that they know of and start a list on the board. For each NGO listed, ask what purpose it serves.

TIP **Provide a list of NGOs or suggest where students can find one. For example, you might find a good list on the Web site of the United Nations. Give students the URL for the page or let them find it themselves using a search engine.**

Exercise A. | Planning a Presentation Explain that students will give a presentation about an NGO based on Internet research. They can pick an NGO from the class list or they may choose another. Arrange time in the computer lab for students to do some online research about the organization.

TIP **If research is done outside of class, encourage the groups to divide the questions fairly so that all of the questions are answered and the work is distributed equally.**

Presentation Skills: Practicing and Timing your Presentation | Go over the information in the box. Write on the board the amount of time students will have for their team presentation and ask them to divide that time equally for each member to present.

Exercise B. | Encourage students to practice their section of the group presentation in advance. Give them time to practice as a group as well. Tell them their presentations should be from eight to 10 minutes and contain visual aids.

TIP **Require visual aids, but be flexible with the type they choose: pictures, posters, PowerPoint, etc.**

TIP **Bring a stopwatch to class and let groups time themselves as they practice their presentations.**

IDEAS FOR... **Expansion**

Videotape the presentations. Evaluate the students using an evaluation form that includes the presentation skills and language taught in Units 1 to 5.

Exercise C. | Presentation Schedule a day in class for presentations. Let students know that even when they are in the audience, they should actively participate by asking questions. Have them review indirect and direct questions before other groups present.

A World of Words

Academic Track
Literature/Humanities

Academic Pathways:
Lesson A: Listening to a Lecture
Discussing Fairy Tales
Lesson B: Listening to a Class
Discussion Session
Giving a Summary

Unit Theme

The study of literature is the study of written works. The works can be of many genres; poetry or fiction are two examples. People's opinions vary on what characteristics a piece of writing needs to have to be considered literature, but one thing most people agree on is that literature has existed in some form since ancient times.

Unit 6 explores the topic of literature as it relates to:

- well-known authors
- understanding sidetracks
- different types of literature
- writing as a profession

Think and Discuss *(page 101)*

5 mins

Everyone has his or her own taste when it comes to literature. Likewise, everyone is entitled to his or her own opinion as to what makes a piece of writing a work of great literature.

- Discuss the questions.
- Initiate the discussion by asking students to list things they like to read. Elicit answers such as *books, magazines, poetry, newspapers,* etc. Accept any reasonable answers.
- Ask students to suggest specific works that they recommend others read. Start the discussion with a question such as: *What are your favorite novels?* Give an example: *My favorite novels are the Harry Potter books. I recommend them because they are well written and it's fun to see the characters develop over time.* Extend the discussion to include examples of each type of reading students mentioned earlier.

TIP **Some students might think they can't participate in the discussion because they don't enjoy reading or they don't read literature. Remind them that there is no wrong answer since it is a personal opinion.**

Exploring the Theme: A World of Words *(pages 102-103)*

15 mins

The opening spread features a library, three authors, and a time line. Ask if anyone would like to read in the library pictured on pages 102 and 103. Begin a discussion about where students like to read literature. For example:

T: Lin, you mentioned you like to read poetry. Where do you go when you want to read poetry?
S: I like to read it in the park because the poems I like are about nature.
T: That's interesting. Jongmin, you read magazines. Where do you like to read magazines?
S: I read them in my dormitory so I can talk about them with my roommate. He likes the same magazines.

IDEAS FOR... Expansion

Have students bring in a picture of a library in a different country or one they have visited. Ask students to share their pictures in small groups and discuss what they like and dislike about each library. Extend the conversation by asking students to compare and contrast their pictures to the picture on pages 102 and 103.

- Discuss the questions.
- Have students read the introductory information.

30 mins

Building and Using Vocabulary *(pages 104-105)*

WARM-UP

The Lesson A target vocabulary is presented in short descriptions of three poets. Remind students that reading the whole sentence is helpful in figuring out the meaning of an individual word. The information that helps explain the word might be anywhere in the sentence.

Building Vocabulary

track 2-12
track 2-13
track 2-14

Exercise A. | Meaning from Context Have students read and listen to the descriptions before matching the words to their definitions.

IDEAS FOR... Expansion

Review the information about making comparisons from Unit 5. Have students form groups and make comparisons about the three writers detailed on page 104. Ask each group to share their comparisons with the rest of the class.

Exercise B. | Go over the words in context and ask students to identify the part of speech of each one. Then have students use that information to help them match words to the correct definitions.

Answer Key

1. external	**5.** published	**9.** influence
2. raised	**6.** insights	**10.** reflected
3. observations	**7.** political	
4. poems	**8.** capture	

Using Vocabulary

Exercise A. | Explain that using new words to ask and answer questions is a good way to help remember them. Ask students to work with a partner to ask and answer the questions.

Exercise B. | Give students time to look at the words in the box. Remind them that words sometimes need to change form in order to correctly complete a sentence.

Answer Key

1. influence	**4.** insight, insights
2. capture	**5.** reflected
3. observation	

IDEAS FOR... Checking Comprehension

Call on individual students to answer a question containing a vocabulary word. For example:

T: Who had a strong **influence** on you?
S: My mother.
T: Why?
S: Because she helped me study.

Use vocabulary items from pages 104 and 105 until each student has had an opportunity to participate.

IDEAS FOR... Expansion

Hold a spelling bee. Divide the class into two teams. Invite a student from each team to the board and give a definition from pages 104 and 105. Students then need to write the vocabulary word or item on the board. Whoever gets the right word and spells it correctly earns a point for the team. Depending on your students' ability, include words from earlier units.

45 mins

Developing Listening Skills

(pages 106-107)

Before Listening

track 2-15

Understanding Sidetracks | Have students skim the box and find the definition of *sidetrack*. Write the definition on the board. Have students follow along as you or a volunteer reads the information in the box.

Explain that noticing the key expressions used to signal sidetracks will help students realize when a speaker has gotten off track as well as when he or she is returning to the topic again. Play the excerpt and then make sure students heard the expressions in use.

Answer Key

As an aside . . .
Getting back to our topic . . .
That reminds me . . .
Getting back to what I was saying . . .

Listening: A Lecture

track 2-15

Exercise A. | Listening for Main Ideas Play the audio again and have students concentrate on the main ideas. Tell them to focus on the left column in the chart and circle the ideas the professor discusses.

Answer Key

Students should circle: Origin of *haiku*, Bashō's early life, What are haikai?, What are haibun?, Bashō's 1689 journey, Bashō's insights

track 2-15

Exercise B. | Note-Taking Play the lecture again and ask students to take notes in the right column.

Answer Key *(Notes may vary.)*

Origin of *haiku*: Came from earlier poetry: haikai

Bashō's early life: studied poetry with famous poet in Kyoto, influenced by Chinese poetry and Taoism

What are *haikai*?: groups of verses or paragraphs, like Shakespeare's—long, with a set structure, haiku developed from first verse of *haikai*

What are *haibun*?: *haiku* followed by prose, books are collections of essays, each begin with *haiku*

Bashō's 1689 journey: walked five months, north of Edo, coast of Sea of Japan, produced masterwork, collection of *haibun*

Bashō's insights: nature, life, death, deeper subjects

After Listening

Exercise A. | Tell students to imagine they have to take the professor's quiz, but that it is an open-notes quiz. Have them use their notes to answer the questions.

Answer Key **1.** a **2.** a **3.** b **4.** c **5.** b

Exercise B. | Give students time to compare answers with a partner.

IDEAS FOR... **Checking Comprehension**

Ask students to think about which questions or details they missed on the quiz. When comparing answers, have students pay special attention to the places in their notes where the missed information can be found. If time allows, play the audio again so students can hear what they missed.

Exercise C. | Discussion Draw attention to the photo of the frog and accompanying *haiku* in the book. Note that the poem in the book is an English translation of a Japanese poem and therefore does not follow traditional *haiku* form. Put students in groups to discuss the questions.

Exercise D. | Critical Thinking Mention that travelers sometimes have problems when they're taking a trip. Encourage volunteers to tell stories about a problem they have had. Then have students think about Basho's masterwork specifically. Have students brainstorm a list.

45 mins

Exploring Spoken English *(pages 108-110)*

Language Function

Let students know that speakers use certain phrases to return to their topic after a sidetrack. Review the expressions in the box on page 106.

track 2-16 track 2-17

Exercise A. | Note-Taking Have students find a partner. Ask each pair to choose Text A or Text B to take notes on. Point out the bulleted information students should focus on.

TIP If necessary, provide more details about style. Style is what helps give the readers an idea about the mood of a story. Style includes sentence forms (e.g., main point followed by clauses, main points in the middle and preceded and followed by clauses), word choice, diction (e.g., abstract, concrete, literal, dense, long), connotation (special meaning conveyed through word choice), punctuation, and/or idioms, clichés, and figures of speech.

Answer Key *(Notes may vary.)*

Text A:

Genre: biography

Setting: Denmark

Author's style: long sentences, varied styles of sentences (main points at the beginning and in the middle), many adjectives and descriptions, literal

Content: describes Denmark and what the Danish islands look like; describes his parents

Text B:

Genre: fiction

Setting: a field

Author's style: very long sentences with many commas, includes quotations, more abstract, more formal

Content: Alice's experience with seeing the White Rabbit, watching it check its watch, following it, and seeing it go down a rabbit-hole

Exercise B. | Making Sidetracks Have students describe their text using their notes. Encourage them to deliberately make sidetracks.

Exercise C. | Discussion In small groups, ask students to discuss the questions.

Grammar: The Simple Past *vs.* The Present Perfect

IDEAS FOR... Presenting Grammar

- Review the simple past tense. Then write three sentences on the board:
  They have studied English for 10 years.
  They have taken an English class three times.
  They have read a lot of magazine articles, so they are ready to read literature now.
- Draw a time line on the board with the present marked in the middle. (See the *Independent Student Handbook* on page 215 of the Student Book for an example of a time line.)

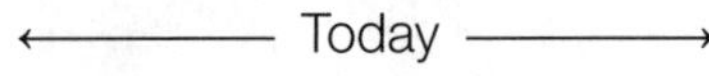

T: These three sentences all use the present perfect tense. In the first sentence, one thing started in the past, but it is still happening today.

- Mark two spots on the time line, one in the past and one above the point indicating the present time. Draw a line between them.

X______X
←——— Today ———→

T: In the second sentence, one thing happened several times in the past before now.

- Mark three spots on the time line all before the present time.

X X X
←——— Today ———→

T: In the third sentence, we're not sure what exact time something happened. We only know that it happened in the past and that it is affecting the present.

- Go over the box in the book.
- Have students write true sentences about themselves for the three situations described by the time lines.

Exercise A. | Make sure students understand the target grammar concept before they begin. Go over the answers as a class. Ask students to explain why they used the past or present perfect in each sentence.

Answer Key

1. lived **2.** have loved **3.** has published **4.** made
5. wrote **6.** haven't read

track 2-18 **Exercise B.** | Play the conversation. Have students find a partner to read with. Give them enough time to reverse roles so each student plays both roles.

> IDEAS FOR... **Multi-level Classes**
>
> Have higher-level students record themselves and analyze what they can do to make themselves sound more like the speakers on the audio.

Exercise C. | Quickly review the rules in the grammar box on page 109. Have students choose whether the statements are true or false. Remind students to pay attention to verb tenses in the conversation and in the statements.

Answer Key **1.** T **2.** F **3.** T **4.** F **5.** T

> IDEAS FOR... **Checking Comprehension**
>
> Ask students to explain why the statements are true or false. Have students discuss how the verb tense is useful to determine when something happened in a sentence.

30-45 mins

Speaking *(page 111)*

Discussing Fairy Tales

Make sure students are familiar with the definition of a fairy tale: a short story that includes fantastic characters such as fairies, elves, or goblins. Ask students if they are familiar with any stories that are considered fairy tales. Introduce Hans Christian Andersen and explain that he was a well-known author of fairy tales.

TIP **Consider showing students a copy of *The Little Mermaid* or another famous fairy tale, especially a version with illustrations, so they have a clear idea of what a fairy tale is.**

track 2-19 **Exercise A.** | Have students read and listen to the synopsis.

Schedule a few minutes to answer vocabulary questions if necessary.

Exercise B. | **Discussion** Ask students if they think they like fairy tales. Have them work with a partner to answer the questions about four of Andersen's tales.

TIP **Bring in pictures or images from the fairy tales to help students visualize the lessons being told in the fairy tales.**

> IDEAS FOR... **Expansion**
>
> Divide students into four groups and assign each group one of the four fairy tales listed in exercise **B**. Have groups read the fairy tale and discern the following details:
>
> - synopsis
> - characters
> - lesson it teaches
>
> Ask each group to prepare a short presentation to present this information to the other groups.
>
> For a more challenging activity, allow students to choose any fairy tale they want to study.

Exercise C. | **Collaboration** Put students into groups of three or four to talk about a fairy tale of their choice. Prepare them to talk about the fairy tale with the rest of the class.

> IDEAS FOR... **Expansion**
>
> Have students prepare and give a short presentation on their favorite book. Ask them to include
>
> - the author's name
> - the title of the work
> - when the author wrote it
> - why the author wrote it
> - a short synopsis
> - why they like it

30 mins

Viewing: Sleepy Hollow *(pages 112-113)*

Overview of the Video | Washington Irving was an American author. He lived from 1783 to 1859. Irving grew up in New York City, not Sleepy Hollow, and he actually wrote *The Legend of Sleepy Hollow* while he was living in England.

Irving's popular story is still widely read today. In the story, Ichabod Crane is a schoolmaster from Connecticut. He and Abraham "Brom Bones" van Brunt both love the same girl, Katrina, from Sleepy Hollow. When a headless horseman chases Ichabod Crane, Crane disappears, leaving Brom Bones as the girl's only suitor.

Before Viewing

Continue to emphasize the importance of activating prior knowledge. Draw students' attention to the photo and map on page 112. Ask the class if anyone has read *The Legend of Sleepy Hollow*.

Using the Simple Past and Present Perfect | Tell students they will read about the author, the setting, and the main characters of the story. Review the verb tenses from earlier in the unit if necessary. Prepare students to explain why each blank needs a certain verb tense.

Answer Key	published, loved, have enjoyed, described

While Viewing

2:56 **Exercise A. |** Play the video for students. Have students choose the correct answer to complete each sentence.

Answer Key	**1.** a **2.** b **3.** b **4.** b

2:56 **Exercise B. |** After students watch the video, give them time to complete the exercise.

Answer Key	**1.** T **2.** T **3.** T **4.** F

TIP **The answer to the fourth question in exercise B may be confusing for some students. If students answer *T*, take the opportunity to review the present perfect rules. The script reads, "We've tried that several times." The use of present perfect shows that this happened several times in the past. Therefore, the correct answer is *F*.**

After Viewing

Exercise A. | Discussion Draw students' attention to the quotation from the video. Give students time to discuss the question.

Listen to the narrator again so students can hear the quotation.

Exercise B. | Critical Thinking Prepare students for the next listening passage by having them write questions. Review the information on direct and indirect questions from Unit 5. Ask students to decide if any of their questions should be rewritten.

IDEAS FOR... Expansion

Have students read *The Legend of Sleepy Hollow*. Tell them to imagine that Washington Irving was going to visit the classroom and that they could ask him questions about the story. Have each student write three questions they would ask the author. Have them think about whether their questions should be direct or indirect.

30 mins

Building and Using Vocabulary *(pages 114-115)*

WARM-UP

Ask students the following question: *If you could start any business you wanted, what would it be?* Have students share their answers in small groups. Then open a class discussion in which students can share their business ideas. Ask them what challenges a new business might have and if those challenges might keep them from pursuing their dream business.

Building Vocabulary

track 2-20

Exercise A. | Meaning from Context Tell students they are going to learn about a woman who owns a bookstore. Ask them to pay special attention to the words in blue as they read and listen to the interview.

Exercise B. | Have students work with a partner to answer the questions. Do not let them use a dictionary unless absolutely necessary. Walk around the classroom to help them answer the questions using context.

IDEAS FOR... Checking Comprehension

Revisit some of the students' business ideas from the warm-up discussion. Have students answer these questions about their own business idea:

Do you think your business would ***eventually*** *be successful? Why, or why not?*

Would there be a ***previous*** *owner?*

Although there is no ***formula*** *for success, what is one thing you would definitely try?*

What kind of ***printed*** *materials would you use to advertise your business?*

Put students in small groups to share their answers.

Using Vocabulary

track 2-21

Exercise C. | Meaning from Context
Tell students they are going to learn about a librarian. Ask them to pay special attention to the words in blue as they read and listen to the interview.

Exercise D. | Have students work with a partner to answer the questions. Do not let them use a dictionary unless absolutely necessary. Walk around the classroom to help them answer the questions using context.

IDEAS FOR... Checking Comprehension

Again, have students think about their ideas from the warm-up discussion.

What do you think you would ***gain*** *from being a business owner?*

If you were giving advice to new business owners, what would you ***mention*** *first?*

Describe an ***accurate*** *piece of advice you've received.*

Do you like any ***contemporary*** *art? Describe it.*

What is a ***contemporary*** *invention that you can think of?*

What was the most recent thing your teacher ***mentioned*** *to you?*

For which subjects in school do you need to be ***accurate****?*

Put students in small groups to share their answers.

Exercise E. | Discussion Ask students to discuss the questions and remind them to think critically.

IDEAS FOR... Expansion

Have students form teams. Ask them to decide on a new business. They can use one of the ideas from the warm-up discussion or they can think of a new business. Have them answer these questions:

What is your business?

How many customers do you want to have eventually?

What is your formula for success?

What do you hope to gain from being business owners?

Ask students to prepare a short presentation and encourage them to use new vocabulary.

Developing Listening Skills

45 mins *(pages 116-117)*

Pronunciation: Review of Question Intonation

Explain to students that if they use the incorrect intonation, people might not be able to tell if they're asking a question. Go over the examples in the box.

Exercise A. | Play the audio and make sure students can hear the difference in intonation.

track 2-22

> **IDEAS FOR... Checking Comprehension**
> Ask students to write some of their own questions. Solicit volunteers to write them on the board. Then ask students to draw the intonation arrows.

Exercise B. | Have students mark the intonation for each question before practicing with a partner.

Answer Key

1. Do you want to go to the bookstore or the library?
2. Are you writing your research paper?
3. Have you read chapter 3?
4. Where did you see him?
5. Would you like to walk or take the bus?
6. How was your presentation?

Before Listening

Review the lecture from Lesson A, page 106.

Listening: A Class Discussion Session

Exercise A. | Listening for Main Ideas Remind students that question and answer periods following a lecture are just as valuable as the lecture itself.

track 2-23

TIP Warn students that the speakers make some "false starts," meaning they begin their question, rethink their wording, and then start their question again, and that two students ask *more than* one question.

> **IDEAS FOR... Multi-level Classes**
> Ask lower-level students to write the key words and ask higher-level students to write as many words as they can.

Answer Key *(Notes may vary.)*

Student 1: *Haibun* both poetry and prose?; Bashō invent *haibun*?
Student 2: How are *haikai* and Shakespeare similar?
Student 3: What is meaning of his frog *haiku*?

Exercise B. | Listening for Details Prepare students to take notes on the details.

track 2-23

Answer Key *(Notes may vary.)*

Haibun: *Haibun* 2 parts. *Haiku 1st*—short poem. Then prose—short essay

Bashō's *haibun*: one of 1st writers to use, wrote a lot, gained reputation as master

Shakespeare: sonnets—long poems w/ set number of verses and lines

Bashō's *haiku*: influenced by Chinese poetry, Taoism, and Zen Buddhism, *haiku* reflected the truth in nature

Exercise C. | Walk around the classroom to make sure everyone has taken accurate notes.

After Listening

Exercise A. | Collaboration Explain that having good notes can help students predict test questions. Ask students to work together to write four questions the professor might ask on the exam.

Exercise B. | Critical Thinking Have groups join together to agree on two questions to put on the exam. Remind students to give good reasons for including their questions.

Exercise C. | Discussion Give students time to discuss the questions.

30 mins

Exploring Spoken English

(pages 118-119)

Grammar: Negative Questions

Exercise A. | Have students choose a partner to practice the conversation with.

Exercise B. | Give students time to answer the questions.

Answer Key

1. Yes.
2. No, but he thinks so.
3. Answers will vary.

Exercise C. | Discussion Have students change the questions to negative questions and discuss the function of each one with a partner.

Answer Key

1. Didn't you send an invitation to the Martins?
2. Aren't you worried about the exam?
3. Don't you wish you lived someplace with a warmer climate?

Language Function

Ask students to describe a time when they have had to persuade someone to do something or change their opinion. Go over the information in the Language Function box. Ask students if any of their situations could have employed the use of negative questions.

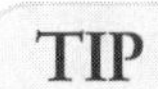

TIP **Review what kind of intonation is needed for this question type.**

Exercise A. | Discussion Give students time to read the information about vacation packages.

IDEAS FOR... Multi-level Classes

If your students are comfortable reading aloud, call on four higher-level students to read the information about the vacation packages for the class.

Student to Student: Staying Neutral | Remind students that they don't have to be negative, and they don't need to be persuaded. They can remain neutral. Go over the phrases.

IDEAS FOR... Expansion

Give each student two index cards (or strips of paper). Have them write a negative question on one and an appropriate follow-up statement on the other. Collect them. Keep the questions and their corresponding statements together. Distribute half of the questions and statements, but give each student only one: either a question or a statement. Have them read it and find their classmate that has the missing piece. After they've found their partner, have everyone read their question and statement. Repeat the activity with the remaining cards.

Exercise B. | Have students choose one vacation package for their group. Walk around the classroom to make sure they are using negative questions correctly.

45 mins

Engage: Giving a Summary *(page 120)*

WARM-UP

Explain that summaries are an important part of academic work. Ask students when they usually see or hear a summary. Elicit answers such as *preceding long pieces of writing, in presentations, when taking notes for a research paper.* Solicit ideas from students about benefits of summaries. Elicit answers such as *saves time, presents the most important information, lets you know what the researchers want you to focus on.* Survey the class to gauge experience with giving summaries.

TIP **Show students sample summaries from academic articles or reports. Point out the length of the complete article or report as well as the length of the summary.**

track 2-24

Exercise A. | Note-Taking

TIP **Groups of three are ideal for this activity.**

Play the news report. Encourage students to take notes in the column of the question they were assigned.

TIP **Depending on the level of your students, spend a little time activating their prior knowledge by asking questions such as the following: *Where is Egypt? What is a mummy? Do you think it would be unusual to find poetry with a mummy?***

Exercise B. | Tell students they will likely have to write summaries in classes.

Critical Thinking Focus: Selecting Relevant Information | Ask students to think about everything that happened to them that day. Define *relevant* if necessary. Ask them if everything that happened is relevant to learning English. Then go over the information in the box and reinforce the idea that only the most important ideas are included in summaries. Ask them what information would be deleted from a summary about their day.

Exercise C. | Critical Thinking Ask students to cross out less important information from their notes.

Exercise D. | Organizing Ideas Ask students to focus on their question and to prepare a summary. Then have them work with their group to write one summary for all three questions.

Exercise E. | Presentation Allow time in class for students to formally present. Ask students to take notes and make comparisons among the summaries. What did they have in common? What differences were there? Were the differences due to the fact that information that didn't need to be included was included anyway? Allow extra time for students to analyze the summaries.

Presentation Skills: Giving a Summary | Go over the information in the box. Have students talk about particular situations in which they've given a summary. If they can't think of anything, spur the discussion by giving a few ideas: *telling a friend about a movie* or *answering your mom's question "How was your day?".*

IDEAS FOR... Expansion

Have students bring in a paragraph or short article about a topic in their field of study. Tell them to imagine they need to summarize this piece of writing for their instructor. Ask them to cross out the information that does not need to be included and to highlight the main ideas. Have them write a short summary.

After Oil

UNIT 7

Academic Track
Interdisciplinary

Academic Pathways:
Lesson A: Listening to a Current Affairs Club Meeting
Giving an Informal Presentation
Lesson B: Listening to a Conversation between Students
Developing Materials for a Promotional Campaign

Unit Theme

The world's consumption of oil is a much discussed and debated topic. Many people wonder what consumers will do when the oil supply runs out. Scientists and companies are exploring a variety of alternative fuel options to have in place before the world's oil supply is completely depleted.

Unit 7 explores the topic of oil as it relates to:

– the history of petroleum
– exploring alternative sources, such as hydrogen and ethanol
– discussing the future
– examining drawbacks

Think and Discuss *(page 121)*

5 mins

Start a general discussion about the world's dependency on oil.

- Initiate the discussion by asking students when they think people became so dependent on gasoline for fuel.
- Discuss the questions in the book.
- Survey the class. Ask students how much gasoline costs in other countries and how much the price has risen in their lifetimes. Write their answers on the board.

TIP **If students don't know information about gas prices in other countries, supply some information about gasoline prices around the world.**

Exploring the Theme: After Oil *(pages 122-123)*

15 mins

The opening spread features a photo of an oilfield in California and information about daily uses, costs, and alternatives of oil.

- Preview the questions with the class.
- Read the three boxes. Make sure students understand the information. For example:

  T: Oil is used for many things. Can you think of other things we use oil for?
  S: The book says we need oil for sports shoes.
  T: That's true. Has anyone heard of something else . . . maybe something not on the page?
  S: I heard you need oil to make candles.
  T: That's interesting. Some people say we need to have alternatives. What alternatives do we have?
  S: Wind power.
  T: Yes. Any others?
  S: Solar power.

- Discuss the questions in further detail.

30 mins

Building and Using Vocabulary *(pages 124-125)*

WARM-UP

The Lesson A target vocabulary is introduced in a matching exercise. Let students know that matching words to definitions reinforces the key vocabulary that will be used throughout the unit.

Building Vocabulary

Exercise A. | Have students work in pairs to match words with their definitions. Allow the use of a dictionary if necessary.

IDEAS FOR... **Multi-level Classes**

Have students work with partners who are at a lower or higher level than they are. The higher-level students can guide the lower-level students in choosing the right answers.

Answer Key	**1.** h **2.** a **3.** i **4.** f **5.** b **6.** j **7.** e **8.** d **9.** g **10.** c

Exercise B. | Understanding Visuals Tell students that understanding visuals is an important part of academic work. Ask them what types of visuals they are familiar with. Elicit answers such as *illustrations*, *tables*, and *graphs*.

Answer Key	4, 1, 2, 5, 3, 7, 6

track 2-25

Exercise C. | Play the audio so that students can check their answers.

IDEAS FOR... **Checking Comprehension**

Ask each student a question that elicits an answer using one of the vocabulary words.

T: What happens when I need to be absent from school?

S1: We have a **substitute**.

T: What happens to your supply of apples after you eat the last one?

S2: It is **depleted**.

T: What is your most important thing to do?

S3: My **priority** is school.

Continue asking questions until everyone has had a chance to participate.

Using Vocabulary

Exercise A. | Have students complete the conversation, using each word only one time.

Answer Key

1. peak	**5.** shift	**8.** enormous
2. deplete	**6.** essential	**9.** extract
3. era	**7.** variety	**10.** priority
4. substitute		

Exercise B. | Discussion Have students role-play the conversation in exercise **A**. Then give them time to discuss the questions. Let them share their answers to question 3 with the class.

IDEAS FOR... **Checking Comprehension**

Ask students to work with a partner to write a dialog incorporating the vocabulary words. Have all the pairs read their dialogs for the class, so students can hear the words used in a variety of contexts. If time is restricted or writing dialogs is too challenging, have students write sentences using the vocabulary.

45 mins

Developing Listening Skills *(pages 126-127)*

Before Listening

Critical Thinking Focus: Considering Viewpoint and Bias | Go over the information in the box. Then ask students to think of situations when speakers may be biased (*sensitive topics such as politics and personal situations*). List these situations on the board. Make a second list of situations where speakers are not usually biased (*fact-based lectures, explaining processes*). List these as well. Ask students how they can tell if a speaker is biased or unbiased.

Making Inferences | Define *inference* and make sure students understand that an inference is an idea based on facts.

Answer Key J, S, J, S

Listening: A Current Affairs Club Meeting

track 2-26

Exercise A. | Listening for Main Ideas Tell students they are going to hear people speaking at the meeting that Sara and Jamie were discussing on page 125.

Answer Key

1. Future Fuels International: works to find substitutes for fossil fuels; Lomax Petroleum: makes a variety of petroleum products
2. Oil production in the United States would peak between 1968 and 1972.
3. Dr. Sparks: will increase for the next 20 years; Dr. Steinberg: peak occurred in 2006
4. The new oil discoveries will be small and difficult to extract.

track 2-26

Exercise B. | Listening for Details Play the audio again and have students listen for details.

Answer Key **1.** 1970 **2.** harder **3.** decrease **4.** small **5.** pessimistic

After Listening

Exercise A. | Critical Thinking Critical thinking often involves making inferences. Advise students to think carefully before answering.

Answer Key L, R

IDEAS FOR... Checking Comprehension

Ask students to explain how they were able to determine the answers to exercise **A**.

Exercise B. | Point out that students have three answer choices for each item.

Answer Key **1.** T **2.** F **3.** M **4.** T **5.** T **6.** M

IDEAS FOR... Checking Comprehension

Ask students to think about the reasons for their answers to exercise **B**. Having students support their answers reinforces their comprehension and leads nicely into the discussion that follows.

Exercise C. | Discussion Give students time to support their answers and discuss any differences of opinion.

IDEAS FOR... Expansion

Have students work in groups. Ask each group to brainstorm a list of professions in which it is best that people be unbiased (*doctor, judge*). Have them brainstorm a second list of professions in which it is best that people be biased (*environmentalist, lawyer*). After a set amount of time, ask students to read their lists to the class.

45 mins

Exploring Spoken English *(pages 128-130)*

Grammar: Reported Speech

IDEAS FOR... Presenting Grammar

- Write the same sentence two times on the board:
  The teacher says we need to practice.
  The teacher says we need to practice.

T: How can I change the first sentence to be a direct quote?

- Write *The teacher says, "We need to practice."*
- Discuss the changes in punctuation and capitalization.

T: How can I change the second sentence to be reported speech?

- Write *The teacher said we needed to practice.*
- Point out the wording and tense changes.
- Go over the information in the book. Make sure students understand the difference between reported speech and quoted speech.
- Open a discussion about when reported speech is used.

Exercise A. | Refresh the students' memories about making inferences before beginning this activity.

TIP Consider having students complete exercise A in three steps. First, begin with a group discussion about what each speaker said. Note that it's not always possible to definitively determine the speaker of each statement and that it's OK if students have different opinions. Second, have students work in pairs to rewrite the statements. Third, have volunteers write their answers on the board. Discuss their sentences and correct them as a class. Review the information in the box on page 128 as necessary.

Answer Key *(Answers may vary.)*

2. He said he started the organization six years ago.
3. She said she was going to have a meeting with the president of the university.
4. He said he had given his presentation in eight countries.
5. She said she would travel to Ireland next summer.

Grammar: Changing Time Expressions in Reported Speech

IDEAS FOR... Presenting Grammar

- Tell students that time expressions may need to change in reported speech.
- Write *yesterday, last week, tomorrow*, and *next week* on the board.
- Ask students to guess how these words and phrases would change in reported speech. Write their guesses on the board.
- Go over the examples in the book. Revisit their guesses on the board to see if they were right.

Exercise B. | Put students into groups of three. Have them exchange roles so each student has a chance to play each role at least one time. When everyone has practiced all the situations, ask the groups to select one role-play to perform for the class.

IDEAS FOR... Multi-level Classes

If higher-level students finish early, challenge them to extend their dialogs with additional information.

Language Function: Reporting What Someone Has Said

Solicit examples of situations when it is necessary to relay information someone said to a third person. Explain that relaying information is a common way to use reported speech.

track 2-27 **Exercise A. |** Have students read the conversation twice so that both students play both roles. Walk around the classroom to answer any vocabulary questions.

Exercise B. | Discussion Explain that a good way to begin incorporating language functions is to identify them in use. Have students use the conversation on page 129 to answer question 1.

Answer Key

1. **Steve:** He said they'd decided to buy a hybrid car.
   Steve: . . . she told Michael she was concerned about the environment.
   Steve: He also said that with four children, they'd been worried about finding a big enough hybrid vehicle.
   Steve: . . . he said it's some kind of a mini-van with three rows of seats.
2. Answers will vary.

IDEAS FOR... Expansion

Ask students to bring in a page of dialog from a television or movie script or another English textbook. Require that the dialog contain at least two examples of reported speech. Have students work with a partner to underline the reported speech. If time allows, have students read their script aloud for the class.

Exercise C. | Ask two students to read the speech bubbles. Give students time to practice with their own conversations. Have volunteers read their conversations for the class.

Exercise D. | Critical Thinking Introduce pie charts as another example of a visual. Have students look back at "The History of Petroleum" on page 124. Talk about the uses of pie charts and direct students' attention to page 216 of the *Independent Student Handbook* for more information.

TIP If students find the first question challenging, have them focus on oil and coal since these two fossil fuels were mentioned in the exercise introduction. Emphasize that guessing is permissible, especially when they can offer a reason for their answer.

Exercise E. | Presentation Have students prepare a short presentation sharing their ideas from exercise **D** with the class.

30-45 mins

Speaking *(page 131)*

Giving an Informal Presentation

Exercise A. | Brainstorming Have students brainstorm a list of ideas for the left column in the T-chart.

Exercise B. | After sufficient time, have students complete the right column.

Presentation Skills: Using an Appropriate Volume | Go over the information in the box. Solicit volunteers to share personal stories about speakers they thought spoke too loudly or too softly. Read each sentence in the box at different volumes and have students vote on whether each sentence is too soft, too loud, or at a normal volume.

Exercise C. | Presentation Point out the speech bubbles. Prepare students to field questions after the presentation. Ask students to be prepared to take notes and ask questions when they are listening to other people's presentations.

Exercise D. | Ask students to review their questions to make sure they used reported speech.

IDEAS FOR... Expansion

Ask students to record themselves speaking at a variety of volumes. Have them play back the audio and determine which one is optimal for giving a presentation.

30 mins

Viewing: Canadian Oil Sands *(pages 132-133)*

Overview of the Video | As oil becomes more difficult to extract, "oil sands" in Canada are now being considered part of the world's oil reserves.

Converting the oil sands into liquid fuel requires a complex refining process and, for many people, the jobs this processing brings to the area are beneficial. On the other hand, obtaining the oil sands means destroying enormous areas of forest. The processing of the sands also generates large quantities of greenhouse gases—more than the typical process of oil production.

Before Viewing

Ask students what they know about oil sands. Explain that the sands are mixtures of several materials; only one is petroleum. Oil sands are found in several countries, but they are especially common in Canada.

Exercise A. | Meaning from Context Draw students' attention to the photos and go over the captions, which are referenced in the questions that follow.

- Have students work together to discuss the questions and figure out the meaning of the words or phrases that are underlined.
- Ask students to define the underlined words and phrases and explain how they determined the answers to the questions.

Exercise B. | Critical Thinking Explain that predicting content actually aids comprehension of the material. Assure students that it doesn't matter if their predictions are correct or incorrect. The important thing is that they're thinking about the topic.

- Give students time to discuss the question and explain their answers.

While Viewing

5:30

Exercise A. | Preview the questions. Then show the video and ask students to choose the right answers.

Answer Key **1.** T **2.** F **3.** F **4.** T **5.** T **6.** F

IDEAS FOR... Expansion

Have students offer opinions about the points of view found in the video. Encourage students to discuss whether each speaker is biased and what the source of his or her bias might be.

5:30

Exercise B. | Considering Viewpoint and Bias After students watch the video, have them decide which topic is the best fit.

Answer Key

Celina Harper: B
Peter Essick: B
Mike Noseworthy: A
Brenda Hampson: A
Steve Kallick: B

After Viewing

Exercise A. | Discussion Ask students to discuss the quotations. Survey the class and find out who found it easy and who found it hard to understand the people's statements. Have students explain why they found it easy or difficult.

Exercise B. | Role-Playing Explain how a debate works and the benefits students will gain from participating in one (*hearing about two sides of an issue, learning reasons for both sides*). Have students follow the directions.

30 mins

Building and Using Vocabulary *(pages 134-135)*

WARM-UP

Prepare students for the topic by asking some general questions about hydrogen fuel. Ask questions: *Have you ever been in a vehicle powered by something other than gasoline? Would you be willing to buy a car that doesn't run on gasoline? Why or why not? How much do you think a hydrogen-powered car costs?*

TIP **Bring in a list of car companies that make hydrogen-powered cars and a list of car models so students can have a better idea of what is available.**

Building Vocabulary

track 2-28

Exercise A. | Meaning from Context Have students read and listen to the information. Remind them to pay attention to the words in blue.

Exercise B. | Explain that students should be able to figure out the answers based on context.

Answer Key

1. g **2.** e **3.** j **4.** a **5.** b
6. i **7.** d **8.** f **9.** h **10.** c

IDEAS FOR... Checking Comprehension

Do a brainstorming activity using the new vocabulary words. Write the following categories on the board: *technology advances (computers, cars), things that burn (paper, wood), types of campaigns (political, advertising), conventional things (classes, cooking), clothing designers (Tommy Hilfiger, Ralph Lauren), places a great distance from your school (answers will vary), manufactured things (cell phones, cars), refined things (sugar, oil), things with sectors (companies, governments), problems that need solutions (mathematical equations, environmental issues).* Have students work in groups to think of two additional items for each category. Give them some ideas by saying, for example, *Sugar is refined and math problems have solutions.* Have a member from each group add answers on the board. Make sure students clearly understand the definitions.

Using Vocabulary

Exercise A. | Review the vocabulary words in the box before students complete the sentences and practice the conversation.

Answer Key

1. conventional **2.** solution **3.** manufacturing **4.** burn
5. refined **6.** distance

Exercise B. | Critical Thinking Give students time to discuss the questions. Ask one student to summarize the answers to share with the rest of the class.

IDEAS FOR... Expansion

Put students in groups. Have groups design a vehicle of the future. (They can use the ideas they discussed in exercise **B.**) Tell them to imagine that they want to promote this car in an effort to get more people to buy it. Give each group a brochure about a car from a local dealership or printed from an online source to use for ideas. Have students write their own brochure and encourage them to use vocabulary from the unit.

45 mins

Developing Listening Skills *(pages 136-137)*

Before Listening

TIP Explain that activating prior knowledge is helpful when preparing to listen to scientific or new information.

Exercise A. | Prior Knowledge Ask students what they already know about ethanol. Give them time (or ask a volunteer) to read the information.

Exercise B. | Discussion Give students time to discuss the questions.

TIP Know if the country you are teaching in uses ethanol. Familiarize yourself with countries that require or heavily use ethanol or ethanol mixtures, such as Brazil, the United States, and Sweden.

Listening: A Conversation between Students

track 2-29

Exercise A. | Point out the notes in the book and challenge students to check for accuracy.

TIP Teach students that this note-taking style is useful when they need to take notes on words and definitions.

track 2-29

Exercise B. | Play the audio again so students can answer the questions.

Answer Key

1. The student missed the part about why the sugarcane waste is burned. Completed notes: heat from burning sugarcane waste used to power mill and get electricity
2. Answers will vary.

IDEAS FOR... Checking Comprehension

Ask students to compare their answers to exercise **B**. See if they have the same information. Open a discussion about what their notes had in common and what was different.

After Listening

Discussion | Have students decide which concern is most important and discuss it.

IDEAS FOR... Multi-level Classes

Pair students who have the same approximate level, so higher-level students can discuss more than one concern if they finish before other students.

Pronunciation: Reduced /h/ in Pronouns

track 2-30

Tell students that when native English speakers talk quickly, the /h/ sound is usually dropped. When that happens, the remaining vowel sounds link to the preceding words. Study the examples in the box. Have students practice reading the examples aloud.

Exercise A. | Have students figure out the words as if the /h/ was not reduced. Then have them practice reading the sentences aloud.

Answer Key	**1.** took him **2.** Has he **3.** Was her **4.** Do his

track 2-31

Exercise B. | Play the audio after students have had time to practice reading the sentences aloud. Have them try to mimic the audio so their reductions sound similar to the audio speakers' reductions.

track 2-32

Exercise C. | Remind students that being able to identify reductions will improve comprehension. Point out that not all the answers have reduced sounds.

Answer Key

1. said her, corn **2.** In her, manufacturing
3. Did he, molasses **4.** told him, cooking

30 mins

Exploring Spoken English

(pages 138-139)

Grammar: Future Time with Adverb Clauses

IDEAS FOR... Presenting Grammar

- As a warm-up, ask students to finish these sentences and write them on a piece of paper:
  Later today, I will . . .
  In one year, I will . . .
  In five years, I will . . .
- Ask students to brainstorm words that imply time. Start the list by suggesting the word *before.*
- Go over the information in the box.
- Draw a time line for each example sentence in the book with a time clause.
- Ask students to revisit the sentences they wrote. Solicit volunteers to read their answers.

Exercise A. | Read the speech bubbles. Have students work together to finish the sentences. Ask volunteers to read their answers aloud.

IDEAS FOR... Expansion

Ask students to write a paragraph about what they plan to do in ten years. Have them use the future tense appropriately.

Exercise B. | Critical Thinking Ask students to think about the questions and develop good answers to share with the whole class.

IDEAS FOR... Expansion

Ask students to write a formal paragraph about their answer to one of the questions in exercise **B.**

Student to Student: Softening Assertions | Present the information in the box. Ask students for examples of situations when they might want to soften their assertion.

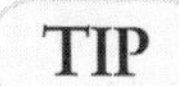

TIP **Reinforce the idea that tone is important when attempting to soften an assertion.**

Language Function: Making Judgements about the Future

Discussion | Give students time to look at the photos and read the captions. Ask students if anyone has ever visited any of the places or seen examples of these power sources somewhere else. Allow time for students to discuss the questions at length.

TIP **Let the discussion proceed without worrying about either softening assertions and adverb clauses for the first two questions. Focus students' attention on adverb clauses for the third question by making it a group writing exercise.**

IDEAS FOR... Expansion

Ask students to research an alternative type of power and find a picture online to bring to class. Have them form groups to create a T-chart for each picture. One side of the T-chart should be benefits of the type of power being used. The other side should detail drawbacks to the type of power. Ask students to choose one of the pictures and accompanying T-charts for the group to share with the rest of the class.

Engage: Developing Materials for a Promotional Campaign *(page 140)*

45 mins

WARM-UP

Explain that many academic fields and careers require development of promotional campaigns. Tell students that the point of a promotional campaign is usually persuasive—they are trying to get someone to do something. Ask them to think of how consumer goods are promoted or advertised. Elicit answers such as *billboards*, *TV commercials*, and *brochures*. Then ask students to focus on not-for-profit organizations (*organizations that are not run with the aim of making a profit*) and which ones have promotional campaigns, what they promote (*fighting disease or poverty, financing research*), and how they do it (*charity fliers, fundraisers such as car washes or blood drives*). Tell students they are going to create a promotional item to present to the class.

TIP **Show students examples of promotional items from local organizations. Include a variety of print and audio material.**

Exercise A. | Present the sample promotional material in the book. Ask students what they liked and disliked about it. See if they have any ideas to make it more appealing.

> IDEAS FOR... **Expansion**
>
> Have students bring a sample of a promotional campaign that they find online. Ask them to compare it to the sample in the book. Have them form groups to share the campaigns they selected.

TIP **Groups of three or four are ideal for this activity.**

Exercise B. | Discussion Have students discuss the questions in the book.

Answer Key *(Answers may vary.)*

1. peat forest and rainforest
2. the ecosystem absorbs little CO_2
3. electric cars: require batteries, varying distance without charging, expenses, recharging time, lack of recharging stations, battery life; hydrogen cars: no large impact on saving gasoline or positively impacting the environment, may produce more emissions, fuel cells not sufficiently developed; solar power: cost of materials and installation, location and weather (cloudy days), unattractive (solar panels on roofs); wind power: noise pollution, weather (wind unpredictability), cost, locations for wind farms, low energy output, negative impact on the environment

TIP **If students participated in the Expansion activity, consider having them work in the same groups. Or, consider having students complete the Expansion activity at this point.**

Exercise C. | Collaboration Tell students it is time to develop their own promotional campaign.

1. Give students time to brainstorm ideas so they have a good list from which to choose. Refer them to the list they started when answering the third question in exercise **B**.
2. After they decide on an energy form, have them brainstorm a list of reasons why it should be supported.
3. Have them choose the best way to present their material.
4. Give them time in and out of class to develop the material.

TIP **If time and resources allow, encourage students to film, record, or develop visuals to go with their promotional material.**

Exercise D. | Presentation Write on the board the amount of time students will have for their presentations. Encourage them to imagine their classmates are the government officials who will decide whether or not to support their research.

TIP **Develop a peer review feedback form for students to use to evaluate each other. Make sure the form includes room for comments about whether or not they, as government officials, would support the research.**

Traditional and Modern Medicine

Academic Track
Health and Medicine

Academic Pathways:
Lesson A: Listening to a Conversation in a Professor's Office
Evaluating Claims about Public Health
Lesson B: Listening to a Conversation between Friends
Preparing and Presenting a Group Summary

Unit Theme

Health science is a science that focuses on the study of the body and how the body functions. Being healthy depends on absence of disease as well as on quality of life. Health science and medicine make being healthy and living longer possible. Health is often dependent on biology as well as on public health organizations, the environment, lifestyles, and medicine.

Unit 8 explores the topic of health and medicine as it relates to:
- traditional and modern medicine
- home remedies
- fighting disease
- evaluating claims

5 mins

Think and Discuss *(page 141)*

The lotus is a plant that grows in hot temperatures. It is native to Asia, and it is harvested for use as food and medicine. All parts of the plant are useful. For example, the seeds are eaten, the leaves are used to wrap food, the stems are used in salads, the rhizomes (*plant stems with roots growing from them*) are eaten and used in herbal medicine, the roots are used in a variety of dishes, and the stamens are used for tea.

- Ask students to list examples of natural medicines (*tea, vinegar*). Write their ideas on the board. Ask them to give examples of medicines from a doctor (*penicillin, aspirin*). Write those in another column.
- Extend the discussion by asking if students have ever used natural medicine.
- Discuss the first two questions.
- Explain that knowing which diseases you are more likely to get based on your DNA is already possible for some diseases. Have students put their advantages and disadvantages for question 3 in a T-chart.

TIP **Prepare a list of common natural or herbal medicines and a list of commonly prescribed medicines in case students aren't familiar with any.**

15 mins

Exploring the Theme: Traditional and Modern Medicine *(pages 142-143)*

The opening spread features a photo of lavender fields and urges students to think about home remedies and modern medicine. Check students' comprehension and activate their prior knowledge.

- Go over the questions.
- Have students read the introductory information.
- Survey the class by asking questions: *How many of you drink green tea? How many of you eat red chili peppers? How many of you eat garlic? How many of you eat ginger?* For each remedy pictured, ask students if they think it works to cure the conditions discussed in the book.

IDEAS FOR... Expansion

After the survey, divide students into four groups and ask them to do some research on the effectiveness of each home remedy. Ask them to share their research in the next class.

15 mins

Building and Using Vocabulary *(pages 144-145)*

WARM-UP

The Lesson A target vocabulary is presented in the context of an article. Explain that although these words are challenging, students should be able to determine their meaning from the context.

- Tell students that most words are learned from context and exercises such as these mimic real-life learning situations.
- Explain that seeing and hearing words improves students' ability to remember new words. Point out that students will hear the article as well as read it so they are exposed to the words in two different ways.

Building Vocabulary

track 3-2

Exercise A. | Meaning from Context
Ask students to read and listen to the article simultaneously.

TIP **Note that in paragraph 2, *revitalisation*, with an s, is the correct spelling in Indian English.**

Exercise B. | Give students time to match the words to their definitions. Challenge students to do this without using a dictionary. Remind students they may need to change the form of the word to match the part of speech.

Answer Key

1. remedies	**5.** cancer	**9.** synthetic
2. promising	**6.** inhibit	**10.** symptom
3. empirical	**7.** restore	
4. crucial	**8.** virus	

IDEAS FOR... Checking Comprehension

Give students the first or second part of a common phrase and see if they can guess which vocabulary word can complete it.
Go around the room until all students have a chance to participate.

T: a natural BLANK
S1: **remedy**
T: Right. How about this one? To BLANK health.
S2: **restore**

Other phrases:
a BLANK of a disease (symptom)
BLANK knowledge (crucial)
a BLANK version of a chemical (synthetic)
to BLANK the growth of BLANK (inhibit/cancer)
a BLANK future (promising)
a deadly BLANK (virus)
an BLANK study (empirical)

Using Vocabulary

Exercise A. | Have students complete the conversation using the vocabulary words.

Answer Key	**1.** virus **2.** symptoms **3.** remedy **4.** restore **5.** empirical

Exercise B. | Give students time to practice the conversation.

Exercise C. | When students finish, ask them to share their answers.

Exercise D. | Remind students that using words in context is an effective way to remember them.

Exercise E. | Consider having students share sentences with the whole class.

IDEAS FOR... Multi-level Classes

Challenge students to use more than one vocabulary word per sentence if they can.

Developing Listening Skills

45 mins

(pages 146-147)

Before Listening

Listener Response: Asking Questions while Listening | Explain that during lectures, it's OK to listen and not respond, but in conversations and discussions, it is necessary to show the listener you are an active and willing participant. Explain that asking questions is a good way to do this. Go over the information in the box.

track 3-3

Exercise A. | Point out the conversation in the book. Play the audio while students follow along.

TIP Have students practice the conversation.

Exercise B. | Discussion Give students time to discuss the questions with a partner. Solicit volunteers to share their answers.

Exercise C. | Ask two students to read the speech bubbles.

IDEAS FOR... Expansion

Give students time to write dialogs of their own using the sentences.

Listening: A Conversation in a Professor's Office

track 3-4

Exercise A. | Explain that students will hear the complete conversation between the professor and the student from page 146. Play the conversation as many times as necessary.

Answer Key

1. He has some questions about her lecture.
2. b. Wow—do those things really make a difference? c. Can medicines actually kill people? d. And are those clinical trials expensive?

track 3-4

Exercise B. | Listening for Details Have students listen again and complete the notes.

IDEAS FOR... Checking Comprehension

Explain that students will use their notes for a discussion. Ask them questions to make sure they have the right information in their notes. For example: *How much do studies cost? What takes a long time? Does the age of the plant matter? Does it matter what time of day the plant is picked?*

Answer Key *(Answers may vary.)*

Problems
1. cost a lot of money
2. approval
3. remedies
   a. subspecies
   b. time of day
   c. old
   d. some other plant

Scientists
1. chemical
2. amount
3. clinical

After Listening

Tell students to use their notes to offer explanations for why it's difficult to develop new medications from plant-based remedies. Ask volunteers to share their answers.

IDEAS FOR... Expansion

Give students time to write a dialog of a visit to a professor's office. In the role-play, one student should act as the student and the other as the professor. The student can ask the professor about an assignment, a book, English, or any other topic the student likes. The roleplay should include questions. Schedule time for the students to perform their roleplays.

Exploring Spoken English

45 mins *(pages 148-150)*

track 3-5 **Exercise A. |** Play the audio and have students follow along. Then give them time to practice.

Exercise B. | Discussion Give students time to discuss the questions.

Answer Key

1. the United States
2. using olive oil, eating vegetables and fruit, exercising every day
3. Answers will vary.

Grammar: Real Conditionals

IDEAS FOR... Presenting Grammar

Prepare students for the challenges of using the conditional. Explain that the conditional is the main grammatical form to use when talking about conditions and results.
Go over the information and examples in the box. Make sure everyone understands.

Ask students to complete these sentences:

If I study English, . . .
I do well on tests if . . .
If you work hard, . . .
I'll . . . if I win a million dollars.

Have the students form groups to make corrections (if needed) to their sentences and share their ideas.

IDEAS FOR... Expansion

Draw students' attention back to the conversation in exercise **A**. Have students underline the real conditionals. Then have them pair up to write a similar conversation about their own countries.

Exercise A. | Critical Thinking Give students time to think of at least two endings for every conditional sentence.

IDEAS FOR... Expansion

Have each pair of students from exercise **A** join another pair to compare answers. Tell them no one should have the same answers. Have them make a list of all their answers and replace any duplicates. Then have groups of four join to form groups of eight and repeat the sharing. Again, tell students no one can have the same answer. For any repeated answers, the group needs to think of a replacement. Have groups share a list of all of the answers to see which group was the most creative.

Exercise B. | Provide enough time for students to ask and answer the questions. For this practice, they could use conditionals in both the questions and the answers.

TIP **Walk around the classroom to make sure students are using the conditional correctly.**

Language Function: Discussing Health

track 3-6 **Exercise A. |** Play the audio and have students follow along. After the audio, ask students to answer the question. Allow time to address any vocabulary questions.

IDEAS FOR... Expansion

Ask students to search the Internet and find another non-governmental organization (NGO) that is working to combat disease or improve health. Have them take notes and bring them to class. In class, put students in groups to share the information.

TIP **Prepare a list of NGOs in case students have trouble finding one on their own. There are several NGOs that work to combat issues such as diseases (*cholera, malaria*), substance abuse (*drugs, alcohol*), poor sanitation (*lack of running water, unsafe food preservation*), and damage to the environment (*air quality, water quality*).**

Exercise B. | Discussion Have partners discuss the questions. Allow time for partners to share their answers for question 3.

Answer Key

1. Answers will vary.
2. Answers may vary.
3. Answers may include nausea, vomiting, skin irritation, or illnesses, such as cancer, from chemicals in water.

IDEAS FOR... Expansion

Ask students to write a short paragraph about what they would do if they were able to start their own NGO.

Exercise C. | Collaboration Tell students to imagine they are members of a team who will work together to battle a public health issue. Go over the instructions with them.

1. Remind students to brainstorm a list of issues first. They can't have too many!
2. Have them choose one issue to work on.
3. Give them time to work on their song titles and lyrics.

TIP **Bring in a copy of the lyrics or play an audio download of one of dos Santos's songs for students to hear. Talk about whether students liked it and whether or not they think it is effective.**

4. Ask them to present their issue to the class.
5. Have them read the song aloud.

IDEAS FOR... Multi-level Classes

Mix students of different levels, making sure the higher-level students are distributed evenly among the groups.

Critical Thinking Focus: Evaluating Claims | Explain that it is important to be able to identify a claim and evaluate it. Even if a claim is true, academic work requires it be supported with evidence.

- Go over the information and examples in the book.
- Present the questions students should ask when evaluating claims.
- Tell students they will use these questions when working on the next exercise.

TIP **As students read the claims on page 151, make a table on the board. Write the four questions from the Critical Thinking box in Column 1 of a table. Then write *Claim 1, Claim 2, Claim 3,* and *Claim 4* across the top of the table.**

30 mins

Speaking: Evaluating Claims about Public Health *(page 151)*

Exercise A. | Critical Thinking Ask volunteers to read the business cards aloud. Put students in groups to evaluate the claims. Bring everyone together for a whole-class discussion. Go over each claim and ask the questions in the box on page 151. Put check marks in the table on the board. Discuss students' evaluations.

Exercise B. | Critical Thinking Have students work together to discuss the claims and decide what type of support is needed.

IDEAS FOR... Expansion

Divide students into six groups and assign each group one of the six claims from exercise **B**. Schedule time in the computer lab or assign students to do online research outside of class to find support for the claim. Have them present their supported claim to the class.

30 mins

Viewing: Wild Health

(pages 152-153)

Overview of the Video | Animals self-medicate using natural items, such as plants, to treat medical problems.

Questions about self-medicating include how animals know when they're sick and how they know what to do. Sometimes their methods have helped advance human medicine.

Before Viewing

Exercise A. | Predicting Content Ask students if they have ever taken care of themselves when they were sick rather than go to a doctor. Ask if any students try to avoid taking medication when they're sick. Give students time to write three predictions about how animals in the wild might cure themselves.

Exercise B. | Using a Dictionary Introduce the words in the box and give students time to match the definitions. Permit the use of a dictionary.

Answer Key

1. preventative	**4.** curative	**7.** avoidance
2. fermentation	**5.** nausea	**8.** ground breaking
3. compound	**6.** lactation	

IDEAS FOR... Checking Comprehension

Have students work in pairs to give examples for the following categories:

- *examples of compounds*
- *how to cure a cold*
- *ways to prevent failing a class*
- *ground breaking discoveries*
- *ways to avoid work*
- *things that cause nausea*

Have students share answers with other pairs of students.

While Viewing

3:48 **Exercise A. |** Play the video and have students take notes so they can complete the exercises.

Answer Key

1. animal self-medication
2. observing, behavior
3. Europe, North America
4. three main

Exercise B. | Let students refer to their notes to answer the questions.

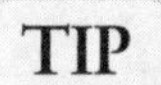

TIP Students may need to watch the video again to complete the exercise.

Answer Key

1. curative measures (curing ailments) **2.** preventative measures (protecting oneself from illnesses)
3. avoidance measures (avoiding toxic plants)

3:48 **Exercise C. |** Play the video one more time if necessary.

Answer Key **1.** d **2.** a **3.** b **4.** c

After Viewing

Exercise A. | Using the Real Conditional Give students time to complete the sentences in their own words.

Answer Key *(Answers may vary.)*

1. If scientists observe animal behavior, they will discover new compounds.
2. If cows want to find the right kind of dirt, they need to travel.
3. If a snow leopard wants to avoid nausea, it needs to eat grass.
4. If we learn more about plants, we will learn more about natural medicine.

Exercise B. | Critical Thinking Tell students to reflect on everything they learned in Lesson A when discussing the questions.

 30 mins

Building and Using Vocabulary *(pages 154-155)*

WARM-UP

Activate students' prior knowledge by asking them what they know about high-tech medicine. Ask what they think of when they hear the term. Elicit answers such as *prosthetic limbs, genetic testing, MRIs, CT scans,* and *robots.*

Building Vocabulary

 track 3-7

Exercise A. | Let students take the quiz and talk about the answers. Draw students' attention to the words in blue.

Exercise B. | Have students read the sentences and complete them using the vocabulary items from exercise **A.**

Answer Key	**1.** devices **2.** transmits **3.** tend **4.** hereditary **5.** consists

 track 3-8

Exercise C. | **Meaning from Context** Have students read and listen to the conversation and note the new vocabulary items.

Using Vocabulary

Exercise D. | Ask students to match the definitions to the words without using a dictionary. Remind students that they may need to change the form of the word to match the part of speech.

Answer Key	**1.** muscles **2.** severe **3.** mechanism **4.** extraordinary **5.** radical

IDEAS FOR... Checking Comprehension

Have students think of a device that interests them. Then have them write answers to these questions:

What is your device?
Does your device transmit anything?
What do people tend to do with it?
What is extraordinary about it?
Is it radical? Why or why not?

IDEAS FOR... Expansion

Have students describe their device from the comprehension activity without saying the name of the device. See if the other students can guess what the device is.

Exercise E. | Tell students to use the context of the sentences to fill in the blanks.

Answer Key	**1.** consists **2.** hereditary **3.** tend **4.** extraordinary

Exercise F. | Give students time to both ask and answer the questions.

IDEAS FOR... Expansion

Focus attention on question 6 of exercise **F.** Give partners time in the computer lab or outside of class to choose a famous person who had a radical idea. Ask them to bring in a number of facts about this person to present to the class. Have them present their facts to the class, including what the radical idea was, but not say the name of the person. See if the other students know or can guess who the person is.

Developing Listening Skills

45 mins *(pages 156-157)*

track 3-9

Pronunciation: Linking Vowels with /y/ and /w/ Sounds

Review the concept of linking and explain that native speakers link vowel sounds with /y/ and /w/ sounds. Go over the examples and listen to the audio.

track 3-10 **Exercises A and B. |** Play the audio more than once if necessary.

Answer Key	**1.** /y/ **2.** /w/ **3.** /y/ **4.** /w/ **5.** /y/

IDEAS FOR... Expansion

Have students think of more linking examples with /y/ and /w/. Write their examples on the board.

IDEAS FOR... Multi-level Classes

Group students of similar levels together. If some groups work more quickly, ask them to write their own sentences on the board as examples.

Before Listening

Self-Reflection | Give students time to think about someone they know who has had surgery.

TIP This topic may be sensitive or emotional for some students. Solicit volunteers rather than requiring everyone to participate in the discussion.

Listening: A Conversation between Friends

Tell students they are going to hear a conversation between friends.

track 3-11 **Exercise A. | Listening for Main Ideas** Play the audio one time.

Answer Key	**1.** b **2.** b **3.** a

IDEAS FOR... Checking Comprehension

Have students use the answers (arthritis, major, and therapy) in their own sentences. If time allows, have them use two of the other answer choices in sentences as well. As a result, students will be able to see the words in other contexts.

track 3-11 **Exercise B. | Listening for Details** Play the audio a second time if necessary.

Answer Key	**1.** week **2.** hip **3.** everyone **4.** six

track 3-11 **Exercise C. | Making Inferences** Review inferences. Play the audio again so students can use the facts to help.

Answer Key	**1.** F **2.** F **3.** T

After Listening

Exercise A. | Discussion Have students share their ideas about the people they heard on the audio.

Exercise B. | Pronunciation Have students mark the linking sounds and practice.

Answer Key

1. He only has to be in the hospital for a few days.
2. If he is in pain, I'll never know about it.
3. . . . the hip will be as good as new.
4. . . . he'll be able to take walks, or travel, or whatever.

Exercise C. | Brainstorming Review T-charts if necessary and then have students complete the activity.

Exercise D. | Allow enough time for groups to come together to compare lists.

30 mins

Exploring Spoken English *(pages 158-159)*

Exercise A. | Prior Knowledge Give students time to think about and answer the questions.

Grammar: Quantifiers with Specific and General Nouns

IDEAS FOR... Presenting Grammar

Go over the information in the box. Explain that quantifiers carry meaning. Point out the scale from 0 percent to 100 percent. Read the examples of quantifiers with general and specific nouns.

TIP Familiarize students with the idea that there are other words besides quantifiers that can make nouns specific. Give examples: *the* and *my*. Elicit other words (*your, those,* etc.).

Exercise B. | Point out that not all quantifiers require the word *of*. Have them determine its use in the sentences.

Answer Key **1.** of **2.** Ø **3.** Ø **4.** of **5.** of **6.** Ø

TIP Ask students why *of* was needed in 1, 4, and 5.

IDEAS FOR... Expansion

Write a copy of the scale from the grammar box on page 158 on the board. Have students write sentences about your school using each of the quantifiers. Give them an example: *None of the teachers in this school are from Cambodia.* Write your sentence above *none* on the scale. Give students time to write their own sentences.

Ask volunteers to write sentences along the scale on the board.

Exercise C. | Give students time to both ask and answer the questions. Allow time for partners to share their answers with the class.

Language Function: Making Suggestions for Home Remedies

Exercise A. | Brainstorming Read the directions to make sure everyone understands the steps.

Student to Student: Ending a Conversation | Explain that native speakers are careful when ending a conversation so as not to sound rude. In order to avoid an awkward ending, they give a signal, an explanation, or suggest a future plan. Tell students to pick an example from each column to form a variety of endings.

Exercise B. | Tell students to work on the conversation they started in exercise **A**. Have them try to use a few real conditionals and quantifiers. Require them to end the conversation politely.

Exercise C. | Presentation Have students perform their role-play for another pair. Allow time for peer feedback.

Presentation Skills: Looking Up While Speaking | Draw students' attention to the Presentation Skills box. Ask students if they have ever seen a presenter who didn't look up at the audience. Ask what they thought about that person's presentation.

IDEAS FOR... Expansion

Give students time to revise their role plays based on their peer feedback. Then have them perform for the class. Encourage them to look up while speaking to their partners.

45 mins

Engage: Preparing and Presenting a Group Summary

(page 160)

WARM-UP

Review the information about summaries. Remind students that summaries are an important part of academic work. Another important component is group work; sometimes students will have to create a group summary. Explain that this presentation will prepare them for such an activity in an academic course.

Refer students to pages 211–213 of the *Independent Student Handbook* for more information on group projects and presentations.

TIP **Groups of five are ideal, but students can double up on tasks if you have smaller groups. If you have six in a group, choose two experts.**

1. Assign students to groups of three to five. Go over the roles. Have students work together to choose the role they want to play.

> **IDEAS FOR... Multi-level Classes**
>
> Consider assigning the roles to students based on their levels. Higher-level students might do well as secretaries or experts. Lower-level students may be effective as the group leader, coach, or manager.

2. Depending on your class schedule, assign a time limit for the presentations and set a presentation date.
3. Let each group choose Option #1 or Option #2.

TIP **Give groups time in class to work together.**

4. Require students to have visual aids for their presentation. Schedule time in the school's computer lab if possible.
5. Remind students that it is a good idea to practice so that they can incorporate the presentation skills they've already learned and make sure their presentation fits within the time limit. Require that each person have a speaking role during the presentation while continuing to attend to his or her specific role.

TIP **Before presentation day, show clips of student or professional presenters giving a summary.**

6. Point out the evaluation form to students in advance so they know how they will be evaluated. Remind students that they will be evaluated as a group rather than as individuals. Explain that 5 is the highest score and 1 is the lowest.

TIP **Consider making copies of the evaluation form for students to evaluate each group. Collect them, without names of the evaluators, to share with the groups.**

> **IDEAS FOR... Expansion**
>
> Before students give their presentations to the class, have them evaluate video clips of students or professionals giving presentations. Ask students to use the evaluation form from the book and remind them this is the same form that you and their peers will use to evaluate their summaries.

The Legacy of Ancient Civilizations

Academic Track
Anthropology/ History

Academic Pathways:
Lesson A: Listening to a Lecture
Discussing Timelines
Lesson B: Listening to a Discussion about a Group Project
Giving a Group Presentation

Unit Theme

Learning about ancient civilizations can be a fascinating process. People who have lived and died before us teach us valuable lessons about how to live—or how not to live—today. The past is still very much alive in many parts of the world. Ancient Celtic culture is celebrated in Great Britain, and modern tourists flock to Cambodia to walk among the ruins of the ancient Khmer civilization.

Unit 9 encourages students to explore anthropology and history as they relate to:
- ancient versus modern times
- ancient civilizations
- the impact of the past on culture
- making comparisons

5 mins

Think and Discuss *(page 161)*

Anthropology is the study of humans. The field studies humans, their ancestors, their behavior, and their differences, among other things.

- Anthropology is often subdivided into different categories. Ask students if they can name any of these categories. Elicit answers such as *cultural, social, linguistic,* or *physical* anthropology.
- Explain that anthropologists often study artifacts found at the sites of ancient civilizations. Ask students if they would like to search for and draw conclusions about ancient civilizations.
- Discuss the questions in the book and ask students to make guesses about the mask.
- Point out Egypt on a map and ask students what they know about its history.

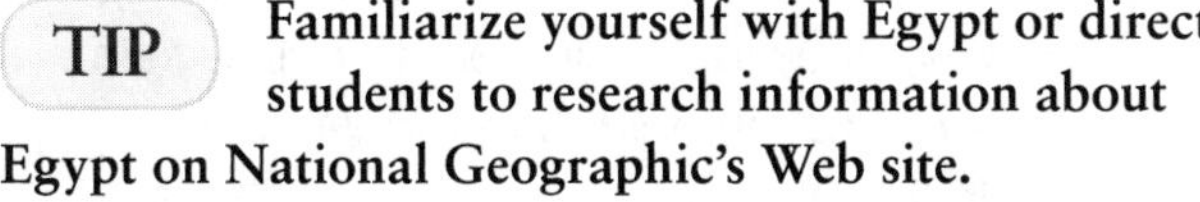
TIP **Familiarize yourself with Egypt or direct students to research information about Egypt on National Geographic's Web site.**

Pronunciation Note
Tell el Sowwah: Tell el **Su**-wah

15 mins

Exploring the Theme: The Legacy of Ancient Civilizations *(pages 162-163)*

The opening spread features information about three ancient civilizations and a photograph of an archeological site in Peru. Make sure students are prepared to discuss these ancient civilizations.

- Discuss the questions on page 162.

IDEAS FOR... Expansion
Ask students to do some research on one ancient civilization they are familiar with or would like to know more about. Ask them to bring in one interesting fact about that ancient civilization.

Pronunciation Note
Choquequirau: chok-uh-keer-**ow**

30 mins

Building and Using Vocabulary *(pages 164-165)*

WARM-UP

The Lesson A target vocabulary is presented in a box and students are asked to identify words they already know. Have a warm-up discussion to help students check more words.

- Ask students about any events they celebrate or that have been celebrated in history. Make a list on the board.

Building Vocabulary

Exercise A. | Using a Dictionary Ask students to check the words they already know. Encourage them to use a dictionary to look up new words. Then ask students to match the words to the definitions.

Answer Key

1. battle	**5.** celebration	**9.** adopt
2. endure	**6.** invade	**10.** ruins
3. rebellious	**7.** defense	
4. surround	**8.** appealing	

IDEAS FOR... Checking Comprehension

Refer back to the list of celebrations on the board. Ask students if any of the vocabulary words can be used to describe any of the celebrations they listed.

Exercise B. | Give students time to complete the chart.

Answer Key

Nouns: battle, celebration, defense, ruins

Verbs: endure, surround, invade, adopt

Adjectives: rebellious, appealing

IDEAS FOR... Expansion

Have students work in groups. Ask them to create a new word chart by converting each vocabulary word into a different part of speech. Give them the example of changing the verb form *invade* to the noun form *invader*. As a class, create a new chart on the board that includes the new word forms students came up with.

Exercise C. | Discussion Give students time to discuss the question.

TIP **Students are probably familiar with English (England), French (France), Spanish (Spain), and Portuguese (Portugal). Let them know that Celtic languages are still spoken in the darker green areas.**

TIP **Some labels, in white, may be difficult to read. They are *Cornwall, Brittany, Galicia, Asturias,* and *Minho.***

Using Vocabulary

Exercise A. | Give students time to fill in the paragraphs with the correct vocabulary items.

Answer Key

Prehistoric Times: ruins, surrounded

Period of Invasions: invaded, battles, rebellious, defenses

Modern Times: endure, appealing, adopt, celebrations

IDEAS FOR... Expansion

Put students in groups. Have them talk about their own culture (its history or one of its celebrations). When they have finished, have students write a short paragraph or summary about what they told their group. Require them to use a certain number of the vocabulary words in their paragraphs.

track 3-12

Exercise B. | Play the audio so students can check their answers to exercise **A**.

45 mins

Developing Listening Skills

(pages 166-167)

Pronunciation: Voicing and Syllable Length

Go over the information in the box. Have students practice or repeat each of the sounds with their hands over their ears so they can hear the difference between them. Play the audio more than once if necessary.

Exercise A. | Play the audio before and after students practice.

Exercise B. | Give students time to identify the short and long vowel sounds. Go over the answers before students practice the conversations with a partner.

Answer Key

1. ice (short), eyes (long)
2. advice (short), advise (long)
3. use (short), use (long)

Before Listening

Prior Knowledge | Tell students to activate their prior knowledge by looking at the photo and reading the caption.

IDEAS FOR... **Multi-level Classes**

Students who finish early can talk together about what they know about Ireland.

Listening: A Lecture

Exercise A. | **Listening for Main Ideas**
The listening passage is an excerpt from a lecture. Prepare students to take notes as they listen.

TIP Inform students that both hard *c* (/k/ sound) and soft *c* (/s/ sound) are correct when pronouncing the word *Celtic.* The audio program uses the hard *c.*

IDEAS FOR... **Checking Comprehension**

Have students compare their answers to exercise **A** with another student. For each answer, have students identify the information from the listening that indicates they have the correct answer (or helps them correct any incorrect answers).

Answer Key **1.** a **2.** b **3.** a **4.** c

Exercise B. | Play the audio again and ask students to identify the words they hear.

Answer Key

1. belief	**4.** backs	**7.** have
2. sad	**5.** safe	**8.** wrote
3. peace	**6.** leave	

After Listening

Self-Reflection | Ask a volunteer to read the information in the box aloud. Address any vocabulary issues or questions before students discuss the questions.

TIP If time allows, have students discuss what they might like about Celtic traditions and whether or not they would like to visit Ireland.

IDEAS FOR... **Expansion**

Play some Celtic music in class. Ask students if they like or dislike it. Assign a future date for students to bring a short recording of traditional music from another country they know well, perhaps their own. Have each student play their recording and tell the class something about the music—for example, what they like about it, at what celebrations it is played, or how long it has been played.

45 mins

Exploring Spoken English *(pages 168-170)*

Grammar: The Past Unreal Conditional

IDEAS FOR... Presenting Grammar

Begin the presentation by giving two sentences in the simple past.

I liked the English class.

I ate pizza for dinner last night.

Review real conditionals from Unit 8. Ask students to make a list of three things they wish they would have done when they were younger. Give an example by saying: *I wish I would have taken dance lessons.*

Explain that sometimes students will need to talk about unreal conditions. Define unreal as something that might have happened but did not happen. Give an example using your list: *If I had taken dance lessons, I might have become a dance teacher instead of an English teacher.*

Go over the information in the box. Make sure students understand that *if* clauses use the past perfect verb tense and result clauses use *would have* and the past participle. Answer any questions.

Ask students to choose one item from their list and write an unreal conditional sentence.

Exercise A. | Prior Knowledge Ask a volunteer to read the information about Lesson A in the book. Give students time to think what could have happened to the Celts.

Exercise B. | Give students time to think of two ways to complete each sentence.

TIP Make sure students' answers are truly unreal. Using situations that are accurate for the context is important while learning the meaning of this form.

IDEAS FOR... Expansion

Ask students to look at the list they made when you were presenting the grammar. Have them exchange their list with a partner. Tell them to imagine they are interviewing each other and that they need to ask questions, such as *What do you think your life would be like if you had (done something from the list)?* Students should answer the interviewers by using the correct grammar. Give them enough time to reverse roles.

track 3-16

Exercise C. | Ask if anyone has heard of Angkor. Draw students' attention to the photo. Then play the audio and have students follow along.

TIP Review the characteristics of World Heritage sites. Information about World Heritage sites can be found at the Web site of the United Nations Educational, Scientific, and Cultural Organization (UNESCO). Photos can be found at the National Geographic Web site.

Exercise D. | Give students time to rewrite the sentences. Check their grammar. Remind students that the *if* clause can be first or last. Review the box on page 168 if necessary.

Answer Key *(Answers may vary.)*

2. If Angkor's engineers hadn't been able to control the water, there would have been serious flooding every year.
3. There wouldn't be 50 large temples at Angkor if the Khmer hadn't built them.
4. The Angkor Wat wouldn't have been built in the 1100s if King Suryavarman II hadn't ordered its construction.
5. Angkor Wat wouldn't have become a UNESCO World Heritage site if it hadn't been rediscovered by the Western world in the late 1800s.
6. If the Khmer Empire had been able to keep control of the Mekong River delta, they could have traded on the South China Sea.

track 3-17

Exercise E. | Give students time to read the conversation or ask volunteers to read it aloud before playing the audio. Answer any vocabulary questions that arise. Give students time to discuss the speakers' regrets.

Language Function: Discussing Conclusions

Critical Thinking Focus: Drawing Conclusions | Go over the information in the box. Make sure students understand the example. Ask them to write another example in their notebooks. Ask volunteers to read their conclusions.

Exercise A. | Have students work in small groups to discuss the information and draw conclusions based on the bulleted points about Angkor. Point out the speech bubble.

Remind students that good conclusions are drawn from all of the information available, not only small pieces of information. Tell them to rely on all the information in this unit.

TIP Have students rely on prior knowledge as well, such as information about World Heritage sites.

Exercise B. | Discussion Give students time to talk about the questions. Ask one group to volunteer to read the answers.

Pronunciation Note
Mekong: mey-kong
Srah Srang: su-rah su-rong

30-45 mins

Speaking *(page 171)*

Discussing Time Lines

Tell students that time lines are used frequently in history books, but also in academic work in general. Ask them to discuss as a class reasons why time lines are used. List the reasons on the board.

track 3-18

Exercise A. | Draw attention to the time line of Carl's life. Have students read and practice the conversation before playing the audio.

TIP Allow students to practice the conversation again, and encourage them to try to mirror the pronunciation used by Rick and Carl in the audio recording.

Exercise B. | Discussion Have students discuss the events on Carl's time line. Prepare them to summarize their answers for the class.

IDEAS FOR... Expansion

Have students write about a negative experience on an index card (it can be real or imaginary). Tell them the activity is anonymous, so they should not put their names on the card. Shuffle the cards and put them in a bag. Ask students to form small groups and have each person pick a card from the bag. Tell them to imagine they need to offer a reason why this negative experience is actually good, or offer advice on what the person should do now. Have them write on the back of the card. Continue to have students choose cards as often as time allows. At the end of the activity, collect the cards and read the negative experiences and the reasons and advice offered.

Exercise C. | Self-Reflection Give students time to make their own time lines.

Exercise D. | Presentation Have students share their time lines in small groups.

30 mins

Viewing: Lost Temple of the Mayans *(pages 172-173)*

Overview of the Video | The Mayan civilization is well known for its strides in language, art, mathematics, astronomy, and architecture. Parts of the Mayan culture can be seen throughout Honduras and Guatemala as well as in parts of Mexico and El Salvador.

Dating back as far as BC 2000, the Mayan culture has been much studied over the years. Some believe that El Mirador, a very old Mayan site, may hold important information about the Mayan civilization.

Before Viewing

Ask students to look at the title and photos and answer these questions:

1. Where is Honduras? Where is Guatemala? Have you ever been to either of these two countries?
2. What do you think of the carvings? Do you think you would like living in El Mirador?

Exercise A. | Prior Knowledge Tell students that the words in the exercise are used in the video. Allow them to use a dictionary if necessary.

Answer Key

1. elusive **2.** chamber **3.** setback **4.** evidence
5. solid **6.** current **7.** commission **8.** suspect

IDEAS FOR... **Checking Comprehension**

Have students form small groups. Ask them to think about a job in which each vocabulary word might be used. Give an example. Say: *I'd list* judge *under* chamber *because judges usually have a chamber, or big room, to work in.* Tell them to use the same parts of speech used in the book's definitions. Ask students to list as many jobs as they can think of.

Exercise B. | Prior Knowledge Have students take the quiz on the Mayan civilization.

Answer Key **1.** b **2.** a **3.** a **4.** b

While Viewing

7:22 **Exercise A. |** After students watch the video, go over the answers to the quiz.

TIP **Note the length of this video clip; it is the longest in the book. Allow enough time to watch the video two times to complete both exercise A and exercise B.**

7:22 **Exercise B. |** Play the video again so students can complete the sentences.

Answer Key

1. between AD 250 and 900
2. how did they achieve so much
3. Mayan kings
4. more personally
5. BC 152 to BC 145
6. pyramid
7. an ancient Mayan king

After Viewing

Exercise A. | Critical Thinking Review the form of indirect questions. Have students develop questions for Hanson.

Exercise B. | Discussion Give students time to share their answers with another group.

30 mins

Building and Using Vocabulary *(pages 174-175)*

WARM-UP

Students are asked to read and listen to information about mummies. Ask students if they have ever seen a mummy in a movie or in a museum. Find out what they already know about mummies.

Building Vocabulary

track 3-19 track 3-20 track 3-21

Exercise A. | Meaning from Context Tell students to pay special attention to the words in blue.

Ask students to talk about which fact they found the most interesting.

TIP Go over the words that are footnoted below the reading. Explain why certain words are highlighted for them to learn while others are included as footnotes. Make students aware that, in general, words that are footnoted are specific to that reading, while words that are highlighted for them to learn are more general and may appear in many types of readings.

Using Vocabulary

Exercise B. | Have students match the definitions to the words.

Answer Key

1. die **2.** distinguish **3.** rational **4.** accompanied **5.** aspects **6.** eternity **7.** tough **8.** inevitable **9.** attempt **10.** exceeded

IDEAS FOR... Checking Comprehension

Call on students to write one question that includes a vocabulary word. Assign words to students so that all words are used. Give an example: *My question would be "What is a tough part of learning English?"* Ask students to answer your question. Give students time to write and then ask their question to the class and solicit answers from classmates.

Exercise C. | Allow time for students to both ask and answer the questions. Encourage them to also use the vocabulary item in their answers.

IDEAS FOR... Multi-level Classes

Pair students of similar levels. If higher-level students finish early, ask them to extend their conversations by adding more details.

Exercise D. | Define collocation and make sure students understand the concept. Give a few examples if necessary (*make progress, heavy traffic, strong smell*).

Answer Key *(Answers will vary.)*

2. There are many different aspects of English. My favorite aspects are pronunciation and speaking.

3. It's my dream to climb Mt. McKinley, so I'll make an attempt next year.

IDEAS FOR... Expansion

Have students form small groups. Ask them to brainstorm a list of other collocations. Have them write their lists on the board. Go over them to make sure they are truly collocations. Then ask students to use the collocations in sentences.

Pronunciation Note

Tutankhamen: toot-en-**kah**-men

Developing Listening Skills

45 mins *(pages 176-177)*

Before Listening

Using Context Clues | Ask students if they have ever missed an important point in a conversation or lecture because they spent too much time struggling with a vocabulary item they didn't know. Talk about how this made them feel.

Point out that they have been learning vocabulary words by reading them in context. Tell them that using context to derive meaning is a vital part of speaking and listening, too. Go over the information in the box. Explain that they shouldn't panic if they miss something they hear. Often they can figure it out based on context.

track 3-22 **Exercise A. |** Tell students that it is common for native speakers to miss parts of a conversation or lecture, especially if it is a new topic or has a lot of new or technical vocabulary. Mention that this listening passage will have two parts missing. The missing parts might be more than one sentence. Play the audio while students follow along in the book.

TIP **Remind students that distractions are another reason why people miss parts of conversations or lectures.**

Exercise B. | Have students analyze the words and phrases around the missing parts of the talk. Tell them to draw conclusions about what the missing information is.

Answer Key	1. b 2. b

TIP **Students may be frustrated that the missing parts are not available for them to read or hear. Emphasize that the objective is to realize that the general idea is conveyed even if every word can't be heard (or understood).**

Exercise C. | Discussion Keep students focused on the transcript. Give them time to discuss the specific information they used to draw their conclusions.

Listening: A Discussion about a Group Project

track 3-23 **Exercise A. | Listening for Main Ideas** The listening passage is a discussion among students about a group project. Alert students that information is deliberately missing and that they need to use the context to determine the answers. Again, there may be more than one sentence missing.

Answer Key	1. c 2. b 3. b

IDEAS FOR... Checking Comprehension

Ask students to give reasons for their answers. At the end of the discussion, point out how they heard a lot of other words and comprehended the main ideas without hearing every detail.

track 3-23 **Exercise B. | Listening for Details** Have students complete the notes in the book.

Answer Key

ancient culture: Celtic
presentation topic: Celtic musical instruments
presentation length: 6–10 minutes
meeting to practice; time: 8:00 A.M. Wednesday
meeting after class at: library

After Listening

Discussion | Have students discuss the questions with a partner.

Remind students they could summarize their answers using T-charts.

30 mins

Exploring Spoken English
(pages 178-179)

Grammar: Comparatives—*The -er, the -er*

IDEAS FOR... Presenting Grammar

Explain that comparatives are used to describe how two things increase or decrease or get better or worse over time. Tell them that the two parts of the sentence must be related. Write these sentences on the board as examples:

The more I learn in English class, the better I do on English tests.

The more I learn in English class, the worse I do on math tests.

Point out that the second sentence isn't logical because what you learn in English class isn't related to your performance on math tests.

Go over the information in the box. Make sure that students understand the different formations.

Open a discussion about academic contexts for which comparatives might be used. Give an example: *History students might compare two ancient civilizations.*

Exercise A. | Have students work together to practice saying the sentences.

Exercise B. | Have students read about the imaginary civilization. Then give them time to create a story about the civilization using *the -er, the -er* comparatives. Have them read their stories to the class.

IDEAS FOR... Expansion

Have students work in groups to create a list of bulleted points about their own imaginary civilization, one in which they would like to live. Then exchange lists with another group. Write comparatives using the information.

Language Function: Interrupting and Holding the Floor

TIP Explain that holding the floor means a person continues speaking despite interruptions.

Student to Student: Interrupting and Holding the Floor | Initiate a discussion about when it might be necessary to interrupt someone who is holding the floor. Talk about when it is permissible to keep holding the floor even when someone is trying to interrupt. Go over the information and phrases in the box.

track 3-24 **Exercise A.** | Have students listen to the conversation and then practice with a partner.

TIP Explain that intonation is important to make interruptions sound polite.

Exercise B. | Tell students to have five-minute conversations. Explain that five minutes is ample time to hold the floor and interrupt.

TIP Bring a stopwatch and let students know when you are starting the clock.

Exercise C. | **Self-Reflection** Have students discuss the questions. Ask them to summarize their ideas for the rest of the class.

45 mins

Engage: Giving a Group Presentation *(page 180)*

WARM-UP

Explain that group work is a large part of academic classes. Ask students to name benefits of group work. Elicit answers such as *sharing the work* and *not being as nervous during presentations.* Solicit stories about past experiences with group work and group presentations. Tell students that they are going to research an ancient civilization and create a group presentation for class.

TIP **Announce the amount of time students will have for their presentation and assign a date for presentations before students get started.**

Presentation Skills: Supporting Your Co-Presenters

Explain that one of the best parts of a group presentation is having support from your team. Stress the point that it requires effort to be a good co-presenter. Go over the information in the box.

Exercise A. | Divide students into groups of three to five.

1. Ask students to assign roles within their groups. Review the responsibilities of each role with the class and refer students to page 160 in Unit 8.
2. Encourage students to brainstorm a list of civilizations or aspects of civilizations as possible topics. Have them narrow their choices to one the whole team agrees on.

TIP **If students don't have time in a computer lab, have a list of possible topics available: China, Mesopotamia, Kush (African), Pompeii, Greece, and Rome.**

3. Remind students that visual aids will be required.

TIP **Allow time in the computer lab if students don't have appropriate resources at home.**

4. Remind students that it is important to practice in order to stay within the time limit and incorporate the presentation skills they have already learned.
5. Tell students that every member of the group is required to speak during the presentation.

TIP **Use the evaluation form on page 160 again. Ask students to add the points given in exercise B as new criteria on the evaluation form. Let them know that this will be the form their peers use to provide feedback on their presentation.**

Exercise B. | Discussion Have students reflect on the planning and presentations after they finish. Give them time to discuss the questions in the book. Have them briefly report their ideas to the class.

UNIT

10

Emotions and Personality

Academic Track
Psychology

Academic Pathways:
Lesson A: Listening to a Radio Interview
Conducting a Survey
Lesson B: Listening to an Informal Conversation
Assessing the Credibility of a News Article

Unit Theme

Psychologists study the mind, examining human behavior and discovering how people's thoughts, beliefs, and experiences shape them. One aspect of psychology is personality—the set of traits that make each person unique. Whether they're introverts or extroverts, happy most of the time or often depressed, there is much to learn about why people feel and act in the ways that they do.

Unit 10 explores the topic of psychology and personality as it relates to:
- emotions and expressing emotions
- how behavior is affected
- discussing past events
- personality types

5 mins

Think and Discuss *(page 181)*

Emotions are associated with personality. They define moods and feelings and describe how people feel. Emotions can be positive or negative. They are often studied in conjunction with personality because they can affect a person's behavior. Ask students to list as many emotions as they can. Get them started by writing *happy* and *sad* on the board.

Draw students' attention to the photo and the first question. Choose a few other emotions from their lists and ask about behavior associated with those emotions.

Extend the discussion by asking if they think people act differently when they experience different emotions. Have them discuss the second and third questions. Ask students to think about people they know with very different personalities. Ask students what might have caused these people's differences?

15 mins

Exploring the Theme: Emotions and Personality *(pages 182-183)*

The opening spread features a photo of young people wearing masks for a festival in Spain. The questions encourage students to think about how money affects happiness. Get students to think about the topic.

- Begin by asking students if they are familiar with the following expressions: *money can't buy happiness*, *love of money is the root of all evil*, and *money makes the world go round.* Ask students what they think each saying means. Have students talk about whether they believe there is any truth to the phrases.
- Have students read the introductory information.
- Discuss the questions.

IDEAS FOR... Expansion

Ask students to do some research about their own country and prepare to tell their classmates what percentage of the people are thriving and what their happiness can be attributed to.

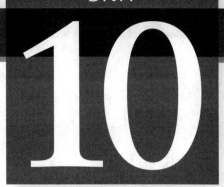

Pronunciation Note Mui Ne: m-oi nee

30 mins

Building and Using Vocabulary *(pages 184-185)*

WARM-UP

The Lesson A target vocabulary is presented in the context of a conversation.

- Before reading and playing the audio, draw attention to the photos and captions. Ask students if they agree that the facial expressions match the captions.
- Survey the class to see if they think culture makes a difference in the facial expressions people make.

TIP **Be aware that some research results suggest that some cultures do express the same emotion with different expressions, contrary to Ekman's research presented in this dialog.**

Building Vocabulary

track 3-25

Exercise A. | Meaning from Context Ask students to read the text and listen to the audio at the same time.

Exercise B. | Discussion Give students time to practice the conversation and discuss the questions. Have them summarize their ideas.

IDEAS FOR... Expansion

Write the names of several emotions on index cards, one emotion per card. Emotions can include those the students listed while working on page 182. Consider including *happiness, sadness, surprise, anger, jealousy, anxiety, fear, nervousness, loneliness, disgust, trust, love, disappointment, relief, frustration, confusion, shame, sympathy,* and so on. Divide students into two teams and give the teams an equal number of cards. Have one member of each team take a card and then make a facial expression to express that emotion. The other team tries to guess the emotion. Explain that the game does not involve any words, only facial expressions. Students take turns showing an emotion with facial expressions while the other team guesses what the emotion is.

Using Vocabulary

Exercise C. | Have students match the words in blue on page 184 with their definitions.

Answer Key

1. basic	**5.** personality	**9.** conducted
2. associate	**6.** trigger	**10.** fear
3. phenomenon	**7.** universal	
4. confirmed	**8.** speculated	

Exercise C. | Give students time to write answers to the questions.

IDEAS FOR... Checking Comprehension

Have students write a new sentence using one of the vocabulary words. Have volunteers write their sentences on the board. As they write, have them omit the vocabulary word, but draw a line where it should be. As a class, have students guess the missing word. Ask the student who wrote the sentence to confirm if students guessed the right word.

Exercise D. | Have students complete the quiz questions.

Answer Key **1.** basic **2.** triggers **3.** fear **4.** associate **5.** phenomenon

Exercise E. | Critical Thinking Give students time to ask each other the questions and talk about their answers.

Exercise F. | Discussion Have students answer the questions. Encourage them to support their answers with opinions and details.

45 mins

Developing Listening Skills *(pages 186-187)*

track 3-26 track 3-27

Pronunciation: Intonation for Thought Groups

Explain that English is spoken in thought groups. Define thought groups as "words that go together." Go over the information in the box. Remind students that they will be asked to identify thought groups and that they should take special note of the falling pitch and slight pause that generally happen at the end of thought groups.

Answer Key

1. Elena has a good personality, / but she doesn't have many friends.
2. We went to the store, / and we bought some fruit.
3. I can't decide between the red shoes /and the brown ones.
4. Do you want to fix the car yourself / or take it to a mechanic?

Before Listening

Predicting Content | Tell students they will hear an interview about fear. Ask students to make predictions about the topic.

Listening: A Radio Interview

track 3-28

Exercise A. | Listening for Main Ideas Play the audio and ask students to answer the questions.

Answer Key

1. radio show host, psychologist
2. whether we learn to be afraid of certain things, or if we inherit something from our ancestors that triggers our fear
3. we inherit a tendency to fear certain things (the same things our ancestors fear), but we also have to learn from others around us
4. his experiment with wild monkeys

track 3-28

Exercise B. | Listening for Details Play the audio again. Have students determine if each statement is true or false.

IDEAS FOR... Checking Comprehension

Ask students to make the necessary changes to turn the false statements into true ones. Challenge students to explain each answer in small groups.

Answer Key

1. T **2.** F **3.** F **4.** F **5.** F

1. no change needed
2. The man's name is Eugene Bateman.
3. The man says that the fear response protected our ancient ancestors from dangers such as hungry lions.
4. The man's example of putting our foot on the brakes in a car is an example of a fear response that happens even before we realize what is happening (or is an example of fear response that keeps us out of trouble).
5. The man says that researchers were able to teach lab monkeys to be afraid of snakes.

track 3-28

Exercise C. | Discussion Play the audio one more time and ask students to pay attention to thought groups as they listen. Give them time to answer the question.

After Listening

Exercise A. | Summarizing Have students summarize the experiment.

Exercise B. | Have students complete and prioritize the list. Ask them to put their rankings on the board. Open the floor to discussion.

Student to Student: Expressing Emotions | Go over the information and words in the box. Note that this information is applicable to both exercises **B** and **C**.

Exercise C. | Discussion Give students time to discuss the questions.

45 mins

Exploring Spoken English *(pages 188-190)*

Grammar: The Past Perfect Tense

IDEAS FOR... Presenting Grammar

Explain that in academic research, it is often necessary to describe two events that happened at different times in the past. In order to make it clear which event happened before the other, we use the past perfect tense.

Ask students to write two things they did before coming to English class. For example: *I ate breakfast. I packed my books.* Ask them to label the sentences in the order they occurred: *(1) I packed my books. (2) I ate breakfast.*

Go over the information and examples of the form of the past perfect in the box. Then continue by discussing the words and phrases *already*, *not yet*, *not ever*, and *never* and the examples. Finally, discuss the simple past tense options and examples.

Have students look at their pairs of sentences and combine them into one sentence using the past perfect tense. Write your example on the board: *I had already packed my books when I ate breakfast.* Ask students for other ways to write the sentence. For example, *After I packed my books, I ate breakfast.*

IDEAS FOR... Expansion

Ask students to repeat your example using the word *before*. Refer to the box on page 188 to show how to form this sentence.

Exercise A. | Read the sentences in the chart. Have students work in pairs to combine the sentences.

Answer Key *(Answers may vary.)*

2. The lecturer had already finished speaking when I arrived at ten thirty.
3. Ken and Rieko had already eaten dinner by the time I arrived at the restaurant.
4. Kim had fallen asleep before the movie ended.
5. Before their parents came home, the children had made a mess.
6. The meeting had already started when Sheila got to work at 10:00.

track 3-29

Exercise B. | Ask students how many times a day they wash their hands, and why. See if they are surprised to learn that there may be psychological reasons to wash their hands. Play the audio and have students follow along before they underline the past perfect.

Answer Key

(Paragraph 2)
had made
had [ranked them]

(Paragraph 4)
hadn't used
had used

Exercise C. | Discussion Provide enough time for students to discuss the grammar of the article in question 1 and the content in questions 2 and 3.

Walk around the classroom to make sure students have the correct verbs underlined.

Language Function: Discussing Past Events

Exercise A. | Critical Thinking Draw students' attention to the photo. Have them work with a partner to brainstorm a list of things the couple had done before 1975. Then have students read the speech bubbles. Have students practice their own conversations using the ideas they brainstormed.

Exercise B. | Give students time to join another pair of students to share answers and check grammar.

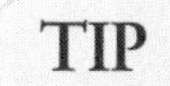

Walk around the classroom to make sure students' use of grammar is correct.

IDEAS FOR... **Expansion**

Ask students to bring in photos of people they know. Have students exchange photos and write sentences about what the people were doing or thinking when the photo was taken. Have students give the photos back and read their sentences to the owner of the photos. They can talk about how many guesses were correct.

Critical Thinking Focus: Assessing the Credibility of Sources | Go over the information in the box. Tell students that having reliable sources is important in academic research.

Exercise A. | Critical Thinking Have students work in groups. Ask them to imagine they are part of a research team. Have them rank the items on the credibility scale.

TIP **Explain that there isn't a right or wrong answer to the ranking exercise. Also, the ranking of the credibility of any source may vary depending on the field of study.**

Exercise B. | Discussion Give students time to share their ideas and discuss the questions.

IDEAS FOR... **Expansion**

Have students bring in an article about a study from their own major. Ask students with similar majors to sit together. Have them rank their articles using the credibility scale. Have them explain their rankings to the other groups.

IDEAS FOR... **Expansion**

Ask students to list Web sites, newspapers, books, or magazines that they read. Make a list on the board. Have small groups decide if each one is a reliable source and give a reason why it is or isn't. Open a class discussion comparing answers and discussing the importance of using credible sources.

30-45 mins

Speaking *(page 191)*

Conducting a Survey

Exercise A. | Make sure students understand what a survey is and mention that surveys are another common way to gather data for research. Have each student follow the directions to create a survey and administer it to three other students.

Exercise B. | Discussion Give students time to analyze their data. Then have them talk about generalizations.

TIP **Point out that a survey of only three people is not valid. Remind students that the objective is to experience the procedure and practice generalizing. To reach valid generalizations, they would need a much larger survey pool.**

IDEAS FOR... **Expansion**

Have students expand the survey by administering it to 10 people outside of the class. Have them compile their data in the form of a pie chart and present it to the class with their conclusions.

30 mins

Viewing: Sigmund Freud
(pages 192-193)

Overview of the Video | Psychoanalysis includes several basic ideas, namely that behavior is determined by *drives* and those drives are irrational and mainly unconscious. These basic ideas are combined with several other ideas and theories in the study of human behavior. Sigmund Freud is considered to be the father of psychotherapy. He believed that one way to study the unconscious mind was through dream interpretation.

Before Viewing

Ask students if they know the names of any well-known psychotherapists or psychoanalysts. Focus their attention on Sigmund Freud.

Exercise A. | Prior Knowledge Announce that the video is about Sigmund Freud. Ask students to list any facts they know about him.

TIP **Since some students may not know much about Freud, have a large-group discussion for other students to share their knowledge.**

Exercise B. | Using a Dictionary Introduce the words in the box to the students and give them time to match them to their definitions. Permit use of a dictionary.

Answer Key	**1.** unconscious **2.** suppress **3.** drive **4.** hallmark **5.** fled **6.** masterpiece

IDEAS FOR... Checking Comprehension

Have students answer these questions with a partner:

What is something that drives you?
What would you flee from?
What is the hallmark of psychotherapy?
What is a masterpiece you have seen?
What emotions do many people want to suppress?
What is something people do unconsciously?

Have them share answers with other groups.

While Viewing

2:31 **Exercise A. |** Play the video and have students see if their ideas about Freud were correct.

2:31 **Exercise B. |** Play the video again and have students mark the statements *true* or *false*.

Answer Key	**1.** F **2.** T **3.** T **4.** F **5.** T **6.** F **7.** F

TIP **Students might think that the fourth statement is true. Point out that the statement uses the word *certain*, but the script uses the word *all*. Therefore, the answer is *F*.**

After Viewing

Exercise A. | Review the form of the past perfect.

Answer Key *(Answers may vary.)*

2. Freud wrote his masterpiece in 1899 after he had named the practice of *psychoanalysis*.

3. Freud turned 81 in 1938 after the Nazis had burned his book.

4. Freud died after his family had fled to England.

Exercise B. | Critical Thinking Ask students to discuss the questions and be prepared to share their answers with the rest of the class.

30 mins

Building and Using Vocabulary *(pages 194-195)*

WARM-UP

Review the process for this activity type. Survey the class to see if they already know some of the words.

Building Vocabulary

Exercise A. | Using a Dictionary Have students check the words they already know and then match them to their definitions.

Answer Key

1. extroverted	**5.** differ	**9.** introverted
2. interaction	**6.** anxiety	**10.** awkward
3. upset	**7.** attribute	
4. charming	**8.** depression	

track 3-30

Exercise B. | Have students read and listen to the information about introverts. Tell them to pay attention to the words in blue.

Exercise C. | Discussion Give students time to discuss the questions. Encourage them to use the new vocabulary words in their answers. Allow time for students to share their ideas for the third question. Encourage them to talk about their own stories and experiences if they're comfortable.

Using Vocabulary

track 3-31

Exercise A. | Have students read and listen to the information about extroverts. Tell them to pay attention to the words in blue.

IDEAS FOR... Checking Comprehension

Have students classify the vocabulary words into a chart titled *Attributes*. Divide the chart into two columns: *Introverts* and *Extroverts*. Have them put the other vocabulary words into the column most likely to be associated with that word.

Exercise B. | Critical Thinking Ask students to share answers and support their ideas.

Exercise C. | Discussion Give students time to discuss the questions. Allow students to share their answers with the class.

IDEAS FOR... Expansion

Have students take an online test or quiz to determine if they are introverted or extroverted. Remind them that most online quizzes are not official or certified tests and that this activity is just for fun. Put them in groups to share their results and talk about whether they agree or disagree with them.

TIP **For students who would like more information, have them read about the Myers-Briggs Type Indicator (MBTI), which is an assessment questionnaire that measures differences based on how individuals make decisions. One section of the MBTI measures introversion and extroversion.**

Exercise D. | Discussion Require that students work with different people for this discussion. Ask them to share their ideas.

IDEAS FOR... Expansion

Tell students to imagine they are psychotherapists. Tell them they have two patients: one who wants to be more extroverted and one who wants to be a little less extroverted. Develop a list of activities for each person to try in order to achieve their goals.

45 mins

Developing Listening Skills *(pages 196-197)*

Before Listening

TIP **Remind students of the Gallup World Poll mentioned at the beginning of the unit. Tell them they can find information about the poll online. Consider playing the video clip about the Gallup poll found on the Gallup Web site.**

Critical Thinking | Put students into small groups to talk about the questions. Have them summarize their discussion for the other groups.

Listening: An Informal Conversation

Ask students to think about how married people they know talk to each other. Let students know they will be listening to an informal conversation.

track 3-32 **Exercise A. | Listening for Main Ideas** Play the audio and have students answer the questions.

Answer Key

1. a work party (Leo's job)
2. the personalities of Leo's colleagues
3. Reba is extroverted. Leo is a little more introverted. (Answers may vary.)
4. meeting colleagues at a restaurant or a sports game to keep a distance between work and personal

IDEAS FOR... Checking Comprehension

Ask students to support their answers with what they understand from the conversation. For example, their answers can begin with "Leo said, . . . ".

IDEAS FOR... Multi-level Classes

Group students of similar levels together to check their answers. If the higher-level groups finish quickly, ask them to list some of the details they remember from the audio or to role-play the conversation as they remember it.

track 3-32 **Exercise B. | Listening for Details** Play the audio again and have students take notes.

Answer Key

Gloria: seems charming, makes anything seem funny

Manager: really nice guy, pretty extroverted, makes people feel comfortable, great social skills

Toby: really introverted, experiences anxiety around a lot of people (especially new people), really nice, good coworker, fine with smaller groups of people

After Listening

Presentation Skills: Role-Playing | Have students read the information in the box. Make sure they understand the rationale for role playing and why it's important to focus on their roles and not worry about being nervous or feeling uncomfortable.

Exercise A. | Planning a Presentation Play the audio again if necessary for students to prepare their presentation.

TIP **Have students work in groups of five.**

Exercise B. | Presentation Have students perform their role plays for another group. Depending on the number of students, role plays could be performed for the class.

Exercise C. | Discussion Give students time to evaluate the role-playing experience.

30 mins

Exploring Spoken English

(pages 198-199)

Grammar: *Used To* + Verb vs. *Be Used To* + Noun

IDEAS FOR... Presenting Grammar

Explain that *used to* is a way to explain something that was true in the past, but that is no longer true in the present.

Tell students not to confuse this with *be used to*. This phrase means the same thing as *be accustomed to*.

Go over the information and examples in the box.

Give students time to read the sentences below the box and decide if a form of the verb *be* is necessary.

Answer Key **1.** are **2.** am **3.** Ø **4.** Ø **5.** Ø **6.** Ø

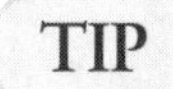

TIP **Ask students why *be* was needed in the first two sentences.**

Language Function: Discussing Study Habits

Exercise A. | Read about Salim's previous study habits aloud or ask a volunteer to read the text.

Exercise B. | Read the speech bubble. Ask students to say their own sentences using information about Salim when he was in high school. Make sure students use correct grammar.

Exercise C. | Read about Salim's current study habits aloud or ask a volunteer to read them.

Exercise D. | Read the speech bubble. Ask students to say their own sentences using information about Salim's study habits now. Make sure students use correct grammar.

IDEAS FOR... Expansion

Put students in small groups. Tell them to imagine they are advisors at a university. Ask them to make a list of study strategies they recommend for someone who wants to go to graduate school. Have them present their lists to the class.

TIP **Bring in a brochure from the advising office of a local college or university to share with the class.**

Exercise E. | Self-Reflection Have students make a list of differences between themselves as they were in the past and themselves as they are now.

TIP **Encourage students to use a T-chart as they work on exercise E.**

Exercise F. | Give students time to share their descriptions.

IDEAS FOR... Expansion

Review Venn diagrams on page 214 of the *Independent Student Handbook*. Have partners each make a Venn diagram about their personality. One circle of the diagram should include details about their personality from 10 years ago. The second circle should include details about the student now. The overlapping circle should include details that are true at both times. Have partners share their diagrams with one another or present their diagrams to the class or a small group.

45 mins

Engage: Assessing the Credibility of a News Article *(page 200)*

WARM-UP

- Ask students what they think *neuroscience* means.
- Read the information in the box at the top of page 200 aloud.
- Open a discussion about what news sources students think are credible. Make a list of any reasonable answers on the board. Elicit names of news sources such as *CNN, Wall Street Journal, Time, Newsweek, New York Times,* or reliable Web sites such as the *American Heart Association* or the *U.S. Census Bureau.*

TIP **Bring in some news articles from newspapers or from online sources that you consider credible for students to reference.**

track 3-33

Exercise A. | Have students read and listen to the news article. Address any vocabulary questions or content issues.

Exercise B. | Critical Thinking Review the credibility factors studied on page 190 of the text. Have students rate the article based on the criteria.

TIP **Remind students they might not have the same answers as everyone else.**

IDEAS FOR... Expansion

Bring in various news articles that you consider both reliable and unreliable. Have students work in groups. Ask them to look at each source and decide if it is credible. Have them exchange articles until each group has had an opportunity to see all the articles. Have groups exchange ideas.

Exercise C. | Planning a Presentation Have students form groups to discuss the article in the book. Tell them they will present their ideas. Give them a time limit.

TIP **Before students present their ideas, show clips of student or professional presenters talking about credible research.**

IDEAS FOR... Expansion

Have students revisit the articles you brought to class and that they feel come from a good source. Have students rate them based on the criteria from page 190 of the text. Ask students to keep their ratings and then exchange articles so that all groups rate all the articles. When everyone has finished, ask students to give their ratings for each article. Make a list on the board ordering the articles with the highest rating first and the lowest rating last. Ask students to explain their ratings. See if everyone agrees on the article that was rated the highest.

Exercise D. | Presentation Have students present their ideas about the article. Require them to make comparisons if appropriate with the groups before them.

CD1

Unit 1: Gender and Society Lesson A

Building Vocabulary

Track 2 A. Meaning from Context Page 4

Kabuki is a traditional form of singing and dancing theater that is still popular in Japan. One unusual characteristic of kabuki is that all the roles of women are played by male actors called *onnagata.* These actors spend many years studying women's behavior and activities, such as sewing. Some people say that the actors are more feminine than real women are!

There are many examples of male actors who play roles of the opposite gender, but the reverse doesn't happen very often. *The Year of Living Dangerously* is a famous movie from the 1980s. It's about an Australian journalist who meets a news photographer during a time of terrible violence. Many people didn't notice that the star who played the role of Billy Kwan, the photographer, was actually a woman. Linda Hunt won an Academy Award for her acting in the movie. She gave Billy Kwan many characteristics that people think are masculine, especially courage.

In the time of William Shakespeare, women were generally not allowed to appear on a theater stage. In Shakespeare's plays, female characters like Juliet (in *Romeo and Juliet*) were played by young boys. Some of them became very famous, like Nathan Field in this picture. When their voices changed and they grew older, these actors had to start playing men's roles.

Developing Listening Skills

Listening: A Lecture

Track 3 A. Listening for Main Ideas, B. Page 7

OK, so today we're going to continue on the topic of how children are socialized. We'll be looking at gender socialization—in other words, how, how children learn their gender roles. Gender is something that we learn—first from our parents, then from our peers, from school . . . and from the culture we live in.

OK, let's start with our parents. Generally, our gender roles are pretty clear to us by the time we're around . . . three years old . . . so how do we, how do we learn these roles so quickly? Well, one way is simply by what our parents say to us. Parents give female children a lot of compliments on how they look—on their appearance, right? We say things like, "What a pretty girl!" . . . or "That's a nice dress you're wearing." Girls might get compliments on other things, too, but they, they soon learn that being feminine has something to do with being attractive or pretty, right? Boys, in contrast, are complimented on what they do. We say things like, "Look how fast little Timmy can run! Good for you, Timmy!" So . . . over time, boys learn that being, being masculine has something to do with their behavior . . . and with being active.

Our peers, when we're children—girls and boys around the same age as we are—also teach us about gender roles . . . and sometimes they're not very nice about this either. . . . They make fun of children who aren't following the rules. . . . Can you remember kids from your childhood who didn't follow the gender rules? . . . Schools continue, schools continue the process of gender socialization. Some schools have separate classes for girls and boys, and, um, of course school uniforms are different—pants for boys, and skirts or dresses for girls. Finally, the culture we live in has a lot to teach us about gender roles.

Track 4 C. Listening for Details Page 7

As you know, one of the first questions when a baby is born is, "Is it a boy or a girl?" We think it's important to know this because when children grow up, their role in the world depends on their gender—at least to some degree. But nowadays, gender roles are changing, and besides, there have always been a few people who are not average, who do not follow the usual gender pattern.

One person from history who did *not* follow her usual gender role was Hatshepsut. Around 150 years before Tutankhamen ruled ancient Egypt as *pharaoh*, or king, Hatshepsut ruled for 21 years as the female king of Egypt. That's right—female *king,* because there was no such thing as a *queen* as leader. A few women had filled the role of leader when their sons were too young to rule, but Hatshepsut stayed in power even after her stepson, Tutmose III, was old enough to rule. And she accomplished a lot while she was king! Up and down the Nile River we can still see the monuments and buildings that were constructed or repaired while Hatshepsut was king. It seems that she did *not* want to be forgotten.

Besides the buildings and monuments, we have a lot of art from the time of Hatshepsut. And what's interesting is that at first, Hatshepsut is shown with female characteristics—she was clearly a woman, but with the clothing and symbols of a king. For example, in one statue, she is seated and has the body of a woman but is wearing the headdress of a king. In later years, we see the reverse. All of the later artwork shows her as a man, with male characteristics. We're not sure why Hatshepsut had her artists do this, but it may have helped her to keep power. It might have been easier for Egyptians to accept a man as king—or at least someone who *looked* like a man.

Lesson A and B Viewing: *Wodaabe*

Before Viewing

Track 5 B. Using a Dictionary Page 12

The Wodaabe *Geerewol* Festival

For most of the year, the Wodaabe are nomadic, moving from place to place to find grass for their cattle. For one week each year, however, it's festival time for the Wodaabe. It's called the *geerewol,* and it's a chance for Wodaabe men to show off for the women.

The *geerewol* is a kind of beauty pageant, and the men who participate wear makeup to emphasize the features that are considered beautiful by the Wodaabe: long noses, strong white teeth, and large eyes, among other characteristics.

The *geerewol* is all about attraction—both physical beauty and charm. While the men dance, the women watch and carefully evaluate the men's appearance. When an available woman finds a man who is irresistible to her, she lets him know with small gestures. With many women watching, the pageant has many winners.

Lesson B

Building Vocabulary

Track 6 A. Meaning from Context Page 14

Boys and Girls Test Their Geography

Question: Timis County is located in the western part of which European country?

Eric Yang knew the answer. "Romania!" he said, and became the winner of the National Geographic Geography Bee. Every year, thousands of young people compete in this international contest of geographical knowledge. Three winners from each country go on to the world championship.

For years, however, the contest's organizers have wondered about a question of their own. An equal number of girls and boys enter the contest at the school and regional levels. Why are so many of the national winners boys? In the United States, Eric's home country, only two girls have won the top prize since 1989.

Track 7 A. Meaning from Context Page 14

Canadian Boys Win World Geography Contest

Three boys from Canada have won the National Geographic World Championship in Mexico City, beating 16 other national teams. The second prize went to three boys from the USA, and the third prize to three boys from Poland. All teams also enjoyed several days of sightseeing in Mexico.

As in the past, most contestants were male, and this year two scientists investigated the reasons for this. They concluded that there is in fact a small gender gap in geography, but they couldn't find the cause. Possibly, boys are taught to be more assertive than girls, or they might feel more pressure from their parents. Maybe boys have a better ability to use maps. Or maybe teachers encourage boys more in geography classes.

Developing Listening Skills

Listening: A Conversation between Classmates

Track 8 A. Listening for Main Ideas Page 16

Mia: Hey, Dylan! Long time, no see!
Dylan: Yeah, it's been ages! I was gone all summer. I had a job working for my uncle, so I stayed with him in Toronto for two months. What about you, Mia? How've you been?
Mia: Great! I just spent the time right here because I was taking a course in summer school. I want to graduate early.
Dylan: Wow, you're really working hard! So, . . . what do you think about this class we're in?
Mia: Oh, I think it's going to be great! It's such an interesting topic—"Gender and Sociology".
Dylan: Hmmph. I suppose. I can see that Professor Henley is very knowledgeable on the subject. But I can also see that I disagree with her about a lot of things.
Mia: Such as . . . ?

Track 9 B. Page 16

Dylan: Well, I think some jobs just aren't good for women . . . like firefighters for instance.
Mia: What? . . . You think women aren't brave enough or something?
Dylan: Hey, I never said that! But, well, they aren't as strong—physically, I mean. Do you think a woman could carry me out of a burning building? Come on, everyone knows men are stronger than women.
Mia: Ha! So, you think you're stronger than the female athletes in the Olympics, just because you're a man?
Dylan: Well, no, of course not. . . .
Mia: Then you can't say that *all* men are stronger than *all* women. . . . Here, let me draw you a graph. . . .
Dylan: What's *that*?
Mia: It's from my summer school class. We had to do some research on gender differences . . . *and* similarities. . . . OK . . . now . . . look at this. . . . This line here shows how it looks if you make a graph of how strong women are, by how much weight they can lift. Here. A small woman *can't* lift more than 20 pounds. . . . And a woman athlete can lift 200 pounds. Right?
Dylan: I don't know, I guess so. . . .
Mia: Now, what about men? Can all men lift 200 pounds?
Dylan: Well, no, probably not. . . .
Mia: Can you lift 200 pounds? Hmmm?
Dylan: [laughter]
Mia: So, maybe a really small man can only lift, oh, 50 pounds. And a really big man can lift 200, so not all men are equal in terms of physical strength either. . . . There are different levels of strength within the genders, too. . . . So, the line for men looks like this. . . . Do you see what I mean? In fact, it's true that *most* men are stronger than *most* women . . . so there is a gender gap when it comes to physical strength. But you can't conclude that *all* men are stronger than *all* women. And if you have to lift, say, 150 pounds to be a firefighter, then some women *can* do the job.
Dylan: Well, I suppose so. . . .
Mia: Besides, most women are smaller than most men. So possibly they can go into smaller spaces to rescue people.

Track 10 C. Listening for Details Page 17

Dylan: It sounds like you just want women to compete with men and take their jobs away. . . .
Mia: No, I don't! There are lots of good jobs that only women used to do, and now men are hired for them, too.
Dylan: Hmm. I can't think of any!
Mia: Well, . . . look at flight attendants. For a long time people thought that only women had the ability to be helpful on planes.
Dylan: Yeah, back when they still used to call them stewardesses, right?
Mia: Yeah! My aunt was a flight attendant—or *stewardess*—when she was young, and she said it used to be just *awful*. They were required to be very thin, and they weren't allowed to keep their jobs if they gained weight! Oh, and they were forbidden to get married, and they had to stop working when they were 32—can you imagine? . . . But now that's all changed, fortunately, and the airlines encourage men to become flight attendants, too. There are lots of men who are flight attendants now.
Dylan: It sounds like a great job to me—traveling every day and meeting so many people. I can't imagine why the airlines didn't want men.
Mia: Well, they thought that all women were more helpful than all men!
Dylan: Now, that's a stupid idea. . . . And hey, men can lift heavier bags for the passengers! Remember? "*Most* men are stronger than *most* women."
Mia: Dylan, you're impossible!

Pronunciation

Track 11 ***Can and Can't*** **Page 17**

Examples:
I can speak three languages.
We can't find our new classroom.

Track 12 Page 17

1. But I can also see that I disagree with her about a lot of things.
2. A small woman can't lift more than 20 pounds.
3. And a woman athlete can lift 200 pounds.
4. Can all men lift 200 pounds?
5. I can't imagine why the airlines didn't want men.
6. Men can lift heavier bags for the passengers.

Unit 2: Reproducing Life Lesson A

Building Vocabulary

Track 13 A. Meaning from Context Page 24

The King Penguin: Challenges to Reproduction

An elephant seal shares South Georgia Island with a huge colony of King Penguins. The penguins have come to the island to reproduce, but space can be a problem. Each penguin must defend its territory, a small area less than three feet (one meter) across.

Although adult King Penguins weigh around 30 pounds (14 kilograms), they cannot always defend their chicks against predators such as this skua. In the ocean, seals and other sea animals sometimes eat penguins.

Cold temperatures also challenge penguin reproduction. This adult penguin keeps its egg warm until its mate returns. Adults may swim and eat for two weeks or more before they return and take over the care of the egg.

Climate change is creating another challenge. Penguin chicks are not independent. They depend on their parents for food. Warmer ocean water means less food nearby, so penguin parents are away for longer time periods and more chicks die.

Developing Listening Skills

Before Listening

Track 14 A. Meaning from Context Page 26

The Penguins of Possession Island

This is not the only documentary film about penguins this year, but it is one of the year's best. In this beautiful nature documentary, King Penguins come to Possession Island to find mates. Most of the footage shows us penguins on land, but some footage shows us penguins in the water.

There is something in this documentary for everyone — except perhaps for young children. Some scenes of penguin chicks being killed by predators are difficult to watch—even for adults.

I was lucky enough to see *The Penguins of Possession Island* in a movie theater, and everyone in the audience liked the film. Don't miss your chance to see it, even if you have to watch it on TV.

Listening: A Conversation about a Documentary

Track 15 A. Listening for Main Ideas
B. Listening for Details Page 26

Man: So, do we have a title yet?
Woman: No, but let's not worry about the title right now. We still need to do *a lot* of work on this film before we have to decide on a title.
Man: That's true. So, do you think they'll show it on the Documentary Channel?
Woman: I don't know, maybe, but they only show really good nature films on that channel, so . . . let's try to make this a really great film!
Man: Good idea. . . . OK, so, let's talk about the Possession Island footage. We have about four, about four hours of film.
Woman: Right. Well, we'll need to include some footage of the adult penguins finding mates. And I really want the audience to see the size of the colony. I think people will find that really interesting.
Man: Yeah, it's huge! And to hear the noise. It's such a noisy place!
Woman: That's true! I don't think many people realize just how huge these penguin colonies are. . . . Hmm, do you think we should include footage of predator birds? I mean, . . . it's so difficult to watch the penguin chicks being killed. Do you think people will really want to *see that*?
Man: It *is* difficult to watch, but it's part of penguin life. We're trying to show some of the challenges that King Penguins face. And defending their chicks against predators is a *serious* challenge for these penguins. It's not easy to watch, but it's, it's a fact.
Woman: All right, then we should also try to show how *cold* the island is, even in the summer.
Man: Sure, we could include some footage of the photographers in their big winter coats to help show that.
Woman: That's a good idea.
Man: And how about some scenes of the island in winter? That would *really* show how cold it is.
Woman: Well . . . yes, but the King Penguins aren't there in the winter. They leave their territories and they don't look for mates during that time of year, so I don't think it's important for the audience to know about winter on the island.
Man: I see what you mean. The film is mainly going to be about penguin reproduction. Having that focus is really going to help us edit our four hours of film footage down to a one-hour documentary.
Woman: Right. That will definitely help us make our decisions on what footage we should use.
Man: OK . . . so, what else do you think we should include? Do you, do you think we should include information on how *big* these penguins are and how much they weigh?
Woman: Yes, good idea. I think that's important information. . . . We also have a lot of footage of penguin parents feeding their chicks. That's important to include, too, since it shows how much work the adults have to do because their chicks are *so* dependent at first.
Man: Good. Hmmm. I don't think we need any footage of the penguins swimming in the water though. They look really beautiful, and they're so *fast* . . . but that doesn't help us tell our story.
Woman: Yes, I agree. Let's not include that.
Man: OK, so it sounds like we have a plan.
Woman: I think so.

Exploring Spoken English

Pronunciation

Track 16 Stress Patterns Before Suffixes Page 28

educate, edu**ca**tion
romance, rom**an**tic

Track 17 A. Page 28

gen**e**tic, gen**e**tic
technical, **tech**nical
repro**du**ction, repro**du**ction

Track 18 D. Page 28
A. Page 29

One type of animal reproduction is called "cell cloning." You probably remember the first cloned mammal? Dolly, the sheep? Well, in that case, scientists took a cell from an adult animal. *Any* type of cell can work because every cell in the body contains genetic information. OK, next, the scientists removed the *nucleus* from the cell. Remember, the nucleus is the part that contains DNA. Then they replaced the nucleus from an adult sheep's *egg* with this other nucleus. In other words, they used a normal egg cell, but all the genetic material in the cell came from that first animal. OK, now—as you know from biology class—egg cells begin to divide and grow when they meet a sperm cell from a male. But in the laboratory, chemicals or electricity can be used. And after the egg cell begins to divide, it can be placed inside the body of an adult female. She becomes pregnant, and if the pregnancy is successful, a cloned baby is born.

Lesson B

Building Vocabulary

Track 19 A. Meaning from Context Page 34

Orchid Question & Answer

Q. Imagine that you're a flower. Like every other living thing, you want to reproduce. But you can't move! How can you get your DNA to another flower?
A. Offer food. This is a great way to trick birds or insects. They think they're just getting a free meal in the form of *nectar*, a sweet liquid. However, they're also carrying your *pollen*—a substance that contains your DNA—to the next flower that they visit.
Q. Nectar is full of calories, so it requires a lot of energy to produce. Is there a less "expensive" way for me to move my pollen around?
A. Absolutely! Many orchids have found fascinating ways to attract insects without offering any food. To do this, they imitate something that the insects want. Here are some ways they do this:

Shelter: Even insects need a place to live. Some orchids resemble insect burrows. The insects crawl in, but since it's not really a good place to live, they leave with pollen on their bodies.
Scents: Insects are attracted to the smell of food, so orchids produce scents that seem wonderful to bugs, but not always to humans. The *Dracula* orchid attracts tiny insects called gnats by smelling like a dirty diaper!
Food: Orchids don't need to offer real food as long as they *seem* to offer food. The *Epidendrum* orchid resembles milkweed, a favorite food of butterflies. Butterflies visit the plant, but all they obtain is pollen to carry away when they leave.
Mates: One of the most common orchid tricks is to offer the promise of a mate. The flower of the *Ophrys* orchid in Italy resembles the wings of a female bee. It even smells like a female bee, so instinct tells every male bee in the area to visit the plant.

Developing Listening Skills

Before Listening

Track 20 Emphasis on Key Words Page 36

Content Words:

*He **told** me he was **finished** with the **assignment**.*
*Is that a **cow** in the **road**?*

Emphasis on New Information:

A: *What did the professor tell you?*
B: *Nothing, because I talked to the **secretary**.*
A: ***Which** secretary?*
B: *The secretary in the **botany department**.*

Track 21 B. Page 36

Leo: Hi, Elena. Are you on your way to the *greenhouse*?
Elena: Hi, Leo. Yes, I am.
Leo: Good. We can walk there *together*. Have you been to the greenhouse *before*?
Elena: I have. It's a *fascinating* place—to me, anyway.
Leo: Oh, I totally agree. They have plants from all over the *world*—even *tropical* plants.

Listening: A Conversation between Classmates

Track 22 A. Listening for Main Ideas
B. Listening for Details Page 37

Leo: Hi, Elena. Are you on your way to the greenhouse?
Elena: Hi, Leo. Yes, I am.
Leo: Good. We can walk there together. Have you been to the greenhouse before?
Elena: I have. It's a fascinating place—to me, anyway.
Leo: Oh, I totally agree. They have plants from all over the world—even tropical plants.
Elena: Right—the greenhouse provides enough shelter for them to grow here, even in the winter.
Leo: Do you know what they're going to show us today?
Elena: I think they're going to show us some epiphytes.
Leo: Epiphytes?
Elena: Yeah. . . those are plants that obtain water from the air.
Leo: Wow, that's a good trick! So they must need a lot of humidity.
Elena: Right. I think most of them live in tropical places.
Leo: Interesting. But our last lecture was about orchids. So, what's the connection?
Elena: Well, I think a lot of orchids are epiphytes. They live high up on trees where there's more light.
Leo: That makes sense, . . . but how can they live on a tree?

Elena: Well, I guess they have some kind of plant parts that attach to the tree. I think it's because there's more sunlight up high, and fewer animals there to eat them.
Leo: And . . . insects can fly, so they can find the orchids up in the trees.
Elena: True. I guess the insects must have strong natural instincts to help them find the orchids in the treetops, and it's a good thing because orchids need their insects. I've actually seen quite a few insects in the greenhouse lately!
Leo: Really? That's kind of surprising. . .
Elena: Yeah . . . I guess the plants attract bugs even when they are indoors. I've read that some orchids are able to trick bugs because they resemble certain kinds of insect burrows.
Leo: Hmm, interesting. I'll have to take a closer look at them. Come to think of it, I have a few bugs in my apartment. And I don't even have any houseplants! Maybe *I* should get an orchid or two.
Elena: Maybe. . . Well, here we are. It looks like there are some people inside the greenhouse already.

Unit 3: Human Migration Lesson A

Building Vocabulary

Track 23 A. Meaning from Context Page 44

1. Erlinda's native language is Tagalog. She learned English in high school.
2. I have a temporary driver's license. I can use it for two months while I take driving lessons.
3. In the 1840s, more than 8 million people emigrated from Ireland to other countries because there wasn't enough food in Ireland.
4. Our university has programs for students who want to study abroad in France or Mexico.
5. There is a large community of Japanese people who live in São Paulo, Brazil.
6. Many immigrants bring traditions from their home countries to their new countries.
7. I'm working in Hong Kong for two years, but my permanent home is Beijing. I'll go back there to live with my family next year.
8. In my city, there is a trend toward hiring more foreign workers in hotels and restaurants. You can see more people from different countries working in those places.
9. Too many people in my country have negative ideas about foreigners. For example, some people think that foreigners don't work hard and that they can't learn our language.
10. His original job was operating a machine in a factory, but then he graduated from a technical college and now he's an engineer.

Developing Listening Skills

Listening: A PowerPoint Lecture

Track 24 C. Listening for Main Ideas Page 46
D. Listening for Details Page 47

Professor: OK, could someone please turn off the lights? Good, thanks. Now, can everyone see the slide? Good. Now, we've been talking about emigration from one country to another. But emigration isn't always from a *country.*

In this first slide, you see a map of the state of North Dakota—in the U.S. We're going to focus on this part of the state—western North Dakota. One hundred years ago, North Dakota had something that many immigrants were looking for. What do you think it was?
Student: Was it farmland?
Professor: That's right. North Dakota had *land,* and that land attracted many immigrants from Europe—especially from Norway and Germany. They left their native countries and moved abroad. In North Dakota, they planted wheat, and they built houses and new towns. Nowadays, however, more and more people are *leaving* North Dakota—especially the rural areas—and moving to other states in the U.S. But before we get to that, let's look more closely at the reasons immigrants left their original countries and *went* to North Dakota in the first place.

This second slide shows one important reason—*trains.* By the early part of the 20th-century, trains had arrived in this part of the country, so travel was easier. And when the railroad companies finished building, they sold their extra land—and they sold it *cheap.* The U.S government was also selling land at low prices, and there were even ways to get land for free! You just had to live on the land for five years, plant some trees, and do a little farming—easy, right?

Well, as you'll see in this next slide, life *wasn't* easy. The family that used to live in this house left a long time ago. That's because after the 1920s, North Dakota had several years of very dry, very windy weather. The economic crisis of the 1930s made things even more difficult, so many farmers had to sell their land and leave.

This next slide is a picture of Corinth in the middle of winter—a town that once had 75 people living in it. One of the six people who still live in Corinth today is a farmer named Melvin Wisdahl. Melvin is 83 years old. And though his two sons are still farmers, Melvin's grandchildren will probably emigrate. That's the trend in North Dakota. There aren't many jobs, and there aren't many people.

But that's not the whole story. This picture was taken at the North Dakota State University in Fargo. And it looks like a nice place, doesn't it? In fact, some people *are* moving *to* North Dakota, but they're moving to the larger cities, not to the small towns.

So, what is happening in the small towns? Well, some people are trying to fight the emigration trend and preserve the old communities. Here, you see the Mystic Theatre in Marmath, North Dakota. Every year, they invite poets to come here for the Cowboy Poets Weekend. That's right—a whole weekend of poetry from writers in the Western states—and it's a big event! Sadly, though, experts think the changes in North Dakota aren't just temporary, they are permanent. They don't think these small towns will grow again. Are there any questions?

Lesson A and B Viewing: *Turkish Germany*

Before Viewing

Track 25 A. Page 52

Moving to Germany

During World War II, many Germans emigrated from their country. Then after the war, when the country was rebuilding and the economy was growing, there was a shortage of workers. So Germany made agreements with several countries to allow workers, mostly men, to live in the country for two years and work at industrial jobs. After two years, the men were expected to return to their home countries, which included Italy, Spain, Greece, and Turkey.

The guest worker program began in 1955 and ended in 1973, when Germany's economic growth slowed. In contrast to the economy, the number of foreigners in Germany continued to grow as family members joined the workers. A new agreement among European Union countries also allowed Italians to enter Germany without any special permission. In addition, a second generation had been born, and those babies were still foreigners according to German law.

Lesson B

Building Vocabulary

Track 26 A. Page 54

1. My last name is Petrov. My ancestors were from Russia.
2. The Aborigines are a minority in Australia.
3. Most of the younger generation in my country can speak English well.
4. Carlos had a very positive experience studying in Beijing. He said his classmates were really friendly.
5. One day, I would like to settle in Canada. It's a beautiful country with lots of opportunities.
6. My family came from Sweden a very long time ago, but we still retain some of the old Swedish customs.
7. Malaysia is the home of many different ethnic groups, including Malays, Chinese, Indians, and tribal people.
8. Some immigrants think that they should try very hard not to assimilate or learn the language of the country they are living in.
9. In the past, there was a lot of discrimination towards people from the southern part of my country. Today, the problem isn't as bad.
10. My grandmother didn't like foreigners, but then she had a doctor from India and she really liked him. That changed her attitude about them completely!

Using Vocabulary

Tracks 27–28 B. Note-Taking Page 55

Track 27
Hmong Americans

The Hmong are an ethnic minority from Vietnam, Laos, and Thailand. In the 1970s, after the war between the U.S. and Vietnam, many Hmong were forced to leave their homes, and a large number of them emigrated to the U.S. to settle permanently. The Hmong were mostly uneducated farmers in their native countries. When they emigrated to the U.S., many of them settled together in small towns and started vegetable farms. They retained many of their native customs and did not learn much English. The Hmong people mainly kept to themselves, but many of the local people did not like having them in their communities. Today, most young Hmong-Americans are bilingual and well educated, but their parents make sure the family retains the traditional culture and customs.

Track 28
Japanese Brazilians

The first Japanese immigrants came to Brazil in 1908, and today Brazil has the largest Japanese community outside of Japan. Japanese immigrants came to work on coffee farms across Brazil. They planned to stay only a few years, make money, and then go home. However, very few returned to Japan. During the 1940s, there were many laws that restricted the activities and freedom of Japanese Brazilians. Life improved for the Japanese Brazilians in the 1970s. They moved into new fields of business and became very successful. Today, only the oldest people in the community still speak Japanese, and the majority of the youngest generation are of mixed-race.

Developing Listening Skills

Listening: A Small Group Discussion

Track 29 A. Using a Graphic Organizer Page 56

Professor Garcia: All right! Now we're going to take our discussion of immigration and emigration to a more personal level. I'm going to have you divide into groups of four. Then I want you to tell your group about someone you know who has emigrated—gone to live in another country—temporarily, or permanently. Does everyone have the chart? In the boxes across the top of the chart, you can write the names of the people in your group. . . . OK . . . here on the left is the information you're going to need. First, you're going to write down *who* emigrated—their name, or their relationship to your classmate. Next, *where* did they come from? And where did they go to? Then . . . *why* did they emigrate? And finally, you're going to take notes about whether they assimilated . . . or not!

Tracks 30–33 B. Listening for Details Page 56

Track 30
Emily: OK, let's get started. . . . Are we all here? Sunisa, Josh, Nasir . . .
Sunisa: And what's your name?
Emily: Sorry! I'm Emily. . . . So, Josh, has your family always lived here in Chicago?
Josh: Well, always since, oh, the 1930s. My grandparents came here from Poland, my dad's parents.
Nasir: Really? Why'd they leave?
Josh: Have you forgotten your history? Poland was a dangerous place then. Everyone knew a war was coming, and my grandparents were lucky enough to get out. They had relatives in Chicago, so they settled in a Polish neighborhood there. Polish church, Polish grocery store, Polish everything. My grandma never really learned English.
Emily: So, they didn't want to assimilate.
Josh: Not really. But then the next generation wasn't interested in Polish customs or anything. My dad and my uncle were crazy about baseball. That's all they cared about. And my grandparents were so unhappy when they didn't marry nice Polish girls!
Nasir: What about you? Are you interested in Polish culture?
Josh: Well, maybe a little. . . . It would be fun to travel there. But like Professor Garcia said, my family is pretty well assimilated. We're just regular Americans. Though we retain some Polish customs, for example we *always* eat Polish food on certain holidays. . . .

Track 31
Sunisa: And, Nasir, you're from Pakistan, right?
Nasir: Yeah, from Karachi.
Sunisa: Did you always live there?
Nasir: Yeah . . . but when I was younger, my dad worked in Saudi Arabia. He was a water engineer, out in the desert there. It was a really good job, and he could come home for a month every year.

Josh: Do you mind if I ask . . . did he earn a lot of money there?
Nasir: Yes, he did. But it was really hard for my mother. Most of the year she was the head of the family, but when he was home, everything changed. And my little sister was born while my father was working in Saudi. She cried every time he came back because she didn't remember him.
Sunisa: That sounds really tough. . . .
Nasir: It was. But he earned enough to send all of us to good schools. And then he started his own engineering firm in Karachi. So in the end, it was a positive thing.
Emily: Do you think it changed your father, . . . living overseas like that?
Nasir: Yeah . . . I think it made him even more Pakistani! After that, he only wore traditional Pakistani clothes, and he never wanted to eat forcign food!

Track 32
Nasir: So, . . . what about your family, Emily?
Emily: Huh! None of them ever did anything interesting . . . well, except for my Uncle Jack. He emigrated from England to Australia back in the 1950s.
Josh: Cool! You can go see your relatives in Australia!
Emily: Mmm, not exactly . . . Back then, Australia was really trying to increase its population. If you wanted to settle there, they gave you a very cheap ticket and promised you a job. Uncle Jack was 26, and he couldn't find a girlfriend. Australia sounded *sooo* much better than England, so off he went.
Josh: And how'd he like it?
Emily: Actually . . . he *hated* it! It's so funny. He didn't like England, but then when he got to Australia, he thought the sun was too hot, and the land was too empty, and the girls were unfriendly . . . and on and on. . . . He worked for a mining company for five years, and of course there were no women there. So one day he just got on a ship and came back. He never got married, and his attitude about Australia hasn't changed. He's been complaining about it ever since. I don't think he had one positive experience there.
Nasir: Well, we read that a high proportion of emigrants actually do return home . . . what did the professor say?
Emily: More than half, I think. . . . Sunisa, what about you? Has anyone in your family emigrated from Thailand?

Track 33
Sunisa: No . . . actually, my ancestors emigrated *to* Thailand, from China. But that was so long ago that no one really remembers, maybe a hundred or two hundred years ago. A lot of Chinese moved to Thailand then.
Nasir: Interesting! D'you know why?
Sunisa: I'm not sure. I think they probably moved because there were too many people in China, in that region. . . . I guess there was just no place for them, and they thought life would be better in Thailand.
Emily: I hope this isn't too personal . . . but is there discrimination against Chinese people in Thailand now?
Sunisa: Not really. We're not exactly a separate ethnic group. So many Chinese married Thais, we're all mixed together. It's not like we're a minority there. . . . Ultimately, we all just became typical Thais, except sometimes our names are a little different.
Josh: So, do the people in your family speak Chinese?
Sunisa: No! Well, actually, my grandma knows a little bit, but she learned it from her friend. I think the Chinese in my country assimilated really well. Usually people don't even know who's Chinese. . . .
Professor Garcia: OK, . . . everyone, almost finished? Next, I want you to discuss these questions that I'm writing on the board. . . .

Pronunciation

Track 34 Fast Speech Page 57

1. In questions, *do* and *did* are reduced (pronounced very quickly) to become *'d.*
   Why did Patty leave?
   Why'd Patty leave?
   Where did John go?
   Where'd John go?
   What time do you wake up?
   What time d'you wake up?
2. Words are linked together and not pronounced separately. We often link:
   - a consonant sound with a vowel sound
     your address, six eggs
   - a vowel sound with another vowel sound
     my uncle, to India
   - the same consonant sound
     a big girl, that town

Track 35 A. Page 57

1. Why'd they leave?
2. Did he earn a lot of money there?
3. You can go see your relatives in Australia!
4. And how'd he like it?
5. D'you know why?

Unit 4: Fascinating Planet Lesson A

Building Vocabulary

Track 36 B. Page 64

1. Ancient people didn't have metal. They used stone tools for farming and hunting.
2. This wall has a crack in it. I can see light coming in from outside.
3. Sophie can't swim very well, so she won't go into deep water.
4. A sharp knife can cut into an apple very easily.
5. After it rains, small streams of water come together and form a river.
6. I almost never eat sweets, so chocolate is a rare treat for me.
7. If you put sugar in a cup of coffee, it will dissolve.
8. This mountain used to be much higher, but wind and rain have eroded it.
9. He's new at this job, but the customers don't seem to notice his lack of experience.
10. Most of the farmers wear hats to protect themselves from the sun.

Track 37 C. Meaning from Context Page 64

It used to be more difficult to reach Jiuzhaigou, with its clean air and clear blue-green lakes, but nowadays, there is no lack of visitors to this national park in China's Sichuan province. Approximately 2 million tourists visit the park each year.

Water is the main attraction of Jiuzhaigou. Rivers flow down from the mountains and form beautiful waterfalls. The park's lakes are not deep, so it's easy to see through the clean water to the bottom, brightly colored with dissolved minerals.

Jiuzhaigou is also a nature reserve, where panda bears and rare bird species are protected. The trees and other plant life in the reserve are also safe as long as this land remains a national park.

Using Vocabulary

Track 38 E. Meaning from Context Page 65

The lakes in Jiuzhaigou National Park were formed by glaciers—huge bodies of ice. Today there are glaciers high up in some mountains, but at other times in the earth's history colder temperatures allowed glaciers to exist in much larger areas.

As glaciers grow and move, they push dirt and stone along with them. This material, along with the ice itself, is sharp enough to erode the land where the glaciers move. In this way, hills can become flat land, and flat land can become holes. Later, when temperatures become warmer and the glaciers melt, lakes are the result.

Glacial ice can become water in another way, too. At the bottom edge of a glacier, cracks can develop and large pieces of ice can fall into the water below. These pieces of ice then melt and become part of the body of water.

Developing Listening Skills

Before Listening

Track 39 B. Page 66

Sherry: How about over here?
Lara: Sure, that looks like a nice table.
Sherry: I saw the most interesting TV show last night.
Lara: Really? What was it about?
Sherry: This cool place in Madagascar—I don't remember the name, but it's a national park.
Lara: Does it have lemurs?
Sherry: Yep, there are lemurs. In fact, lemurs are one of the few kinds of animals that can live there because the place is so pointy.
Lara: The place is *pointy*?!
Sherry: It really is!
Patron: Oh, excuse me.
Lara: No problem.
Sherry: It's all limestone, and over time, the stone's eroded and formed thousands of sharp peaks and very deep cracks and canyons—it's just incredible.
Lara: Wow! It sounds fascinating.
Sherry: It *really* is! You should watch it if you get the chance. I think they're showing it again on Thursday night.
Lara: Sorry . . . I need to get this. It's my daughter.
Sherry: That's OK.
Lara: Thanks. Hello?

Listening: A Documentary

Track 40 A., B. Note-Taking, C. Using a Graphic Organizer Page 67

Lara: OK, It's starting.
Narrator: Journey to the Tsingy de Bemaraha—Madagascar's unseen paradise.
Doreen: Mom . . . what's this?
Narrator: Located in the western part of Madagascar, the Tsingy de Bemaraha is home to some of the rarest species on Earth. Plants and animals are protected here; first, because the Tsingy is a national park, but more importantly because it's almost impossible for people to go there.
Lara: It's a show that my friend told me about. I really want to watch it. Doreen, could you close that window?
Doreen: Sure. ... Mom, I think I'm going to take a walk.
Lara: All right.
Narrator: The name of the park means, "place where one cannot walk barefoot," and in fact, you need more than a good pair of shoes to enter the Tsingy. The stone peaks at the top are almost as sharp as knives. Down below in the deep canyons, there are caves and water to deal with. This is no place for the casual tourist.

On the other hand, this dramatic landscape is an advantage for the plants and animals that live in the Tsingy. Here white lemurs can easily jump from peak to peak, looking for trees in the canyons below and eating leaves. Insects, lizards, and frogs live here, too, and all of them are free from the effects of human beings.
Lara: You're back already?
Doreen: Yeah. It's raining.
Narrator: In other ways, however, the lack of people visiting the Tsingy is a problem. Tourism was once a very important part of Madagascar's economy, but political violence and other problems now keep many tourists away, and in the Tsingy, the rock formations are simply too difficult for most tourists to reach. Without tourists, there is a lack of money coming into the region. That means little money for research, so scientists aren't sure how climate change, for example, is affecting the Tsingy. . . .
Narrator: There is still much to learn about this fascinating place.

Lesson B

Building Vocabulary

Track 41 A. Meaning from Context Page 74

World Heritage

In 1887, a Maori chief gave Tongariro's three sacred volcanoes and the land around them to the government and people of New Zealand, thus creating the country's first national park. It has been named a World Heritage site twice—first on the basis of its natural beauty. In addition, its cultural importance to the Maori was sufficient to earn the park World Heritage status.

Film Location

New Zealand's landscape is varied. It has dramatic features such as volcanoes, but also rolling green hills and beautiful lakes, so Peter Jackson had many options when he was choosing locations for his *Lord of the Rings* films.

Ring of Fire

The Ring of Fire is an area with numerous earthquakes and active volcanoes. New Zealand sits on the Alpine Fault, where the edges of the Australian Plate and Pacific Plate move sideways past each other. The movement of the plates along the fault line leads to earthquakes, and the release of hot material from under the earth's surface leads to volcanic activity.

Invasive Species

In the 19th century, European immigrants began to arrive, along with foreign animals and plants. These species are a threat to

New Zealand's native species. Cats, Australian possums, and even rats kill and eat native birds. Plants such as European heather and North American pine compete with native plants. To restore the balance of nature and encourage the survival of native species, much work has been done to kill the invasive species brought in from other parts of the world.

Tourism

The most popular ski areas on North Island—with their roads, ski lifts, hotels, and shops—are on Mount Ruapehu. This kind of development would not be allowed in a national park today, but the ski areas date from 1913, and they do bring money to the area. Staff members at the Department of Conservation are constantly trying to find compromises in park management that will keep skiers happy and protect the environment at the same time.

Developing Listening Skills

Before Listening

Track 42 A., B. Page 76

Lençóis Maranhenses National Park

The name of this national park means the "bedsheets of Maranhão," the state in Brazil where the park is located. From the air, the park's white sand dunes do look like sheets drying in the wind, and it's the wind that gives the dunes their half-moon shapes. However, this park features a lot more than sand. Green and blue pools of water are left behind by the rain, fishermen go out to sea in their boats, and local people take care of herds of goats.

So is the Lençóis a desert, or a seascape? Is it a park, or a place where people live? In fact, it's not a true desert because it receives around 42 inches (120 centimeters) of rain each year. Yet sand dunes as far as the eye can see, along with the lack of trees and other plants, suggest a desert. The park also has 90 residents—people in two villages who change their routines with the seasons. They raise chickens, goats, cattle, and crops such as cassava, beans, and cashews during the dry season. When it rains, residents go out to sea and live in fishing camps on the beach.

Pronunciation

Track 43 Intonation for Choices and Lists Page 76

Do you prefer the aisle or the window?
My favorite colors are yellow, blue, and red.

Track 44 C. Page 77

1. We have coffee, tea, and lemonade.
2. Do you think the salary they're offering is sufficient, or will you ask for more?
3. We could stay home, or we could stay out late, or we could compromise.
4. Would you rather go to Spain or to Portugal?
5. She's going to Korea, Japan, and China.

Listening: An Informal Conversation

Track 45 A. Listening for Main Ideas
B. Listening for Details Page 77

Woman: We should make some decisions about our vacation trip. August is only three months away.
Man: OK. How do you like my idea? I think a vacation in New Zealand would be great!
Woman: Well, I think New Zealand is probably a beautiful place. But there isn't much to do there besides go hiking. That's not something I want to do every day for two weeks. After all, I'm constantly on the go when I'm at home.
Man: We wouldn't do it every day. We could definitely plan to relax on the beach for part of the time.
Woman: But it's winter in New Zealand in August. That's one of the coldest months.
Man: Oh, right. But let's keep New Zealand as an option. Let's either go to New Zealand or to Australia.
Woman: All right. I'll try to keep an open mind, but I've been thinking a lot about Australia. There are a lot of things to do there, so we could find a nice balance—some hiking for you and some golf for me.
Man: Can you play golf in Australia in August?
Woman: Sure, you can. In fact, they even have some winter golf specials, so prices are better.
Man: That's nice, but golf specials shouldn't be the basis of our decision about where to go.
Woman: All right. Then what should be the basis of our decision?
Man: Well, um, things like beautiful scenery. Scenery that we never see here in Japan.
Woman: I know, you're thinking about the Tongariro National Park again, aren't you? I know it looked cool in the movies, but we have plenty of volcanoes right here in Japan.
Man: It's not, it's not just volcanoes, though. . . . Listen to this. "The park features native bird species including the rare blue duck, a bird known by the Maori name kaka, and the New Zealand robin, which seems to have no fear as it hops around the boots of hikers. I guess they must not see human beings as a threat. Oh, . . . and there are interesting towns at the edges of the park, like National Park Village. Maybe we could stay there for a night or two, if we go.
Woman: Hmmm. That does sound pretty nice. How about a compromise?
Man: Sure. What do you have in mind?
Woman: How about, how about a week in New Zealand hiking and then a week in Australia playing golf and relaxing.
Man: Yes, that sounds good. I like that idea.
Woman: Good. Me too. . . .

 **CD2**

Unit 5: Making a Living, Making a Difference Lesson A

Building Vocabulary

Track 2 C. Page 84

Cooperatives, or co-ops, are different from corporations or other business enterprises in several ways. First, they're made up of members who are also the owners of the cooperative.

In the case of an agricultural co-op, a number of farmers may decide to cooperate and sell their products together, rather than separately. As co-op members, the farmers make decisions democratically. They also share their wealth among themselves. Instead of going to stockholders and executives, profits in cooperatives are returned to their members, who may also share machinery and borrow money from the co-op.

Perhaps the most important benefit of co-ops is the pooling of farm products because large quantities may be more attractive to buyers.

Farmers in agricultural cooperatives are a diverse group. They can be found in numerous countries, and they produce everything from cotton and soybeans to flowers and fruit.

Using Vocabulary

Track 3 G. Page 85

Peruvian Weavers: A Profitable Cottage Industry

In the Andes Mountains of Peru, people in the village of Chinchero, not far from Cusco, were living in poverty. Their agricultural products—potatoes, barley, sheep—were not bringing in much money.

That's when the women of Chinchero became entrepreneurs. They started the Chinchero Weaving Cooperative, and they began selling their traditional handmade textiles to tourists. The women may not earn a lot of money for their work, but at least the money they make stays within the cooperative and within the community.

Starting a co-op was an effective way for villagers in Chinchero to bring in more money. However, co-ops are not the answer for every cottage industry.

Before deciding to start or join a cooperative, home-based industries need to assess their situation carefully. If a small business is already doing well, it may have the customer base it needs. It may not want to spend time going to co-op meetings and money on co-op dues. On the other hand, joining together with others can be the answer for businesses that are struggling.

Developing Listening Skills

Before Listening

Track 4 A. Page 86

Snake Hunters Find Cure for Joblessness

Most people run away when they see a poisonous snake—but not the Irulas of India. For generations, the Irulas made their living catching wild snakes. The snakes' skins were sold and made into luxury goods such as handbags and boots.

Then in 1972, the Indian Parliament adopted the Wildlife Protection Act, and the basis of the Irula's economy was suddenly illegal. Some Irulas got jobs as farm laborers, but many found themselves out of work.

The solution came in 1978 with the creation of the Irula Snake Catchers Industrial Cooperative Society, whose members use their snake hunting skills to catch snakes. However, the snakes are no longer sold for their skins. The cooperative has found a better use for the dangerous snakes.

Listening: A Guest Speaker

Track 5 A. Listening for Main Ideas
C. Listening for Details Page 87

Speaker: Good afternoon and thank you for inviting me to speak. My name is Marsha Nolan, and I'm the director of Worldwide Co-op. I hope, I hope that some of you have heard of our organization? Worldwide Co-op exists to support cooperative enterprises of all kinds, and today, today, I'd like to give you some information about a co-op in India. It's an unusual co-op since it was formed in response to wildlife protection measures. Since all of you here are members of wildlife organizations, I know you'll be interested in this.

All right. The story. The story begins in 1972. That was the year that India took a major step in wildlife protection. So far, so good, right? Well, the Wildlife Protection Act wasn't so good for a small tribe called the Irulas, who made their living catching snakes, such as the Indian cobra, which were, which were sold for their skins. Even before 1972, the Irulas lived in relative poverty, . . . despite being some of the only people in India with the necessary skills to catch poisonous snakes. After 1972, . . . things went from bad to worse.

What happened next, however, could serve as a model for many places. The Irulas became entrepreneurs. With more than 30,000 deaths from snakebites in India each year, there is a huge demand for venom. It's used to produce antivenin—the only known cure for poisonous snakebites. The Irulas knew how to handle cobras, so they decided—they decided to cooperate and work together. They formed the Irula Snake Catchers Industrial Cooperative Society, . . . and they were back in the snake business.

These days, the Irulas catch snakes just as they've done for generations, but now, they carefully milk the snakes' venom before returning them to the wild. The snakes they catch are not killed, and the Irulas earn more money from the venom than they used to get for the snakes' skins. Even better—the co-op members are all owners, they are all owners, so there's no longer a "middleman" getting rich from the Irulas' hard work. . . . All of the wealth generated by the sale of venom stays in the Irula community.

The reason I'm telling *you* all of this is simple: The ideas behind the Irulas' co-op can be used in *many* places. After all, the Irulas have found an effective and sustainable way to use wild animals their own benefit. Instead of being killed, the snakes are staying alive, and they're benefiting people in more than one way.

Now, I know that I'm speaking to a *diverse* group of people. The different species that you want to protect can't all be milked for their venom. . . . But what all of you *can* do is to assess *your* situation. If endangered animals in your country are being killed and sold, it's important to understand the *reasons*—the economic benefits that come from killing the animals. You might find another way, some other way, for people to earn even *more* money than before by *not* killing the animals.

If you need help with any of this, Worldwide Co-op has many information resources. . . . So, please feel free to visit the Web site, send an email, or give me a call.

Exploring Spoken English

Track 6 D. Page 88

1. Imported to the U.S. from Japan in 1876, kudzu grows from large underground tubers that can weigh almost 300 pounds (136 kilograms).
2. During the 1930s, the U.S. government planted 70 million kudzu seedlings.
3. Kudzu was such a popular plant that at one time, the Kudzu Club of America had 20,000 members.
4. Kudzu can cover as many as 150,000 acres of land each year.
5. Currently, kudzu covers around eight million acres of land in the U.S.

Lesson B

Building Vocabulary

Track 7 A. Meaning from Context Page 94

Margo: What are you reading?
Walter: It's a letter from a charity organization. I've never heard of them before, but listen to this: "Just 10 years after our *Schools for Kids* program began, there has been a 27 percent drop in the rate of poverty among people in the region." That's pretty impressive!
Margo: Sure. I mean, less poverty is a good thing. Are you thinking of sending them money?
Walter: I'm thinking about it. After all, I have a pretty good job, and this is a good concept—invest in education now, and there will be less poverty in the future.
Margo: That does seem like a good idea.
Walter: Do you give any money to charities?
Margo: Yes, there's one called Heifer International where you send enough money for a farm animal, like a chicken or a goat. The animal provides eggs or milk to a poor family, and if the animal reproduces, the babies are given to another poor family.
Walter: That makes a lot of sense. Good nutrition is such a fundamental human need.
Margo: It is indeed.

Track 8 D. Meaning from Context Page 94

Title: *Just Give Money to the Poor: The Development Revolution from the Global South*
Authors: Joseph Hanlon, Armando Barrientos, David Hulme
Review: Traditionally, help for poor people has come from large organizations such as Oxfam and WHO, and it has been in the form of complex projects such as dams, irrigation systems, schools, and hospitals. In this book, authors Hanlon, Barrientos, and Hulme present evidence in favor of a simpler approach. According to their data, making small, regular payments directly to poor people provides a better outcome—in other words better living conditions—than the large, complex projects provide.

Hanlon et al. describe "cash transfer" programs in a number of countries where poverty is a major problem. People in need receive a small amount of money, sometimes as little as five to ten dollars each month, and they use the money in any way they choose. Almost always, the authors say, poor families make very responsible decisions about using the extra income, buying more or better food, buying a school uniform so a child can attend school, or saving a little each month to start a small business.

Developing Listening Skills

Pronunciation

Track 9 Contractions Page 96

There's no hospital in the town.
There was no hospital in the town.

Some Common Contractions:

With *be:*
I am, I'm;
you/we/they are;
you're/we're/they're;
he/she/it is, he's/she's/it's;
Linda's at the library.

With *have/has:*
I have, I've (you've/we've)
he/she/it has, he's/she's/it's
They've always wanted to go scuba diving.

With *will:*
I will, I'll (you'll/he'll/we'll/)
She'll tell us when it's time to leave.

With *would:*
I would, I'd (you'd/she'd/they'd/)
We'd rather not have the party here.

Listening: A Class Question and Answer Session

Track 10 A., B. Pages 96–97

Female Professor: OK, let's get started. Today is our question and answer session with our guest speaker, Donald Yates, who has quite a bit of experience with charity organizations. This is your chance to have some of your questions answered, so let's not waste any time. Mr. Yates?
Guest Speaker: Hi, everyone. I, I'd like to start by thanking you for inviting me here. I'm always happy to get out of the office. Your professor's right. . . . I've worked for several charitable organizations over the years. Now I'm more interested in cash transfer programs, so that's what I'm doing my research on now. Who'd like to ask the first question?.

Track 11 C., D. Note-Taking. Page 97

Female Professor: OK, let's get started. Today is our question and answer session with our guest speaker, Donald Yates, who has quite a bit of experience with charity organizations. This is your chance to have some of your questions answered, so let's not waste any time. Mr. Yates?

Guest Speaker: Hi, everyone. I, I'd like to start by thanking you for inviting me here. I'm always happy to get out of the office. Your professor's right. . . . I've worked for several charitable organizations over the years. Now I'm more interested in cash transfer programs, so that's what I'm doing my research on now. Who'd like to ask the first question?

Female Student #1: Yes, um with cash transfer programs, do you, do you know whether people really use the money for important things? I mean, it seems like people might not spend the money responsibly.

Guest Speaker: A lot of people ask me that, but according to my research, people living in poverty make *very* good decisions about how to spend their money. They almost never buy things they don't need. Instead, mothers buy things for their children—school uniforms or notebooks—even medicine. Or a farmer might buy a new tool to help with the harvest. With cash transfer programs, poor people themselves decide what they need the most, so the outcomes of these programs have been very good. Yes?

Male Student #1: Yes, sir. Can you please explain why you don't ask people to work for the money? I guess, I'd be afraid that if people, people got their payments for nothing, they wouldn't use the money well.

Guest Speaker: Well, the fact is, most people who are living in poverty are already working *very* hard. . . . We're talking about mothers with children, families with crops to take care of, working people with two or three jobs. . . . For them, a little extra cash is very much appreciated! They're not going to waste it on something they don't need. Next question?

Female Student #2: I'd like to know who makes decisions about the money. I mean, you can't give money to everyone—someone has to decide who should get it.

Guest Speaker: Well, in cash transfer programs, money is given to as large a group as possible—often to governments, in fact. Or the same payment might be made to every adult in a certain village. The idea is that financial decisions are made *locally.* Charity organizations that come in from outside might not be the best people to make those decisions. Time for one last question. . . .

Male Student #2: I, I was wondering how communities get things like new schools and roads. I mean, people need those too, . . . but you can't buy them with small amounts of cash.

Guest Speaker: That's really the fundamental question—what works best when it comes to fighting poverty? Many people in the world understand the concept of giving a little money to charity if you can and letting the charity figure out what to do with it. And that might be the best way to get the really big projects done. On the other hand, I've heard of villages pooling their money to build new irrigation systems, so we're really just starting to learn what works best.

Unit 6: A World of Words
Lesson A

Building Vocabulary

Tracks 12–14 A. Meaning from Context Page 104

Track 12
Matsuo Bashō, Japan, ca. 1644–1694

Bashō is famous for his *haiku,* short poems with three lines. Each line in a *haiku* has a set number of syllables—seven in the first line, five in the second, and seven in the last line. A *haiku* does not need to rhyme, but it should capture a moment of one's life. Nature is often the subject of a haiku, but the meaning can be as much about human emotion as the external world. Bashō's most famous book, *Narrow Road to a Far Province,* was published after a long journey on foot.

Track 13
Robert Burns, Scotland, 1759–1796

Robert Burns's first book, *Poems, Chiefly in the Scottish Dialect,* was published in 1786—just one year after the first of his 14 children was born. The book contained Burns's observations of the lives of ordinary people. He watched them doing farm work, going to church, and falling in love, and his humor and insights on everyday life made him a very popular writer. Robert Burns only lived to the age of 37, but he continues to have an influence on writers today.

Track 14
Anna Akhmatova, Ukraine, 1889–1966

Anna Akhmatova—poet, translator, and literary critic—was born in the Ukraine, but spent much of her life in Russia. Much of her writing was political, and many of her poems, including the well-known *Requiem,* reflected the difficulties that Russians faced during the time of Joseph Stalin and World War II. Family life was also difficult for Akhmatova, who married three times, and whose one child was raised by grandparents. Akhmatova is remembered for her original writing style as well as her ideas.

Developing Listening Skills

Before Listening

Track 15 Understanding Sidetracks Pages 106–107
A. Listening for Main Ideas
B. Note-Taking

Professor: Welcome back, everyone. Are you all ready for the essay exam next week?
Professor continues: OK, "no comment," I guess. Well, today's, today's lecture on the poet Bashō could be a big help to you. As we discussed last time, Bashō is known today for his *haiku.* But did you know that *haiku* came from an earlier form of poetry called *haikai*? . . . That's what Bashō was writing in the early part of his career.

Now, we don't know a lot about Bashō's early life, but we do know he studied poetry with a famous poet in Kyoto. We also know that Chinese poetry and the principles of Taoism had their influence on Bashō. As an aside, my wife and I spent several weeks in Japan right after, right after we got married, and we went to the area where Bashō was born. . . . We got to see the Ueno Castle—an amazing, *amazing* place! It was built before Bashō was born, so it's something he would have seen, too. It gave, it gave me some real insight into 17th-century Japan.

But getting back to our topic, *haikai* poems are groups of verses, verses or paragraphs, you could say, all linked together. They were more like the poems of Shakespeare, for example—fairly long, they were fairly long and with a set formula, or structure. The short *haiku* form developed from the . . . from the first verse of the *haikai,* and Bashō had enough *haiku* published to get pretty famous. . . . He soon had his own writing school in Edo, now called Old Tokyo, and that became known as the Bashō School.

That reminds me—Bashō was not the poet's family name. He got the name Bashō from a—from a species of *banana* tree that was planted near his house!

OK, getting back to what I was saying, the *haiku* developed from the longer *haikai,* but Bashō's most famous books are not collections of *haiku.* They're, they're in a form called *haibun,* which is a *haiku* followed by prose. The books are kind of like collections of essays—each essay beginning with a *haiku.* Bashō wrote these books, he wrote these books while he was traveling, and he did a lot of traveling.

In 1689, Bashō walked for *five months* through the villages and mountains north of Edo and along the coast of the Sea of Japan. . . . During this journey, Bashō produced his masterwork, *Narrow Road to a Far Province.* The modern poet Miyazawa Kenji said this about the book, "It was as if the very soul of Japan had written it." The book is a collection of *haibun,* and Bashō's writing reflects the everyday problems of travel, like lying awake at night, lying awake at night in a bed full of fleas, with a horse making noise outside. . . . Honestly, that's what he wrote about! But the book is also full of insights into nature, life, and death—pretty big themes. He is able to turn his observations on the outside world—on the external world into very insightful comments on deeper subjects.

Exploring Spoken English

Tracks 16–17 A. Note-Taking Page 108

Track 16
Published in 1847, The True Story of My Life *by well-known fairy-tale writer Hans Christian Andersen, begins with his birth:*

My native land, Denmark, is a poetical land, full of popular traditions, old songs, and an eventful history, which has become bound up with that of Sweden and Norway. The Danish islands are possessed of beautiful beech woods, and corn and clover fields: they resemble gardens on a great scale. Upon one of these green islands, Funen, stands Odense, the place of my birth[. . .] Odense is the capital of the province, and lies 22 Danish miles from Copenhagen.

In the year 1805 there lived here, in a small, mean room, a young married couple, who were extremely attached to each other; he was a shoemaker, scarcely 22 years old, a man of a richly gifted and truly poetical mind. His wife, a few years older than himself, was ignorant of life and of the world, but possessed a heart full of love.

Track 17

Published in 1865, Alice's Adventures in Wonderland *by Lewis Carroll begins with a day in the life of Alice, the story's main character:*

So she was considering, in her own mind (as well as she could, for the hot day made her feel very sleepy and stupid), whether the pleasure of making a daisy-chain would be worth the trouble of getting up and picking the daisies, when suddenly a White Rabbit with pink eyes ran close by her.

There was nothing so *very* remarkable in that; nor did Alice think it so *very* much out of the way to hear the Rabbit say to itself, "Oh dear! Oh dear! I shall be too late!" (when she thought it over afterward, it occurred to her that she ought to have wondered at this, but at the time it all seemed quite natural); but, when the Rabbit actually *took a watch out of its waistcoat-pocket,* and looked at it, and then hurried on, Alice started to her feet, for it flashed across her mind that she had never before seen a rabbit with either a waistcoat-pocket, or a watch to take out of it, and, burning with curiosity, she ran across the field after it, and was just in time to see it pop down a large rabbit-hole under the hedge.

Grammar: The Simple Past vs. The Present Perfect

Track 18 B. Page 110

Amanda: Have you decided what your research paper is going to be about?
Tyler: Not yet. I'm interested in Akhmatova's poetry, but I don't know much about it.
Amanda: Maybe the professor can recommend some good sources of information. Yesterday she said we could go to her office for help any time today.
Tyler: But I'm also interested in fiction. Have you read anything by Isabel Allende?
Amanda: No, I haven't. She's a modern-day novelist, isn't she?
Tyler: She is, and she's really popular. Her books have been translated into a lot of different languages, including English.
Amanda: That's lucky for you since you don't speak Spanish!
Tyler: Very funny. The problem is—I haven't read any of her books either, and I don't think I have enough time before the paper is due.
Amanda: Didn't the professor say something about books of literary criticism? Maybe you can just read *about* Allende.
Tyler: I'd still have to do a lot of reading.
Amanda: Well, sure—it's a research paper.
Tyler: I think I'll go with the poet, and I think I'll go to the professor's office now.
Amanda: Good ideas. Now I need to decide on *my* topic . . .

Speaking: Discussing Fairy Tales

Track 19 A. Page 111

Narrator:
Andersen's *Little Mermaid* is the daughter of the Sea King, and she must wait to get married until her older sisters have been married—and she has a lot of older sisters! When it's finally her turn, she goes to the surface of the sea, rescues a prince from drowning, and falls in love. She's not human, however. In fact—she has a tail, so marriage to the prince seems unlikely. It turns out that in order for the mermaid to become human, the prince must love her with all his heart and marry her, and she must give up her beautiful mermaid voice in order to lose the tail.

The fairy tale doesn't end the way you might expect. The prince does get married, but to a human princess, and the little mermaid becomes a spirit, one of the "daughters of the air," as a reward for her good deeds as a mermaid.

Lesson B

Building Vocabulary

Track 20 A. Meaning from Context Page 114

Q: You're the owner of a successful bookstore. What's the secret of your success?
A: Well, there's no magic formula that works for everyone. I bought this bookstore from the previous owner over 20 years ago. Eventually, a store like mine builds up a customer base. I know a lot of the customers by name, and some of them come in every day.
Q: What challenges do bookstores face nowadays?
A: As you know, in the digital age, almost everything my bookstore sells is available online. Instead of buying printed media like books and magazines, people can download them onto their electronic devices. The same goes for music. When was the last time you bought a CD?
Q: Do you have any regrets?
A: Absolutely not. You have to be fearless and follow your dreams. Otherwise, you might get to the end of your life and feel as if you haven't really lived.

Using Vocabulary

Track 21 C. Meaning from Context Page 115

Q: You mentioned that you're a librarian at a public library. Tell us more about that.
A: That's not quite accurate. I do work at a public library part time, but I also work at a university library, and I teach a class once a week. Everyone has access to the materials at the public library, whereas only students and staff can use the university library.
Q: I see. And do you think it's fair for taxpayers to have to pay for the public library?
A: I used to wonder about that, but I've gained some insight since I've been working there. The public library really does make the city a better place, and taxpayers don't mind paying for that.
Q: Are people reading contemporary authors these days, or do they prefer the classics?
A: Both, really. They read the contemporary authors when their books are first published, but the older authors will never go out of style. They've already stood the test of time.

Developing Listening Skills

Pronunciation: Review of Question Intonation

Track 22 A. Page 116

Yes/no questions:
Is this information *accurate*?
Have you talked to the *professor*?

Questions with *wh-* words:
Where was the article *published*?
Why are you *comparing* them?

Questions with two or more choices:
Do you prefer to read *poetry* or *prose*?
Will you write your paper on *Bashō, Burns*, or *Akhmatova*?

Listening: A Class Discussion Session

Track 23 A. Listening for Main Ideas Page 116
B. Listening for Details Page 117

Professor: OK. . . . Well, this is our last discussion session before the exam, so—a word to the wise—now is the time for you to ask your questions about Bashō. You'll remember, you'll remember that in my last lecture, I told you a little about Bashō's life, and also about the forms of poetry and prose that he wrote.
Student #1: I have a question.
Professor: Great.
Student #1: You mentioned a form of, um , writing called *haibun.* Would it be correct . . .
would it be accurate to say that *haibun* is both poetry and prose?
Professor: Yes, that's correct. A *haibun* begins with a *haiku,* which is a short poem. That's followed by prose—a short essay that contains the writer's observations about life.
Student #1: So, did he, did Bashō invent the *haibun*?
Professor: He didn't *invent* it, but he was one of the first writers to *use* the form, and he wrote a lot of *haibun.* Eventually, Bashō gained a reputation as a real master of *haibun.* OK . . . other questions?
Student #2: Yes, I was, I was wondering . . . you mentioned that an older form of Japanese poetry called *haikai* was similar to Shakespeare's poetry. Could you explain that?
Professor: Sure . . . I'm glad you asked about that. . . . I didn't want to confuse anyone, because even though Shakespeare was a contemporary of the early Japanese poets who wrote *haikai,* they didn't have any, they didn't have any influence on each other. In other words, the Japanese poets were not reading Shakespeare's poems, or vice versa.
Student #2: So, how are they similar?
Professor: The *haikai* were longer poems, and they followed a very specific formula. Each verse had a certain number of lines, and there was a set number of verses in each poem. As an aside, the *haikai* came from a previous form called *renga.* That was really formal poetry, whereas *haikai, haikai* were for the common people to read. But getting back to our topic, Shakespeare's sonnets were also fairly long poems with a set number of verses and lines.
Student #3: Can I, can I ask a question?
Professor: Absolutely! That's what we're here for.
Student #3: Well, I have to admit that I don't really get . . .
I don't really understand Bashō's *haiku.* I mean . . .
so, a frog jumps into the water . . . *and*?
Professor: That's a good question, and it takes us back to Bashō's influences. Remember—he read a lot of Chinese poetry, and he learned about Taoism. He thought that nature had lessons to teach us if we sat quietly . . . if we just sat quietly and listened. He also studied Zen Buddhism. He was a deep thinker, and for him, the *haiku* reflected the truth that can be found in nature. Does that help?
Student #3: Well . . . maybe it's because I'm not Japanese.
Professor: That could be. Bashō's *haiku* are well loved in Japan. Just about every person I met there knows at least one Bashō *haiku.*

Engage: Giving a Summary

Track 24 A. Note-Taking Page 120

Ancient Greek Poems Found with Egyptian Mummy

More than 2000 years ago in Egypt, a roll of paper with extensive writings was wrapped around a body that was being mummified for preservation. It's the oldest surviving example of a Greek poetry book, according to scholars who have studied it. It's also unusual for its length and the well-preserved state of the remaining text.

The writings are by a Greek poet named Posidippus, who wrote epigrams—short poems written to remember a person or an event. The epigrams offer new insights into daily life in ancient Greece, covering events such as official dedications, shipwrecks, and sports.

Peter Bing, an associate professor of classics at Emory University, said the scroll "provides us with the earliest detailed evidence of how an editor—perhaps the poet himself—organized a poetry collection."

But how did Posidippus's poems end up wrapped around a mummy in Egypt? Kathryn Gutzwiller, a professor at the University of Cincinnati, said the practice was not unusual for that period. In the third century BC, "mummies were placed in a kind of papier-mâché casing, for which old papyri were sometimes used," said Gutzwiller.

Greek and Egyptian cultures became connected after the death of Alexander the Great in 323 BC, and Posidippus was associated with the Ptolemies, the Greek rulers who inherited Egypt after Alexander's death.

Unit 7: After Oil Lesson A

Building Vocabulary

Track 25 C. Page 124

In a geological era 300 to 400 million years ago, sea plants and animals died and their remains fell to the bottom of the ocean.

The remains were covered with sand and silt. Heat and pressure under the sand were essential in making the remains into petroleum. Oil wells extract the petroleum from under the sand and silt rock. The petroleum is used to make an enormous variety of products. Some scientists think that our supply of oil has reached a peak and will be depleted in the future. Many people now believe that scientists are right and shifting to substitutes for petroleum is an important priority.

Listening: A Current Affairs Club Meeting

Track 26 A. Listening for Main Ideas Page 126
B. Listening for Details Page 127

Ron Steinberg: Thanks for coming, everyone. I'm sure you all have other things to do with your free time, . . . but our topic tonight is an important one. I'm Ron Steinberg, and I'm the president of Future Fuels International. We're, we're a group of scientists working to find substitutes for fossil fuels of all kinds. Tonight, though, I'm going to try to answer some of your questions about the peak oil theory.

Before we. . . before we get started, it turns out that you get *two* speakers this evening instead of one. Dr. Leila Sparks from Lomax Petroleum is also here, and I'll let her introduce herself. Dr. Sparks?

Leila Sparks: Thank you, Ron. . . . As Mr. Steinberg mentioned, I work for a company that makes a variety of petroleum products. Naturally, oil is essential for our company, so we're also concerned about the world's oil supply being depleted. One difference, though . . . well, the main *difference* between Mr. Steinberg and me is that our scientists tell us there are still enormous amounts of oil to be found. We're pushing for more exploration to find those new oil wells.

Ron Steinberg: All right. . . . Well, before we take your questions, I'll do a quick introduction to the peak oil theory. First off, we know . . . scientists will tell you that oil is a *non*-renewable resource. Oil was formed in a different era of Earth's history, so once we deplete the supply of oil we have now, that's it. The theory of *peak* oil came from Dr. M. King Hubbert.

Back in 1956, Hubbert used mathematical models, and he thought, he predicted that sometime between 1968 and 1972, the United States would produce as much oil as it was ever going to produce. In other words, that would be the *peak* of U.S. oil production. . . . In fact, oil production in the U.S. has been declining since 1970, so Dr. Hubbert was right. The U.S. is still extracting oil, but the oil wells are in hard-to-reach places . . . places like Alaska or the Gulf of Mexico, and as the *level* of oil in those wells goes down, it takes a lot more work to *extract* it, too.

Male Student: Can I ask a question?

Ron Steinberg: Absolutely. That's what we're here for tonight.

Male Student: I'd like to know what Dr. Hubbert's models have to say about the *world's* oil supply.

Leila Sparks: I can answer that one. In fact, engineers tell us that oil production will probably continue to increase for the next 20 years or so. So that means, they're saying we have some time to make the shift from oil to other fuels, and to find good substitutes for plastic and other petroleum products.

Ron Steinberg: Actually, your facts may be out of date. The latest reports say that peak oil production probably occurred in 2006. If that's true, it means that the oil supply will be *decreasing* while the world demand for oil is *increasing*. Expect higher prices, folks.

Leila Sparks: Hmmm. I hadn't heard those figures, Ron, but in any case, finding more oil is a high priority for all of us.

Female Student: I have a question. What if, what if there's oil somewhere that nobody knows about yet? Wouldn't new discoveries change the situation?

Ron Steinberg: That's a good question, and no doubt there *is* oil that hasn't been discovered yet. The problem though is that all the enormous, easily discovered oil fields were found years ago, so new discoveries will be pretty *small*, or the oil will be difficult to extract, like it is in the oil sands in Canada.

Leila Sparks: You sound pretty pessimistic, Ron. . . . I have more hope that the world's scientists will figure this thing out, and Lomax Petroleum will go on making quality products for a long, long time.

Ron Steinberg: Well, I hope you're right, Leila, but just in case you're not, . . . we need to act quickly to conserve the oil we have and to find other energy sources for the future.

Exploring Spoken English

Track 27 A. Language Function Page 129

Grace: Who was that on the phone?
Steve: It was Michael. He said they'd decided to buy a hybrid car.
Grace: *They* decided? I thought Laura loved fast, powerful cars.
Steve: She does, but she told Michael she was concerned about the environment.
Grace: Well, that sounds like a good change.
Steve: I agree. He also said that with four children, they'd been worried about finding a big enough hybrid vehicle.
Grace: Did they find one?
Steve: Yes, he said it's some kind of a mini-van with three rows of seats.
Grace: That sounds perfect. Maybe we should think about getting a hybrid.
Steve: I think I'd rather wait for hydrogen cars. Those don't use any gasoline at all.
Grace: True, but where are we going to get hydrogen fuel?
Steve: Actually, there are already some gas stations in Germany that sell it.

Lesson B

Building Vocabulary

Track 28 A. Meaning from Context Page 134

Hydrogen Fuel Question & Answer

Q: Will there be cars that are powered by hydrogen in the future?
A: Yes, in fact, there are hydrogen vehicles now. Engineers have designed them to either burn hydrogen in an engine, or to react with oxygen in fuel cells to run an electric engine.
Q: What are some of the advantages of hydrogen vehicles?
A: Unlike conventional gasoline or diesel-powered vehicles, hydrogen vehicles produce no carbon emissions. In addition, compared to electric cars, hydrogen cars can go a much longer distance before they need refueling, and the refueling process takes minutes instead of hours. Hydrogen fuel cells can also power larger vehicles such as buses.

Q: Are there any problems associated with hydrogen vehicles?
A: Unfortunately, there are. Although hydrogen doesn't need to be refined from crude oil like gasoline does, it does need to be manufactured. At present, it's manufactured either from natural gas or by using a lot of electricity. In places where electricity comes from fossil fuels such as coal, hydrogen isn't a great advantage—especially since hydrogen currently requires more energy to produce than it provides to the vehicle.
Q: Does that mean hydrogen vehicles might not be the energy solution that the transportation sector is looking for?
A: Maybe not right now, but eventually, technological advances should make hydrogen vehicles more practical and more efficient. Recently, a group of vehicle manufacturers and oil companies launched a campaign to convince more people to drive hydrogen cars. If more people buy the cars, there will be more reasons to develop new technologies and solve the problems.

Developing Listening Skills

Listening: A Conversation between Students

Track 29 A., B. Page 136

Student #1: I thought that was an interesting lecture today.
Student #2: So did I. Wasn't ethanol one of Professor Anderson's research subjects?
Student #3: I believe she said her research was on corn ethanol—the best way to transport it, or something like that.
Student #2: That sounds right.
Student #1: But you know . . . there was one thing I didn't understand. It was about the sugarcane refining process. . . . If they burn the sugarcane waste, doesn't that release CO_2 into the air? How is, how is *that* a solution to the problem of global warming?
Student #3: Actually, I don't think she said it was burned.
Student #2: It *is* burned. The machinery at the mill is designed to burn plant material. Then the heat from burning is used to power the mill and generate electricity. To me, that seems *way* better than using conventional fossil fuels like coal or natural gas.
Student #1: OK . . . I must have missed that part.
Student #3: So, here's the part I don't understand: In her presentation slides, Professor Anderson showed them manufacturing different kinds of sugar, like white sugar and brown sugar. So where does the molasses fit in?
Student #1: I, I've got that in my notes. The molasses is the liquid that's left over after they separate the sugar crystals from the, from the sugarcane juice. It's the stuff that gets *fermented* to make ethanol.
Student #3: Got it.
Student #2: OK, but what was that guy's question? Did he ask what they used to do with the molasses before they started making ethanol? I didn't catch that part.
Student #1: She told him it used to be used in cooking a lot more than it is now. It was cheaper than sugar.
Student #3: There might have been some advances . . . in sugar-making since then because it's pretty cheap now.
Student #1: Yeah, you could be right.

Pronunciation

Track 30 Reduced /h/ in Pronouns Page 137

Examples:
give + her sounds like "giver"
Please give her the message.
is + his sounds like "izzes"
Is his brother here?

Track 31 B. Page 137

1. His parents took him to the doctor's office.
2. Has he finished the project yet?
3. Was her presentation good?
4. Do his friends live in Jakarta?

Track 32 C. Page 137

1. I believe she said her research was on corn ethanol.
2. In her presentation slides, Professor Anderson showed them manufacturing different kinds of sugar.
3. Did he ask what they used to do with the molasses before they started making ethanol?
4. She told him it used to be used in cooking a lot more than it is now.

 **CD3**

Unit 8: Traditional and Modern Medicine Lesson A

Building Vocabulary

Track 2 A. Meaning from Context Page 144

New Respect for Old-Fashioned Medicines

Using plants as natural remedies for health problems is nothing new. In fact, almost two-thirds of the earth's population still relies on the healing power of plants. For them, nothing else is affordable or available. Plant-based medicine has also captured the attention of many scientists, who are studying plants' ability to restore health and fight diseases such as cancer.

In India, where many people talk about their symptoms with a traditional healer instead of a medical doctor, Darshan Shankar has created the Foundation for Revitalisation of Local Health Traditions. He says that preserving the knowledge of these healers is as crucial as conserving the plants they use. "The world has realized it should be concerned about saving biodiversity. But cultural knowledge is just as important."

Nat Quansah, an ethnobotanist who lives in Madagascar, studies plants such as the rosy periwinkle. A synthetic version of the active chemical from that plant is now produced in laboratories and made into drugs that inhibit cancer growth. Quansah knows about hundreds of other promising plant species that could be the basis for future medicines.

Jim Duke, now retired from the U.S. Department of Agriculture, still teaches and writes about medicinal plants such as chicory, which contains chicoric acid—a chemical that may someday be used to fight a deadly virus. Duke says that empirical studies of medicinal plants are needed. "We can use science to test plants, to find what works best. The issue is how to use science to get the best medicine, be it natural or synthetic."

Developing Listening Skills

Before Listening

Track 3 A. Page 146

Professor: First of all, it costs a lot of money to develop any new drug, and then to do empirical studies on it and get government approval. It's just a long, expensive process.
Student: Sure, but isn't it worth it if the new drug can save lives?

Listening: A Conversation in a Professor's Office

Track 4 A., B. Listening for Details Page 147

Student: Hi, . . . Professor Sullivan?
Professor: Hi, Patrick. Come on in.
Student: Thanks. I wanted to . . . to talk to you about this morning's lecture.
Professor: Good. Have a seat. What would you like to know?
Student: Well, in the lecture, you talked about some really promising medicinal plants, like chicory, and . . . and some others, I think. And, um, . . . also about those two anti-cancer drugs that are made from rosy periwinkle.
Professor: Well, actually, they're made from a synthetic chemical, . . . but it's the same chemical that's in rosy periwinkle.
Student: OK, so . . . basically, what I'd like to know is . . . why they're not studying *hundreds* of plant species looking for the next great medications.
Professor: That's a good question, and the answer's pretty complicated. First of all, it costs a *lot* of money to develop any new drug, and then to do empirical studies on it and get government approval. . . . It's just a long, expensive process.
Student: Sure, but isn't it *worth* it if the new drug can save lives?
Professor: Yes, but there's more to it. . . . With traditional remedies, there are a lot of variables. Imagine that a drug company learns about a plant that's supposed to inhibit the action of a virus—like the chicory plant, for example. They do experiments with the plant, and nothing happens. It turns out—afterwards—that they picked the wrong sub-species of the plant, or they picked the plant at the wrong time of day. . . . *Really*! . . . The plant chemicals can actually be different in the morning than they are at night. . . . Or, or maybe the plants were old instead of young, or . . . some other plant was growing nearby . . .
Student: Wow . . . do those things really make a difference?
Professor: They *can*. The crucial thing to remember is that scientists need to know exactly *which* chemical from the plant is active, and they need to put a standard amount of that chemical in each tablet or injection, and they need to make sure it won't kill anybody.
Student: Can medicines actually kill people?
Professor: It's possible. . . . That's why they have studies to find out what the medicines will do. . . . They might start with rats and mice, but eventually, they need to do large clinical trials with human beings.
Student: That makes sense. And are those clinical trials expensive?
Professor: Absolutely, and they take time, too.
Student: Well, I guess I can understand the problem, then. It's a shame though, . . . with plant species going extinct and all. I mean, one of those plants could . . . might be the cure for some disease, and we'll never know about it.
Professor: You could be right.
Student: Well, I need to get to the library. Thanks for taking the time to talk to me.
Professor: No problem at all . . . anytime. See you in class.

Exploring Spoken English

Track 5 A. Page 148

Nico: Hi, Bill. What's up?
Bill: I'm reading an article about olive oil.
Nico: Really? What does it say?
Bill: It says that olive oil can prevent heart disease and some cancers.
Nico: I've heard that before, and of course we make and use a lot of olive oil in Greece.
Bill: Maybe if I use more of it, I'll live a longer, healthier life.
Nico: Maybe, but you know—olive oil isn't the only reason Greek people are healthy.
Bill: Yeah? What are some other reasons?
Nico: We eat a lot of vegetables and fruit—every day. And exercise is built into our lifestyle. The weather is good, so we walk everywhere, and in my family at least, we love to dance.
Bill: I see what you mean. Here in the U.S., I take the bus most places, especially in winter.
Nico: There you go. But at least you get to hang out with a Greek person.
Bill: True. Maybe that will make me healthier.

Language Function: Discussing Health

Track 6 A. Page 149

Fighting Disease with a Guitar

As a child in Mozambique's Niassa Province, Feliciano dos Santos caught the polio virus from the dirty water in his tiny village. "When I was young," he recalls, "I never believed I would grow up, get married, have children, drive a car, and live such a full life. . . . "

These days, Santos and his band *Massukos* use music to spread messages of sanitation and hygiene to some of the poorest, most remote villages in Mozambique. Their hit song, *Wash Your Hands,* is part of a public health campaign created by Santos's non-governmental organization (NGO), Estamos. The project has successfully convinced villagers to install thousands of sustainable EcoSan latrines, dramatically improving sanitation and reducing disease throughout the region.

Santos's NGO also works on programs to install pumps for clean water, conduct health studies, and combat a new cholera epidemic. Says Santos, "Clean water is a basic human right, yet so many don't have it. I'm using my music to be the voice of people who have no voice."

Lesson B

Building Vocabulary

Track 7 A. Prior Knowledge Page 154

Quiz: High-Tech Medicine

1. The human genome consists of more than one million genes.
2. By looking at your genes, doctors can determine which hereditary diseases you will tend to get.
3. People who lose an arm or leg can get a device called a *prosthesis* that helps them to walk or lift things.
4. Prosthetic arms or legs can be operated by signals that the brain transmits to the device.
5. New technology allows patients to re-grow lost fingers and toes.

Track 8 C. Meaning from Context Page 154

Lily: I just saw the most extraordinary thing on television.
Charles: What was it?
Lily: It was this woman who had a severe injury and lost her arm.
Charles: What's extraordinary about that? It sounds terrible.
Lily: It was, but I haven't gotten to the extraordinary part yet.
Charles: OK, go on.
Lily: This woman didn't have enough muscles left to operate most prostheses. But luckily, they've come up with a radical new solution to the problem.
Charles: Sounds interesting. Did they reattach her arm?
Lily: No, they couldn't do that. But they gave her a prosthesis with a mechanism that receives signals from her brain. She just thinks about moving the synthetic arm, and it moves!

Developing Listening Skills

Pronunciation

Track 9 Linking Vowels with /y/ and /w/ sounds Page 156

Examples:
I am.
We always
So easy
Who is

Track 10 A. Page 156

1. She is not going skiing this weekend.
2. Who else missed class today?
3. He asked a good question.
4. They did two other blood tests.
5. Three of his friends are sick.

Listening: A Conversation between Friends

Track 11 A. Listening for Main Ideas Page 156
B. Listening for Details Page 156
C. Making Inferences Page 157

Teresa: Did I tell you my father is having a hip replacement next week?
Aiden: No, what's the matter with his hip?
Teresa: He has a lot of pain in his hip—from arthritis. It must be hereditary because everyone in my family gets arthritis when they get older.
Aiden: Yeah, it's very common—unfortunately, . . . but isn't hip replacement a pretty radical surgery?
Teresa: No, not really. ... I mean, it's *major* surgery, but it's fairly simple and it's over in a few hours.
Aiden: I see. So what does the surgery consist of? What do they have to do?
Teresa: Well, they remove part of the bone at the top of the leg, and they put in a, a device—a metal device. . . . It has a ball and a socket, just like a real hip joint.
Aiden: Hmmm . . . And then how long is the recovery? Will, will your dad be in a lot of pain?
Teresa: He'll be in a hospital for a few days, and then he needs physical therapy for six weeks to make the leg muscles strong again. . . . There will be some pain, . . . but it shouldn't be too severe.
Aiden: That's good.
Teresa: Definitely, but even when something is wrong, my dad tends to pretend that everything is fine. . . . If he *is* in pain, . . . I'll never know about it.
Aiden: My father is the same way.
Teresa: The extraordinary thing is . . . after the surgery and the recovery, the hip will be as good as new. He'll need to be careful, of course, but he'll be able to take walks, or travel, or whatever.
Aiden: That's great. I hope it goes well for him.
Teresa: Thanks.

Unit 9: The Legacy of Ancient Civilizations Lesson A

Using Vocabulary

Track 12 B. Page 165

Prehistoric Times: The Celtic languages spoken today date back at least 3000 years, and Celtic people have lived on the European continent much longer than that. Stone structures and the ruins of buildings and villages provide some information about the early Celtic people. Recent archaeological discoveries tell us that the well-known Stonehenge monument is surrounded by buried human remains. Archaeologists now think the site may have been a cemetery for a powerful family.

Period of Invasions: First the Romans, then the Vikings, Normans, Anglo-Saxons, and English all invaded Celtic lands. Over the centuries, numerous battles were fought, and the Celtic people became known for their rebellious nature and strong military defenses. The legends of King Arthur may be based on a real king who fought against the Anglo-Saxons, and William Wallace, the subject of the Hollywood movie, *Braveheart,* was killed by the English in 1305 after years of fighting for Scottish independence.

Modern Times: Today, Celtic languages and customs endure. Around 2.5 million people say they speak a Celtic language, and many modern people find ancient Celtic culture very appealing. Some adopt religious traditions, while many others participate in Celtic celebrations such as Beltane, which signals the beginning of summer.

Developing Listening Skills

Pronunciation

Track 13 Voicing and Syllable Length Page 166

Examples:
leaf, leave
hat, had
advice, advise

Track 14 A. Page 166

1. belief, believe
2. pat, pad
3. device, devise
4. safe, save
5. tap, tab

Listening: A Lecture

Track 15 A. Listening for Main Ideas, B. Page 167

Professor: Before we get started, just a reminder that there's a holiday on Monday, so no class that day. OK. Today we're continuing with our topic—the Celtic, people of Western Europe. . . . Last time, we talked a lot about the foreign invaders, the foreign invaders and the rebellious response of the Celtic people in every case. Today, we're going to focus on what endures—Celtic languages, archaeological sites, music, and a belief system based on the seasons—the seasons of the year—and the natural world.

Let's start with some of the archaeological sites. . . . Many of them are the ruins of structures that were built for defense—a sad reminder that times of peace were repeatedly interrupted by invasions and battles. I'd like you . . . I'd like to show you an example of the type of defense that the Celtic people of Ireland needed. In this slide, you see Dun Aengus in the Aran Island, where this thick, high, stone wall surrounds enough land for a pretty large village to inhabit—at least for a while. And on this side—well, let's say the people inside the wall didn't have to watch their backs! *Nobody* was going to climb up there from the sea, so the people inside were safe as long as the invaders didn't get past that wall, and they themselves didn't leave.

Let's turn now to language—another part of the legacy of the ancient Celtic people. . . . OK, by now you know what I mean when I talk about language extinction, and unfortunately, two of the six modern Celtic languages are nearly extinct. Both Cornish—once spoken in Cornwall—and Manx, the language from the Isle of Man, today, are spoken by only a few *hundred* native speakers.

It's quite a different case with Welsh and Irish Gaelic, which between them have over a million speakers. . . . What's, what's really unusual here is that when most languages become extinct, that's it—they're gone for good. They don't come back. But thanks to language revival efforts and a new interest in this area's ancient roots, many people now read newspapers, or, or listen to radio programs in a Celtic language, . . . and the number of speakers has actually grown!

Now let's talk a little about other aspects of Celtic culture, and why, in the 21st century, people seem to find it so appealing. . . . First off, I don't need to tell you about the music and the dancing. They're probably loved by more people in the world now than they ever were in ancient times. And although the very early Celtic people never wrote a *book*, storytelling was—and still is—an essential part of Celtic life. Some of the most respected modern writers have come from Ireland and Scotland—James Joyce . . . Robert Louis Stevenson . . . the list goes on.

What might be the biggest surprise about this cultural comeback is that some people have adopted Celtic religious traditions. The Celtic calendar was lunar—based on the cycle of the moon—and many of the important Celtic celebrations had to do with the time of year. You may have heard of some of these celebrations before . . .

Exploring Spoken English

Track 16 C. Page 169

Angkor Quick Facts

- In Southeast Asia, a short period of monsoon rains is followed by months of drought.
- The engineers of ancient Angkor designed a complex system of reservoirs and waterways to control flooding, support rice production, and provide transportation.
- Beginning around AD 900, every major king of the Khmer empire had a temple constructed at Angkor. The largest and best-known of the 50 temples is Angkor Wat, now a UNESCO World Heritage site and an important tourist attraction.
- By the early 1600s, the wealth of the empire had shifted from rice production to trading by sea.
- In the early 1700s, Vietnam took control of the Mekong River delta, and Angkor no longer had river access to the South China Sea.

Track 17 E. Page 170

Paolo: What a great vacation. I'm so glad we decided to go to Angkor Wat.
Harold: I agree. It would have been so easy to stay a few more days in Thailand. But if we hadn't gone to Cambodia, we wouldn't have seen such a marvelous place.
Paolo: That's true, but it is a shame we didn't go to see the wildlife sanctuary.
Harold: Seeing the sanctuary would have been nice, but if we had gone there, we would have missed that beautiful sunset in Angkor.
Paolo: That was incredible! I got some great pictures.
Harold: You know, you really should have brought your good camera.
Paolo: If I had brought that one, I would have been worried about losing it. It's a really expensive camera.
Harold: That's a good point. And my camera wasn't working, so if you hadn't brought yours, we wouldn't have any pictures at all.
Paolo: This old camera has never let me down.
Harold: All in all, it was a really good vacation, wasn't it?
Paolo: One of the best.

Speaking: Discussing Timelines

Track 18 A. Page 171

Rick: Which of these events had the biggest impact on your life?
Carl: They all had a big impact, but the academic award was especially important.
Rick: Really? Why was it so important?
Carl: Well, I grew up in a small village. If I hadn't won that award, I wouldn't have gotten a scholarship to a private high school in the city.
Rick: Wow—good for you! That's quite an achievement.
Carl: Thanks, but there were some negative experiences as well.
Rick: Like what? Everything on your timeline seems good.
Carl: Actually, working for my aunt's company wasn't a good experience. I really didn't know what I was doing.
Rick: But if you hadn't had that bad experience, you might not have realized that you needed to study business.
Carl: That's a good point. Now that I'm studying for a master's degree in business, I'm learning all kinds of things that would have helped me back then.
Rick: You see? Your past has gotten you where you are today.
Carl: Right, and I hope that this degree helps me to run my own business someday.

Lesson B

Building Vocabulary

Tracks 19–21 A. Meaning from Context Page 174

Track 19
This mummy of an ibis reflects a time in the past when millions of these birds lived along the Nile River. Getting the mummy out of the jar is tough because of the dried mud that surrounds it, but to Egyptologist Salima Ikram, it's worth the work. The popularity of the animal mummy exhibit that she's working on at the Egyptian Museum in Cairo has exceeded expectations. Visitors of all ages line up to look at the carefully preserved mummies.

Track 20
The Egyptian Museum in Cairo is home to some of the world's best-known mummies, including that of King Tutankhamen, his parents, and his grandparents. Ancient Egyptians knew that death was inevitable—all living things eventually die—but in an attempt to make the afterlife as comfortable as possible, mummies were accompanied by things they would need in the future; in other words, for all eternity. Much of the art and other valuable objects at the museum were found in Egyptian tombs.

Track 21
This mummy of a cat wearing a painted face mask stands next to a cat-shaped wooden coffin with a mummified kitten inside. The items buried with ancient Egyptians represented important aspects of their daily lives—everything from furniture to cooking oil. They believed that in the afterlife, these items became real and useful to the dead person. That idea may not seem rational nowadays, but ancient Egyptians didn't distinguish between human needs before and after death. They even mummified pieces of meat to represent the food the dead person would need.

Developing Listening Skills

Before Listening

Track 22 A. Page 176

Speaker: The Abydos site was really interesting because of the contrasts, but also the similarities, among the mummies we found there. Beginning around 5000 years ago, Egyptian kings and queens were buried there along with food and luxury items to enjoy in the next world, and in some cases, their pets . . . . she must have loved it very much because the gazelle was carefully wrapped in special cloth strips, and the mummy was placed inside a special gazelle-shaped coffin. Then in another part of the site, we found . . . . He was buried a couple of thousand years later, and he didn't have the valuable art and furniture that the kings and queens had, but that dog was as well-preserved as any mummy and was lying at its master's feet.

Listening: A Discussion about a Group Project

Track 23 A. Listening for Main Ideas Page 177
B. Listening for Details Page 177

Megan: We should get going on our project. We still need to choose our topic, and then divide the work . . .
Tyler: How long is our presentation supposed to be?
Megan: The minimum is six minutes, and it can't exceed 10 minutes.
Alana: OK. Now, which culture do we want to learn more about? I thought the animal mummies were really interesting.
Hassan: They were interesting, but I've studied ancient Egypt before. Maybe some aspect of Celtic culture? Like the music?
Megan: That sounds good to me. But first, . . . if I'm going to be the group leader, Alana, would you be the secretary?
Alana: I'm always the secretary. I'd rather do something else. . . . How about the expert? I'll do some of the research, and I'll answer questions from the audience.
Tyler: I could accompany Alana to the library to look for information.
Megan: Good, and could you be the secretary as well?
Tyler: No problem. I'll attempt to take notes that everyone can read.
Hassan: And I'll volunteer to be the coach.
Megan: That's great. Thank you. Let's see . . . we have a couple of tough decisions to make. . . . Good. It's settled, then. The study hall at the student union, at eight o'clock on Wednesday morning.
Alana: That sounds pretty early, but it's the only time we can all get together. Hassan, remember to wear a watch so we can time ourselves.
Hassan: No worries. I always wear a watch, and it has a second hand.
Megan: OK, this is going pretty well. Everyone has a job to do, and we all like the topic of Celtic music, right?
Tyler: The topic is good, but it's very broad. Narrowing it to something more specific is probably inevitable.
Hassan: Right, like Celtic musical instruments or something.
Alana: Hey, we could make some . . . Maybe one that shows an Irish harp, and another that shows both Irish and Scottish bagpipes so our audience can learn how to distinguish the two kinds.

Hassan: That's a great idea, and I know where we can find some good photos to use.
Megan: OK, it sounds like we have a plan. Can everyone go to the library after class so we can get started?

Exploring Spoken English

Track 24 A. Page 179

Joel: And then he told me that he had some tickets to the basketball game, so I said . . .
Antonio: If I could just add something . . .
Joel: I'm almost done—so I said I could go to the game with him!
Antonio: And speaking of the game, did you hear that it's been cancelled? They said that . . .
Joel: Um . . . did you say, *cancelled*? I can't believe it!
Antonio: It's true. The other team couldn't get here, or something.

Unit 10: Emotions and Personality Lesson A

Building Vocabulary

Track 25 A. Meaning from Context Page 184

Max: What's the matter? You look like you're sad.
Abigail: I'm reading a newspaper. How can I look sad?
Max: I'm just reading your facial expression. I learned that when people experience basic emotions, like sadness or fear, you can see it in their faces.
Abigail: But I'm Indonesian, and you're Canadian. Maybe we make different facial expressions to express the same emotions.
Max: Well, that's the interesting thing. Back in the 1800s, Charles Darwin speculated that our facial expressions, like smiling when we're happy, are a universal human phenomenon.
Abigail: So was he right? Do we all make the same facial expressions?
Max: We do. Around 40 years ago, a psychologist named Paul Ekman confirmed Darwin's theory. He conducted an experiment, and the results showed that people across cultures make the same facial expressions to express the same emotions.
Abigail: So it doesn't matter which culture we come from?
Max: Right. He also wondered whether the things that trigger our emotions might be universal.
Abigail: Interesting. So are the things that cause our emotions the same for everyone?
Max: The answer is—yes, and no. Certain things are universal, like a sudden movement in our field of vision triggers fear, for example.
Abigail: That makes sense. A sudden movement could signal danger so maybe we react because of our instincts.
Max: Right, but some things don't trigger the same emotion. For example, one person could associate the smell of the sea with something positive, like a vacation.
Abigail: And another person might associate the smell with a sad time in their lives.
Max: Exactly!
Abigail: And I suppose that those emotional triggers might have to do with personality as well.
Max: You're probably right.

Developing Listening Skills

Pronunciation

Track 26 Intonation for Thought Groups Page 186

What kind of **car** did you buy?
I bought a used **sedan**.
It's better to give than to receive.
The Johnson's baby wasn't afraid of snakes before that day.

Track 27 Page 186

1. Elena has a good *personality,* but she doesn't have many *friends*.
2. We went to the *store* and we bought some *fruit*.
3. I can't decide between the *red shoes* and the *brown ones.*
4. Do you want to fix the car *yourself* or take it to a *mechanic*?

Listening: A Radio Interview

Track 28 A. Listening for Main Ideas Page 186
B. Listening for Details Page 187
C. Discussion Page 187

Radio Host: Welcome back to Talk Radio ten ninety-four. I'm your host, Nancy Morales, and we're talking today with Dr. Eugene Bateman, a psychologist from the National University. Good morning, Dr. Bateman.
Guest: Good morning, Nancy. Thank you for having me.
Radio Host: Thank *you* for being here. . . . Now, your research area is the human fear response, or more specifically, the question of whether we *learn* to be afraid of certain things, or if we inherit something from our ancestors that triggers our fear.
Guest: That's right, Nancy, . . . and we're talking about our distant, *distant* ancestors—people who lived a long time ago—tens of thousands of years ago. Back then, reacting quickly to something like a, like a falling rock or a hungry lion was a good quality in a human being. . . . It meant that he or she was more likely to survive, more likely to live long enough to have children, and more likely to pass on their genes to their children.
Radio Host: OK, but people today don't have to deal with *hungry lions* very often. So, what does the fear response do for *us*?
Guest: Well, it still keeps us out of trouble and helps us to survive. Imagine that you're driving a car, and the car in front of you suddenly stops. There's a series of events that takes place in our brains that makes our bodies react—in this case, by putting our foot on the brakes—that takes place before we even realize what is happening. It all happens much faster than our conscious thought processes.
Radio Host: That sounds like a pretty useful phenomenon. . . . Does it confirm that we *do* inherit our knowledge of what to fear from our ancient ancestors?
Guest: Yes, and no. . . . Some interesting experiments were conducted with monkeys that were raised in a laboratory. These monkeys had *zero* experience with being outdoors, right? So they—the researchers—showed the monkeys some snakes.
Radio Host: And were the lab monkeys afraid of the snakes?
Guest: Not at all, at least—not at first. Then the researchers showed the monkeys videos of wild monkeys having a fearful reaction to snakes. After that, the lab monkeys became afraid of snakes too as they learned to associate the sight of a snake with a fearful reaction.
Radio Host: So they learned the fear from the wild monkeys, in a sense.
Guest: That's right, but here's the interesting part. When the researchers changed the videos so that the wild monkeys

appeared to be afraid of flowers, the lab monkeys developed no fear of flowers at all!
Radio Host: Huh . . . smart monkeys.
Guest: Exactly, and that's where the inherited aspect of fear comes into the picture. What we inherit is a *tendency* to fear certain things—the same things our ancient ancestors feared. On the other hand, we have to learn from others around us as well; otherwise, the fear response doesn't occur.
Radio Host: That *is* very interesting. Fear seems like such a basic response. It wouldn't have occurred to me that we would need to learn it from anyone. And is it the same for people as for monkeys?
Guest: It seems to be, yes, but that's exactly the question that my research is hoping to answer.
Radio Host: Then I wish you luck with your research. Ladies and gentlemen, Dr. Eugene Bateman.
Guest: Thank you. Thanks very much, Nancy.

Exploring Spoken English

Track 29 B. Page 189

Hand Washing Wipes away Regrets?

If you have to make a tough decision, research suggests that you should wash your hands afterwards. The research was conducted at the University of Michigan in the U.S. by Spike W.S. Lee and Norbert Schwarz, who asked student volunteers to participate in what they thought was a consumer survey.

The students were asked to rank 10 music CDs in order of preference. Then the researchers let them choose between the fifth and the sixth CD to take home as a gift. Once the volunteers had made a decision, some students chose to evaluate a liquid hand soap by washing their hands, while others just looked at the bottle. The students who didn't wash their hands later ranked their chosen CDs higher than they had before, but students who did wash up ranked the 10 CDs in basically the same order as before.

This phenomenon is called post-decisional dissonance. "You want to feel that you made the right choice, so you justify it by thinking about the positive features of your decision," Lee explained.

The researchers conducted a similar survey in which they asked people to choose a jam without tasting it first. People who hadn't used an antiseptic wipe expected their chosen jam to taste better than the rejected one. Those who had used the wipe thought the jams would taste about the same.

It's as if hand washing in any form "wipes the slate clean" and removes the need to confirm that we've made the right choice, Lee said.

Lesson B

Building Vocabulary

Track 30 B. Page 194

Introverts

Modern psychology offers many models to explain personality types, but nearly all of them include two terms made popular by Carl Jung in the early 20th century: *introverted* and *extroverted*. These two personality types have very different attributes, and while almost everyone has some aspects of both types in their own personality, one type is usually stronger.

In general, introverted people prefer activities they can do alone, such as reading or playing video games. They may feel awkward in social situations, where they're worried about how they should behave. In some cases, they may even feel enough anxiety about social situations to avoid them altogether. For most people, however, having an introverted nature simply means they prefer to have less frequent social contact with smaller numbers of people.

Using Vocabulary

Track 31 A. Page 195

Extroverts

Extroverted people differ from introverted people in several ways. Extroverted people thrive on interaction with others and feel energized at social gatherings such as large parties. Politicians, teachers, and business managers are often extroverted. They may be very charming in order to attract people to interact with, or they may be overly talkative and so outgoing that people become uncomfortable around them.

Extroverted people may become upset when they lack human contact on the job or in their social lives, and in more serious cases, feelings of being alone can lead to depression. In these cases, psychological counseling can give extroverted people insights into themselves and ways to manage their feelings.

Developing Listening Skills

Listening: An Informal Conversation

Track 32 A. Listening for Main Ideas
B. Listening for Details Page 196

Leo: So, did you enjoy the party?
Reba: I did. It was really nice to meet all of the people you work with. They're a big part of your life, after all.
Leo: Yeah, sometimes *too* big a part, maybe.
Reba: Oh, come on. They seem like pretty nice people—especially Gloria. She said "hi" to me right away. I thought she was really charming. . . . I loved the story she told us about her car accident. That was pretty funny.
Leo: Right . . . she can make anything seem funny. I guess all of my coworkers have their positive attributes.
Reba: Like your manager. . . . When you got a little bit upset about the food arriving late, he made sure everyone knew it wasn't Gloria's fault. I mean, she may have chosen the caterer, but *they* brought the food late, not her.
Leo: Yeah, that's true. He's always doing things like that. He's a really nice guy . . . he's pretty extroverted, so he likes to talk to everyone. And if somebody is feeling awkward, he says something to make them feel comfortable. . . . He's got great social skills, which I guess is part of the reason why he's such a good manager.
Reba: That *is* an important quality in a manager. But what about Toby? I tried to talk to *him* at one point, but he, he just walked away. It seemed like he was avoiding any kind of interaction. Is he just really shy or something?
Leo: Yeah, Toby is really introverted, and I think he experiences a lot of anxiety when he's around a lot of people, especially new people. He's really a nice guy though and a good coworker, and he's fine with smaller groups of people—like when we go out for lunch together. He's fine then.
Reba: I see. All in all, it was a good party. I had fun.
Leo: Good, I'm glad. I had fun, too. And now that you've met the people I work with, maybe we can do things with them sometimes.

Reba: Yeah, should we invite some of them over for dinner some time?
Leo: Well, that might be too much. But I'd enjoy meeting them at a restaurant for dinner or going to a soccer game together, or something like that.
Reba: So, you don't want them coming to our house?
Leo: You got it. I'd rather keep at least a *little* distance between my work life and my personal life.

Engage: Assessing the Credibility of a News Article

Track 33 A. Page 200

Making Music Boosts Brain's Language Skills

Do you have trouble hearing people talk at parties? Try practicing the piano before you leave the house. That's because musicians—from karaoke singers to professional cello players—are better able to hear targeted sounds in a noisy environment.

"In the past 10 years there's been an explosion of research on music and the brain," Aniruddh Patel, the Esther J. Burnham Senior Fellow at the Neurosciences Institute in San Diego, said today at a press briefing.

Most recently, brain-imaging studies have shown that music activates many diverse parts of the brain, including a part of the brain that processes both music and language. Language is a natural aspect to consider in looking at how music affects the brain, according to Patel. Patel states that like music, language is "universal, there's a strong learning component, and it carries complex meanings."

According to study leader Nina Kraus, director of the Auditory Neuroscience Laboratory at Northwestern University in Illinois, the brains of people with even casual musical training are better able to generate the brain wave patterns associated with specific sounds, whether musical or spoken. In other words, musicians are used to "playing" sounds in their heads, so they've trained their brains to recognize selective sound patterns, such as spoken words, even as background noise goes up.

Unit 1: Wodaabe

Narrator:
For 51 weeks of the year, the Wodaabe, a nomadic African tribe, eke out a living on a parched strip of land in West Africa.

In the 52nd week, they dance. This is far more than an ordinary dance, though. Part beauty pageant and part mating ritual, this dance is part of a seven-day festival that gives the men in the tribe the opportunity to show off for the women. For Wodaabe men, this is the time to weave the web of enchantment. For psychologists, the Wodaabe festival provides insight into the impact of appearance on attraction and social behavior.

All the Wodaabe—but especially the men—pride themselves on their physical beauty. Light skin, thin lips, a long nose and jaw-line. . . . The Wodaabe consider these to be the ideal features, and they accentuate them with carefully applied makeup.

Wodaabe Man:
If a man puts black color on his lips, it makes his white teeth stand out, and this is very attractive to women. If a man puts yellow on his face, it brings out his charm and personality and makes him irresistible.

Narrator:
The first part of the dance, known as the *yaake*, begins in the late afternoon. The dancers face the setting sun so its golden rays will enhance their beauty.

The object of the *yaake* is to make oneself as irresistible as possible to the group of eligible women who are monitoring every move and expression.

The three most beautiful women of the clan act as judges. They express their approval of certain dancers by a tap on the chest without making eye contact. It is taboo for them to look directly at those they find attractive. The *yaake* ends just before sunset. Slowly the dancers disperse to prepare for the night's festivities.

After a rest period, preparations for the second part of the dance begin—the sacred dance of physical beauty called the *geerewol*. Unlike the *yaake*, in which the men are evaluated on charm and personality as well as looks, the *geerewol* dancers will be judged on the basis of beauty alone. Only the most handsome men dare to compete.

Normally the *geerewol* would be danced throughout the night, but a drought has shortened the supply of drinking water, so the Wodaabe elders call a halt to the dancing shortly before midnight. By then, many of the members have paired up. The women have chosen the men they find most attractive and appealing.

Shortly after sunrise on the final night, the Wodaabe prepare to leave the celebration site. After a week of dancing, they are once again nomads.

Unit 2: Turtle Excluder

Narrator:
The warm waters off the Gulf of Mexico are home to many different kinds of endangered sea turtles. One species, the Kemp's Ridley sea turtle, is still very much in danger of extinction. But the population is making a gradual rebound thanks in part to a group of marine researchers in Texas.

Shanna Lynne Baker, Fishery Biologist:
Welcome to the national fishery sea turtle facility.

Narrator:
Marine biologist Shanna Lynne Baker says, as the smallest species of sea turtle in the world, the Kemp's Ridley needs all the help it can get.

Shanna Lynne Baker:
They are an integral part of the ecosystem; they've been around for millions and millions of years—ever since the dinosaurs—and really it's the humans' fault why their numbers are going down and we have sort of a responsibility to make up for that.

Narrator:
The turtle population along the Gulf Coast is making its comeback thanks in part to the invention of a new technology for fishing nets called the T.E.D (T-E-D), or turtle excluder device.

Shanna Lynne Baker:
This is the actual turtle excluder device right here. How this works is this funnel shape over here is called an accelerator funnel and what it does . . . it passes a large quantity of water through a small area and that causes the water to move really fast and starts a current through here, so everything is being pushed through this area up against these bars. Anything smaller than the spaces between these bars like shrimp and small fish go through the bars and on toward the back of the net where they are caught in the back. . . . Anything larger than the spaces between these bars is designed for turtles, but it also works for sharks and large fish because the current is pushing on them and the bars are kind of slanted towards this opening here at the bottom. . . . This flap right here will be held shut by

the water pressure, but as soon as anything gets down inside there, it opens it up and the turtle can escape and go up to the top to breathe and the flap will close behind them.

Narrator:
In the past turtles were often caught in a variety of fishing nets. And while the problem still exists today, U.S. shrimp fishermen are now required by law to use the new device. Some fishermen who use the device complain that having holes in their nets can cause them to lose a significant percentage of their catch. But biologists say the new nets can also work in the fishermen's favor.

Shanna Lynne Baker:
They generally catch more shrimp through the season because this doesn't just exclude the occasional turtle—it excludes anything large in the back of their nets so they can pull their nets for a lot longer before they fill up and they get a higher percentage of actual shrimp that they can keep each time.

Narrator:
Biologists at this facility are putting a lot of hope in the success of the turtle excluder device, but they've also developed other research efforts that have boosted the Ridley population, like captive breeding. With every healthy turtle, the species is one small step farther from extinction.

Unit 3: Turkish Germany

Narrator:
It has the look and the sound of Istanbul. But this Turkish community is in Germany. In a country learning how to prosper with a diversity it didn't want. After the devastation of World War II, Germany needed help to rebuild and so invited Turkish guest workers. Both Germans and Turks believed the arrangement was temporary.

Ozcan Mutlu, Member of Parliament, Berlin:
But that was a lie. It was a life lie, I say. Because no one returned.

Narrator:
Turks like to say that the Germans sent for workers, but got human beings. And the human beings became a vibrant community. Two hundred thousand in Berlin, 2 million in all of Germany. A third generation of German Turks is now being born, but many Germans still think of them as foreigners.

Ozcan Mutlu:
This is one reason why these people kept their ties to the home country, and why they still identify themselves as Turks.

Narrator:
Turkish fears grew when the Berlin Wall fell and the government focused on reunification rather than the needs of minorities.

Ozcan Mutlu:
Turks say the wall came down, but it came down on the heads of the Turks.

Narrator:
There is a rich Turkish cultural tradition in Germany. But though the cultural border between peoples here has grown more distinct, both Germans and Turks are trying to bridge it.

This is a pioneering public school called Rixdorfer. Students from both cultures are taught side by side in both languages. The costs are higher than average, but so is the success.

Marion Berning, Rixdorfer Elementary School, Berlin:
If you put money in the small kids, in the younger kids, you don't have much problems when they are older.

Narrator:
Marion Berning hopes that what she sees here is the shape of the future.

Marion Berning:
They don't see the difference between the Turkish and the German. And so they have no problems with foreigners. They are not foreigners. They are kids.

Unit 4: The Giant's Causeway

Narrator:
This stone walkway on the coast of Northern Ireland is one of the country's most important tourist centers—the Giant's Causeway. It's a special place of science and legends. Many visitors come each year to see Northern Ireland's first World Heritage site. For some people, these 40,000 pieces of basalt are a natural formation. For other people, the Giant's Causeway is the home of a giant named Finn MacCool. In the past, Hill Dick was a tour guide. He tells the legend of Finn MacCool.

Hill Dick, Former Tour Guide:
Finn was one of the great characters in Irish mythology or, if you like, Irish fact.

Narrator:
Dick then tells a story about how Finn was angry with a Scottish giant who lived 25 miles across the sea. So Finn decided to go to Scotland. He was not a good swimmer, so he used rocks from volcanoes to build a road to

Scotland, and he called it the "Giant's Causeway." Is the story of Finn MacCool true? Well, perhaps—if you use your imagination. But not everyone agrees. Scientists like geologist Patrick McKeever have their own story. They say that a volcano made the Giant's Causeway about 60 million years ago. That was a very long time before humans ever lived in this beautiful part of the world. McKeever talks about how he thinks the Giant's Causeway was made.

Dr. Patrick McKeever, Geologist:
The lava that was erupted was erupted very, very quickly and the flows were very, very thick.

Narrator:
He then explains that the lava was a bit like wet mud on a hot day. The mud becomes dry and shrinks, or gets smaller when it dries. McKeever says that a similar condition with the lava made the many-sided columns. Visitors have been coming to the Giant's Causeway and the nearby Irish coast since the 1800s; these people don't have to believe in the legend—or the science—to want to come to this interesting place.

Dr. Patrick McKeever:
You can weave your own story around it. You can look at a rock and say, "That reminds me of something . . . that looks like something. . . ."

Narrator:
Each year, many tourists and children visit the Giant's Causeway and hear the legends. These people—and their interest—may help the legend of Finn MacCool live for a very long time.

Unit 5: The Business of Cranberries

Narrator:
As dawn breaks over the countryside, Mary Brazeau Brown is already starting her day.

Mary Brazeau Brown, Owner of Glacial Lake Cranberries:
Ready to go for a walk, Holly girl? Let's go.

Narrator:
Early morning is her time to focus and get ready for the busy day ahead. The calm of sunrise won't last long . . . not with a family to take care of inside.

Mary Brazeau Brown:
Coffee cake time . . .

Narrator:
And a passion waiting right outside the door.

Mary Brazeau Brown:
When people would ask me what I wanted to be when I grew up, I knew all along there were two things that I wanted to do. Be a mom and work outside. You're going to work, and I'm going to work.

Narrator:
Life has worked out just as she planned. Mary's office is this 6100-acre cranberry marsh . . . one of the largest and oldest in Wisconsin.

Mary Brazeau Brown:
I can't resist. This particular system was established back in 1873. . . . Some of the vines out here are over 70 years old. . . . They were here before me, and they'll be here after me.

Narrator:
As owner of Glacial Lake Cranberries, she oversees every aspect of the business . . . and today the long-awaited fall harvest has just begun.

Mary Brazeau Brown:
Harvest is a great time of year because you work for it all year long.

Narrator:
The marsh sits in Cranmoor—a tiny town that produces more cranberries inland than anyplace in the world.

Mary Brazeau Brown:
This area where we are is all part of old Glacial Lake Wisconsin and it's very flat, high water table, acid conditions, lots of sand, and cranberries are native to this area. Cranberries are one of North America's native fruits.

Narrator:
Here, 14 families, each with its own legacy, have been harvesting this crop for generations. Mary herself is a third generation cranberry grower. When the berries ripen to a glowing red in early fall, it's time to flood the beds. . . . The berries are knocked from their vines by machines called beaters . . . and they float to the surface to be corralled. Mary keeps a cautious eye on the weather. . . .

Mary Brazeau Brown:
Tomorrow morning you'll say, "Yeah this is fall." Yeah, I know it.

Narrator:
A hard frost could wipe out an entire crop. When the berries are in danger of freezing, the irrigation system is turned on to keep water flowing over the vines and the temperature from reaching damaging levels. These sprinklers could be the difference between a bumper crop and a bitter harvest.

Mary Brazeau Brown:
And the forecast for this week is cold all week so we'll probably not only be up tonight but tomorrow night and who knows how long.

Narrator:
Because the cranberry crop is so dependent on water. . . . large systems of reservoirs, ditches, and dikes are needed to keep an adequate supply ready at a moment's notice.

Mary Brazeau Brown:
. . . And it's a wonderful time of year, but it's so reassuring because it tells me that we're doing something right and when we're doing something right for the wildlife, then we're doing something for us. And whether you're a mom to kids or a mom to the cranberry vines or the loons or the northern harriers, it's a great job to have.

Unit 6: Sleepy Hollow

Narrator:
Nestled in the hills of New York's Hudson River Valley lies the town of Sleepy Hollow . . . a place where a spooky legend meets modern-day life. Dutch settlers came here in the 1600s to farm, trap, and fish. At this historic manor, you can still experience life as it was in the 17th and 18th centuries. It's a fun place to visit, but it's the tale of a gangly schoolmaster and a headless horseman that really put Sleepy Hollow on the map.

Jonathan Kruk, Storyteller:
Now dwelling in these parts, in a tenant house, was a certain schoolmaster by the name of Ichabod Crane.

Narrator:
American author, Washington Irving, visited this area as a boy, and is believed to have based *The Legend of Sleepy Hollow* on people and places right in this town. Bill Lent knows everything there is to know about the legend, showing tourists where the famous characters are buried.

Bill Lent:
And when he was writing the book, he remembered the name on the stone, Katrina Van Tassel. Lead female character in *The Legend of Sleepy Hollow.*

Narrator:
As the story goes, Ichabod Crane fled across this bridge . . . racing to escape the headless horseman close behind.

Jonathan Kruk:
Ichabod urged his horse, Gunpowder, on, "Come, come," but the horse needed no further urging as he took off and headed down to get to that churchyard bridge.

Narrator:
Every year Sal Tarantino plays the headless horseman in the town's Halloween festival.

Sal Tarantino, Headless Horseman:
The hardest problem is a real jack-o-lantern. We've tried that several times. A good-sized jack-o-lantern with the right candle in it weighs about 20 pounds. And to hold that out on your arm and try to control the horse at 40 miles per hour in the dark doesn't work too well.

Narrator:
Irving did not actually write the legend here in Sleepy Hollow. But he loved the area so much, he returned as an adult to live on this 24-acre estate right on the Hudson River. And nearly two centuries after Irving wrote *The Legend of Sleepy Hollow,* the history and landscape of this place still inspire. And the legend lives on. . . .

Jonathan Kruk:
If you listen, you'll hear the unmistakable clattering of hooves of the headless horseman . . . beware . . .

Unit 7: Canadian Oil Sands

Narrator:
We head now on assignment with *National Geographic Magazine* to document this changing landscape. Late into the night . . . flames flare over the landscape. This mining operation continues 24 hours a day . . . 365 days a year . . . extracting oil from just beneath the surface of what was once Canadian wilderness.

Celina Harper, Resident:
I could just cry when I see what, what they have done to our land. You just see, that's all you could see, just as far as you could see. Nothing, just nothing—not even one, one stick. Not even one tree standing.

Narrator:
This is Canada's boreal . . . one of the largest forests on earth. It's Northern America's nesting spot for billions upon billions of birds that migrate across North America . . . and even as far as South America. It's also the site of something called "Oil Sands" . . . a naturally occurring mix of sand and a thick form of petroleum known as bitumen. Bitumen must be heavily processed before it becomes crude oil . . . then turned into gasoline and diesel fuels. This section of northern Alberta has the largest amount of oil sand in the world . . . and some estimates suggest Alberta's oil reserves are comparable to those of Saudi Arabia. But to get to this oil . . . Canada has been strip mining large sections of former wilderness. *National Geographic Magazine* photographer Peter Essick journeyed to Ft. McMurray to capture the changing landscape.

Peter Essick, National Geographic Photographer:
You can take pictures of the wilderness part, which is sort of the trees and the muskeg which hasn't been developed, and then you can take a picture of some of the mining, the big trucks . . . but I was trying to show some ways you could see sort of the connection between sort of the wildlife or the nature and the mining.

Narrator:
First the forest is cut down . . . top soil is removed and the sand collected by enormous shovels. It's then carried by dump trucks to a processing facility. Each truck can carry almost 400 tons of oil-rich sand. After processing . . . the synthetic crude is shipped via pipeline to refineries in the United States. Canada has been extracting oil here for almost a century . . . but higher fuel prices in recent years . . . and new processing technologies . . . have led to a major oil boom. This part of Alberta has been completely changed.

Mike Noseworthy, Resident:
You're looking at high-rent costs, high food costs, high fuel costs.

Brenda Hampson, Truck Driver:
It's just money and it's all over the place and the jobs are all over the place. In Alberta there is 10 jobs for one person.

Narrator:
People's lives have been changed . . . some for the worse but many arguably for the better.

But conservationists say the landscape is also being changed—for the worse. They worry that stripping the boreal forest of thousands of square miles of forest is hurting a major ecosystem. Some argue that destruction in the boreal forest is a major contributor to global warming. The forest is so enormous that it helps control the earth's thermostat. Its wetlands and bogs absorb carbon . . . helping cleanse the atmosphere of the greenhouse gases that contribute to higher temperatures throughout the world.

Steve Kallick, Pew Environment Group
This is the peat. It's spongy and there's no strength to it. This is the accumulated carbon from millennia. It's been exposed now to the surface, the protective cover has been removed, and all the carbon that has been stored has come back out into the atmosphere. Development across the boreal is going to continue to do this. We don't know how much, we don't know what the ultimate result is going to be.

Narrator:
Already temperatures here are climbing . . . while there's been a corresponding drop in rain and snow. But the country is not planning to stop oil-sand processing anytime soon. Dozens of companies are planning nearly 100 more projects . . . worth 100 billion dollars. Canada is working to reduce the amount of greenhouse emissions . . . and to take back land that's been stripped in the mining process. But some conservationists hope large sections of the boreal forest will be set aside and protected from future strip mining.

Steve Kallick, Pew Environment Group
By having a large underdeveloped area where wildlife can move and adapt to change, we may be able to protect them from one of the worst impacts of global warming. As climate change is affecting their habitat, they'll be able to migrate to other areas if we set aside millions and tens of millions of acres of large intact natural landscapes.

Narrator:
It would seem the needs of humans . . . wildlife . . . and the planet's thermostat are in conflict in this oil-rich region.

Unit 8: Wild Health

Narrator:
Have the sniffles? Feeling under the weather? Have an ache or a pain? Then generally, our first stop is the drugstore. But this luxury is only allowed to humans. It may not surprise you to learn that the rest of the

species that inhabit the planet come up with some very interesting ways of self-medication. Deep in the English countryside, animal behaviorist Cindy Engel studies a new form of biology called zoopharmacognosy—or animal self-medication. Cindy's dedicated the last few years of her life into compiling all of her research into a new book.

Cindy Engel, Animal Behaviorist:
I often have people asking me whether it's just instinct, and the answer is no—the ability to seek out a well-balanced diet is incredibly complicated, and they are adjusting it moment to moment.

Narrator:
Engel suggests there may be examples where humans, having studied animals' self-medicating, have come across benefits ourselves in drugs or chemical uses.

Cindy Engel:
Early medicine was based on observing the behavior of sick animals. It's relatively recently that we've stopped looking. Chimpanzees have already shown six or seven new compounds previously unknown to science, many of which are incredibly important for human medicine.

Narrator:
Engel's book has received enormous interest in scientific communities across Europe and North America. She's concentrated on three main areas of animal self-medication. First are curative measures, whereby animals have the ability to cure contracted ailments. Second are preventative measures, whereby animals take positive action to protect themselves from illness or parasites. And lastly are avoidance measures, where animals have the knowledge or insight to avoid toxic plants and select the right food to keep themselves on a healthy diet. Cows, for instance, have certain ways of improving their self-health.

Cindy Engel:
Cattle have got a special type of stomach—they have to ferment the tough fibrous material in the grass. And fermentation requires a really carefully balanced level of acidity, and clay will, being alkaline, will help balance acidity for the fermentation process. And this is not an unconsidered part of the cow's ecology and behavior. Some species will travel long distances just to get to the right type of dirt.

Cindy Engel:
Wildebeests, in Africa, are probably the best example. They will migrate to the volcanic ash floor. It contains these essential minerals for lactation.

Narrator:
Observing wild animals self-medicating is something that's very rarely seen, but during Engel's research she came across some groundbreaking video footage.

Cindy Engel:
This snow leopard was being treated for a bladder infection. She lives in San Francisco Zoo, and she had to go on a course of antibiotics, and antibiotics can cause nausea, and all the while she was suffering from nausea, she was eating grass continuously. And of course, when the antibiotics stopped, so did the grass eating.

Narrator:
So, in an attempt to combat the effects of this man-made antibiotic, this wild animal has resorted to self-medication by way of a good dose of grass. Whether it is buffalo eating mud to combat parasites or primates using plants to eliminate stomach infections, animal self-medication, or zoopharmacognosy is an area of biology that's sure to attract much more attention in years to come.

Unit 9: Lost Temple of the Mayans

Narrator:
In the middle of the Central American country of Guatemala, archaeologists are finding new evidence about the ancient Maya civilization. They're discovering a Maya world that may have existed long before scientists thought it did. Under the leaves and earth of the Guatemalan jungle, the secrets of this new discovery may lie under one of the biggest pyramids ever built: the great pyramid of Danta. Archaeologist Richard Hansen is traveling to the site of the pyramid. He suspects that the area called Mirador may have information about the origins of one of the world's greatest civilizations. He thinks that it may unlock the secrets of the early Maya. The culture that is thought of as "Classic Maya" grew across Central America between AD 250 and 900. However, archaeologists are now discovering a Maya civilization that existed 1000 years before the classic period, in the preclassic period. Most of the remains of this newly discovered culture lie under the earth in the Mirador region. They may be near an ancient city that has been lost for hundreds of years: El Mirador. Hansen has worked for more than 20 years at El Mirador. During that time, he has been trying to solve the mystery of the early Maya. Who were they and how did they achieve so much? Hansen hopes to find the answers by digging under the pyramids.

Richard Hansen, Archaeologist:
Well, this is the third level of the great pyramid of Danta at El Mirador, the largest pyramid at the site. It sustains for nearly a half a mile on platforms below us here, and a . . . probably one of the largest pyramids in the world.

Narrator:
The Danta pyramid was built during a time that many people consider to be basic and simple. But if the early Maya were so simple, how did they build a structure that was as complex as the Great Pyramids of Egypt? According to Hansen, the kings of the Maya were as important as the ancient Egyptian kings.

Richard Hansen:
The person that commissioned this building was not a simple chief, living in a grass hut. This was a king on the order of Ramses and Cheops.

Narrator:
Hansen dreams of finding these kings from the beginning of Maya time. He hopes that their tombs will reveal who they were. Most archaeological discoveries focus on the physical evidence, or outer signs, of the power and influence of the kings. Hansen says that there's not a lot of knowledge about them as people. He feels that the work that archaeologists are doing in Mirador may help scientists get to know the kings more personally. Hansen is especially interested in one of the smaller pyramids of El Mirador.

One of the stones in the pyramid has a large jaguar paw with three claws on it. Hansen believes that this could be a temple; the tomb of an important king who ruled from 152 BC to 145 BC during the preclassic period. The king's name means "Great Fiery Jaguar Paw."

Richard Hansen:
This may be a symbol of this, that's why this building is so interesting to us, because it's possible that this king could be buried here.

Narrator:
Is the Jaguar Paw king buried in the temple? Hansen wants to find out. He's brought in the newest technology in underground imaging systems to do this. This special equipment sends electrical currents through the ground. These currents determine whether the ground is solid, or if there's an opening. The system then creates a map of what's under the soil. Will the imaging system show an empty room? If it does, it might be a place where there's a king's tomb. After three hours, the mapping expert has a result.

There is an open space under the pyramid that's about 11 meters under the earth. It's approximately eight meters long by two meters wide. That's just the right size for a king's tomb!

Richard Hansen:
So, it's definitely there?

Mapping Expert:
Yeah. So the shape may be different because the elevation change.

Narrator:
Hansen may soon uncover a major archaeological discovery.

Richard Hansen:
It's exciting, yeah. This is exciting.

Narrator:
Hansen's team begins to dig. It's a challenging project. There's a lot of rock and earth to move.

Richard Hansen:
We've gotten about 13.5 yards into the building now, and that represents about 22 cubic yards of rock that we've brought out of there.

Narrator:
Hansen and his team dig deep into the Jaguar temple. He's determined to prove that Great Fiery Jaguar Paw really existed all those years ago. The digging continues for some time. Finally, they arrive at the place where the equipment showed a space that might be the king's tomb. The team could be just a few minutes away from finding the tomb of Great Fiery Jaguar Paw. The team finally breaks through, but there's disappointment waiting on the other side. There's nothing behind the chamber wall.

Richard Hansen:
There should have been a chamber or something on the other side of this wall. This has . . . um . . . is a setback. There should have been something there. So, the fact that it's not there, tells us that the . . . the elusive Kan kings are still elusive.

Narrator:
Does this mean that the mystery of the early Maya kings is just a story after all? Hansen doesn't think so. He still feels that they're real, and he's not content to give up easily. He's preparing to dig at another pyramid next year. Perhaps then this archaeologist will achieve his goal of seeing the tomb of an ancient Maya king. Maybe he will finally find what he's looking for in the lost temples of the Maya.

Unit 10: Sigmund Freud

Narrator:
On May 6th, 1856, Sigmund Freud was born in what is today the Czech Republic. And 150 years later . . . the man known as the founding father of psychotherapy is still generating controversy. It's the city of Vienna, where the family moved when Sigmund was a young child, that's most associated with Freud. He received his medical degree here in 1881 and began studying the human brain. But over time, Freud became fascinated by something he couldn't see or touch—the human mind. In the 1890s, Freud began developing the theories behind the practice he named *psychoanalysis.* He believed that all human beings have an unconscious portion of the mind. In the unconscious, strong sexual and aggressive drives struggle against the mind's attempts to suppress them. Freud believed that dreams were one way to look into the unconscious . . . and to discover a person's deepest desires and fears. Using his own dreams and those of his patients, Freud published what is widely considered his masterpiece, *The Interpretation of Dreams,* in 1899. In the process, he helped make psychology a hallmark of the new century. In 1938, when Freud was 81, the Nazis annexed Austria. They had already burned Freud's books in Germany, labeling them the product of Jewish science. Freud fled to England that same year, and died the next autumn, on September 23rd, 1939. Today, fewer than 5000 patients in the U.S. are treated with Freud's method of psychoanalysis . . . a type of therapy where patients explore the workings of their unconscious over the course of five to six years. His methods as a doctor may be in decline . . . but as a theorist, Sigmund Freud succeeded in changing forever the way that people think about the human mind.